MW00877455

ASHES

a story about cigarettes,
cremation and hope

Mala Mukherji

The names of some of the characters and locations have been changed to protect the privacy of the participants in this story. Specific recollections may differ due to individual perceptions and faded memories.

ISBN: 9781490374680

Copyright 2013 by Mala Mukherji
All rights reserved.

Library of Congress

Mukherji, Mala
ASHES: a story about cigarettes, cremation and hope

For Ma

Contents

PART TWO
Cremation

PART THREE
Hope

Prologue

Dad and I lifted the top from the square metal canister that held a plastic bag of Mom's ashes. When I looked inside, the absence of the vibrant, burgundy sari she had been wearing surprised me. I knew the sari had burned with her body, but the dullness of her remains betrayed the strength of her presence.

Two of Mom's brothers and one of her sisters gathered around the canister Dad held. Together, they ran the soft powder through their fingers, placed the white-gray ash to their lips and wept their good-byes. Unhindered tears landed in pools on their necks. Dad, my brother Raj and I watched them for many silent moments. When they finished, we all embraced.

Dad chose one of the many barges waiting by the river's edge for the three of us to board. Under a clear sky, the thin, dhoti-wearing driver rowed us over the Ganges River. A slight wind blew and the September sun shone warm yet mild.

To my right, Dad perched on a sliver of a bench. Raj laid back on the bow of the boat, resting his head on his folded arms. "Look up, Mala!" he said.

When I did, I saw a single strip of a rainbow. A couple of weeks prior a psychic had told us that Mom would communicate from the other side in that form.

"I don't believe it," I said.

Raj and I began to sob.

"What's going on?" Dad asked.

Raj pointed to the rainbow above us. "Someone told us Mom would come to us as a rainbow." Raj bent his head and gulped down a sob. "She's here with us." I'd hated Dad my whole life, but when his tears joined ours, the hard edges of my hatred softened.

We floated in the middle of the river for a long while. I glanced back to the shore several times to find Mom's sister and brothers on the river's edge, while Dad looked lost in thought and Raj focused on the rainbow that did not dissipate or move.

Much too soon, the light breeze on the water stopped. A film of sweat rose over my face and body. The Calcutta heat pierced our sacred space and forced the inevitable. We had to let Mom go.

"Dad, should we do this?" I asked.

He nodded his head heavy with pain and lifted the canister onto the bench beside him.

With a sigh, Raj kneeled in front of Dad. Each of us took handfuls of ash and dropped them in the gently lapping river. In between my fingers, I found a dusty identification slip, which stated Mom's name, cremation date and number. That, I tucked into my backpack.

With each release of the powder, I whispered over and over, "You're free, Mom. You're free." She no longer bore the burden that broke her body. She escaped a life torn between India and America, her children and her marriage.

When Dad lifted the bag from the canister to release the last of the powder stuck in the bottom corners, a surprise gust of wind blew them all over me and only me. I was covered in her. My black skirt turned gray, and the hair on my arms shimmered. I watched the ash create a paste with my sweat. I hoped it was Mom's way of telling me that she was free, but a part of me.

I didn't want to move beyond that moment on the river. I didn't want to change my skirt or shower off that paste. With the ceremonies completed, all I had left was a life without her. A life I didn't think I could survive.

My hand shook when I wiped my tears beneath my sunglasses. The river stilled to a hush. I looked up to find the rainbow, but it had disappeared, like Mom's ashes into the water.

PART ONE

Cigarettes

CHAPTER ONE
Split

A giant, unspoken worry filled my childhood. My parents didn't understand how America worked, and I could tell by the way they looked at each other with terror when seemingly small choices presented themselves. Each of their faces tightened, Dad clenched and unclenched his jaw, and Mom's eyes grew wide, while her thin eyebrows lifted a little. They didn't speak of their uncertainty, only showed it.

They got those looks when I joined the swim team, before my first parent–teacher night and when I had to choose between Girl Scouts and Camp Fire Girls at my new school. Yet, not when they built our new house.

Two and a half months after my sixth birthday and a year after Raj was born, we moved from our townhome in West Covina to a house in Covina. My parents hired an architect, who rendered beautiful, exact drawings of their dream home. Over several months, we took many trips to the bare dirt lot and watched the new house come to life. I didn't want to leave our old home, my school or friends. Mom said it was a much bigger house in a far nicer area. I wasn't sure what she meant but knew there was no choice but to go with her.

The sun began to set by the time the movers unloaded all of our belongings from their truck into our new home, which sat up a steep hill past two pale stone entry walls, which read "Covina Heights" in black, wrought iron script. Our driveway pitched short and sharp. Mom was nervous about driving her car into the garage for the first several years that we lived there. Dad teased her about it until she died.

He teased her often about how she did things and what she said. Most of the time she laughed with him but every now and then her lips pressed into a hard line, and she either gave him a look of disgust or snapped back. It was hard to tell what would get to her. The teasing about the driveway didn't. That is, unless Dad tried to instruct her on how to maneuver it.

"Turn the wheel, turn the wheel!" he yelled many weekends standing on the driveway while she left to go on an errand. "Oof, you're going to hit the ice plant I just put in."

"I do it without you everyday. Leave me alone," she said from her open window.

Mom unpacked the kitchen, while Dad stood close to her—ten inches taller and looked out the window at the snow-covered San Bernardino Mountains in the distance. I walked back and forth from them to my new room uncertain of what to do. I kept my ear tuned to the eight, bright gold bangles Mom wore on her right wrist, which chimed in their own song with any shift of her arm. They told me where she was.

From the doorway of the kitchen, I heard Dad say to Mom, "Hey, can you believe it? We came to America by ourselves and made it. We built our own house." He laughed. "Can you think what our families would say?" His thin frame puffed with pride. It seemed odd to hear Dad satisfied. I mostly knew him by his yelling or the tinkle of ice in his Cutty Sark scotch on the rocks, which he poured from a large green bottle everyday when he returned from work.

"It's nice," Mom said and continued to fill the kitchen cabinets with her deliberate, imperceptible movements. She glided from box to cabinet with so little effort that Dad didn't seem to notice that she was doing all the work.

Before my new school, Badillo Elementary, I never realized that my skin was darker than the other kids'. None of my friends in my old neighborhood, school or swim team had said anything about how I looked. That's why the first attack surprised me.

I chose Girl Scouts over Camp Fire Girls, because the older girls in their green uniforms and sashes with plentiful patches looked festive and important. I'd never joined a club at school, because my swim team practiced every afternoon. I was excited to try it. Before anyone could initiate into Girl Scouts, we had to spend one year as a Brownie.

Mom bought me my Brownie uniform, although I knew she had to convince Dad. She didn't work, and he worried about money, because we didn't have a lot.

Dad yelled about it, especially every other Saturday when he wrote bills at his desk in his den. His company paid him on the fifteenth and on the last Friday of the month. He marked those days with "PAYDAY" in a red pen on the calendar, which hung to the left of his desk. On those Saturdays, he opened a silver can of Coors Light beer before lunch. We avoided him after the first click of the tab pulled from the can let out a hiss.

Everyday after Mom picked me up from school, I waited in the garage while she took small, careful steps down our driveway to the mailbox. On the Tuesday before my first Brownie meeting, Mom opened an envelope and waved a letter in my direction. The song of her bracelets sounded.

"There's a notice that all new Brownies have to wear their uniform to school on meeting days," Mom said.

"Does it say why?" I thought the Girl Scouts wore their outfits and sashes from pride not obligation.

"No, but you should do what this says." She held the letter out to me. "Do you want to check?"

"No, I don't need to." I bristled inside. I hated being told what to wear. At swim meets, I felt silly when our whole team wore matching sweats and bathing suits.

That Thursday, I took my crisp, new uniform out of its plastic bag and laid it on my bed. The Brownie outfit looked stiff and bland. The orange, snap tie seemed out of place, the jumper too dull to call brown. I didn't want to wear it the whole day. I liked my clothes loose and soft.

After I put on the uniform, I hesitated to look in the mirror above my dresser. It felt scratchy. The jumper was shorter than I liked, and my legs felt exposed. None of my shoes matched it. I chose some plain, white tennis shoes but wasn't happy with the results.

Mom met me at the front door and must have sensed my discomfort. "You look nice." Mom didn't give many compliments.

"You think so?"

"I guess." She shrugged her shoulders. "Is that what it should look like?" She'd never seen anyone in a Brownie uniform either.

After she dropped me off at school, I went straight to the classroom to put my lunch in my desk. Before the first bell and at recess and lunch, I played with Cindy and Debbie. They were in second grade and hadn't joined Brownies. Cindy danced ballet every afternoon. Mom said that Debbie's parents were weird, although I didn't know why she thought so.

I felt uncertain in the short jumper and silly tie. I wanted to wait at my desk, instead of looking for Cindy and Debbie. Once a few other kids came in to leave their lunches, I realized I'd look strange staying inside.

On the playground, I always avoided the dodge, tether and handball games. I was scared to get hit in the face with a ball. Cindy and Debbie didn't like those games either. We usually met out in the field to compare each other's new lipglosses.

On my way out to the field I noticed a group of the boys from another class playing handball on the court closest to me. The tallest one pointed at me and said to the others, "Hey, look at her."

I felt a knowing knot in my stomach when three of the boys walked toward me. Like when Dad came home from work in a bad mood. Although vulnerable in the ugly uniform, I stood where I was.

The tallest boy strode ahead of the others and stood no more than two feet in front of me. He smiled back at his friends, which revealed two buck front teeth. "Gross. You're a brownie in a Brownie uniform. You look just like poop." He crinkled his face and turned to his friends, who laughed in encouragement. "I bet you smell like it too," he said. White milky paste painted the corners of his mouth and I thought that he was gross.

Other kids from all grades heard their laughter, gathered around and created a blur in front of me. I felt confused. I looked down at the muted brown jumper dress against my brown legs with horror. They were right. I was brown. How had I missed something so obvious?

I hoped that I didn't smell like poop but couldn't be sure. I wanted to hide but had no way to escape. I waited in shame until they stopped, which they did at the ring of the first bell.

I ran to my seat with my head down and stared at my legs beneath my desk.

My heart raced as I searched my life for a clue as to how this could have happened. How no one had told me that my skin was disgusting. What was I going to do if I smelled like poop?

The chlorine in the pool from practice should've rinsed it off. I swam everyday and took a shower after. I bent my head down beneath a wall of my hair to sniff the back of my hand. It smelled like the chlorine that never rinsed off, no matter how much soap I used. I didn't feel any better. Maybe I couldn't smell myself.

I peered down my row and saw that everybody else's hands were light and white. Lighter than our desks. My brown hand jumped from the peach-colored, light wood desk and buried itself in my lap. It was dark and different from everyone else's. I was ugly.

I stayed in the classroom for the rest of the day. I asked the teacher if I could eat lunch at my desk. I didn't lie when I told Cindy and Debbie that my stomach hurt. I pretended that I was invisible in my seat, and no one bothered me the rest of the day.

After the last bell rang and everyone left, I went out the rear sliding doors of the classroom and took the long way, around the back of the school, to find Mom's maroon Volvo station wagon. Because we were going straight from the Brownie meeting to swimming, mom brought my swim bag so that I could change at the pool for practice. Raj and my bag were in the back seat.

I noticed for the first time that Mom's and Raj's arms and hands were brown like mine and not white either. I couldn't tell Mom what happened at school. I didn't want her to know that she and Raj were ugly too. I didn't want her eyes to widen in worry.

I took a deep sniff and felt relieved that they didn't smell bad. Raj smelled like the powder in his diaper and Mom like her flowery perfume. I loved her smell.

The first Brownie meeting was held at the house of a girl from a different class at my school. We ate cookies while the Brownie troop leader told us things I couldn't hear.

I didn't care what she said. I wanted to get to swimming and change out of that stupid uniform.

At the pool in the locker room, I found a quiet corner far from the big kids and shed the brown fabric. I looked down at my legs, arms and stomach. My belly was lighter than my legs and arms. Afternoon practice in our outdoor pool created the lines of my swimsuit on my body. Even my lighter belly was still brown, a more yellow brown. My hands, arms and legs looked like the crust I didn't eat on toast.

On the pool deck, I inspected every person on our team. Not one of them had brown skin. They were tanned but white. I wondered if they thought the same things the boys at school thought. I put my head down and couldn't smile or wave when other kids said hello. I didn't hesitate to jump into the cold water for the first time in the two years since I joined the team. It felt good to bury my body in the pool and forget about my skin.

I didn't discuss the problem of my skin with anyone, except Skippy and God. A few months after I turned three, we got Skippy from a lady at Dad's work whose dog had puppies. He was a gray and white cockapoo with floppy, folded ears and bangs that grew over his eyes. Every few weeks, I held him while Mom cut his bangs straight across above his eyebrows, like she cut mine. Skippy looked shy afterwards and ran to his place on the patio behind the kitchen. Mom and Dad didn't want him in the house. I put him in the garage when it rained.

Although I'd never spoken out loud to God, the night after my first Brownie day began my ritual. Mom and Dad didn't discuss God, but Mom said, "Someone watches everything." I think I got the idea to pray watching people do it on T.V.

Every night, without knowing how, I talked to God in whispered prayers into my pillow. I never doubted that the Someone Mom spoke about heard me. I begged God to turn my skin white and my hair blond. I prayed that God make me pretty. Even as my prayers went unanswered, I prayed harder.

I had to talk to the Someone. Skippy couldn't tell me how to fix it, and I couldn't discuss my problem with anyone that I knew well. If I told Mom, I'd hurt her feelings. If I told Dad, he'd yell and blame Mom and me. The other people I saw wouldn't understand. The kids at school, on my swim team, the teachers, my parents' friends, Uncle Stan, Aunt Kathy and their girls, were white.

Dad met Stan Burk and his wife, Kathy, in 1970, when he and Uncle Stan were posted by their company in Bullhead City, Arizona. They had four daughters, who were between eight and thirteen years older than me. When not at swim meets, we often went to their house in West Covina on the weekends. I was close to their youngest daughter, Rosalie, but the oldest one, Lily had a boyfriend and wasn't around much. Mindy and Missy, the twins stuck together and didn't include Rosalie or me in stuff they did. I never called their parents anything other than their false familial names.

I met our family in India when my parents took me there to celebrate my third birthday. Although most of the trip blurred in my mind, I remembered the love rained on me by our family and that I liked India more than America. I loved the food, the noise of the city and the constant presence of my cousins, aunts, uncles and grandparents. Everyone either lived in the same house or close enough to come over for most meals. I spent more time with Mom in India, because other people cleaned, cooked, and did the laundry. I secretly wished we could've lived there instead.

I often wondered why my parents left our family, why they came to a place where we were so different and alone, even with Skippy and the Burks. A few months after my first prayers to become white and before Dad got home from work, I asked Mom why.

Mom started dinner while I sat at the kitchen counter and watched. She didn't like us in the kitchen with her, but I loved to see how she took various plastic bags filled with vegetables from the fridge, spooned spices out of a round tin container, and created a many-course meal of any ethnic origin.

"How come you guys didn't go back to India after Dad was done with grad school?" In 1968, after Mom ruled out the east coast due to its cold weather, Dad came to America to attend graduate school at U.S.C. She followed him several months after his school started. I was born nine months after she arrived.

Mom moved from the stove to the sink where she'd left the cut vegetables. She grabbed the cauliflower and threw them into a pan with heated oil. When the wet vegetables hit the oil, they popped. Mom jumped back and stirred them with an outstretched arm. "Why do you ask so many questions all the time?" she said.

"I don't know. It's fun there."

She turned the heat down on the cauliflower and looked around the kitchen. "Life's not fun." She began to rip the skin from the raw chicken in the sink. When I didn't respond, she looked back at me.

I shrugged my shoulders.

Mom washed her hands and wiped them on the towel next to her. She exhaled with a loud whoosh and returned to the stove in front of me. "Okay, what're you asking me?"

"Why didn't you guys go back?"

"I guess we thought that you'd have more chances here. India's different." She fiddled with the small diamond ring on her left hand. "It's harder for everyone, especially women."

"How?" Mom required step-by-step questions to reveal information. "Women don't get jobs as easily."

"But you told me that your aunts were doctors." I wanted to be a doctor like them until I realized that blood scared me.

"Yeah, they were, but that's not common."

"Why not? They did it." I hated when a hidden layer of a story revealed itself after I relied on the first version.

"There's a lot of pressure for a woman to marry young. Your Mejo Mashi [her middle sister] was very, very smart. A top level student, but she married a doctor instead of becoming one."

"Is she sad about not being a doctor?"

"No, she says she's happy." Her words fell flat. It didn't sound like Mom believed it.

"What'd you want to do?" I'd never thought of Mom with a job. "I always wanted to have kids, to be a mom like I am now."

"You didn't want a job?" I wouldn't have wanted to ask Dad for money like she did.

"This is my job."

"But–"

"I like staying at home, taking care of you guys. It's important for a mom to pick her kids up from school, to be there for them." She looked to the sink worried with the thought of how much she had left to do to finish dinner and read my mind. "More important than more money for us."

"Lots of moms work."

"We're not American." She said American like it tasted badly. "This is how your Dad and I wanted you guys to be raised."

"What do you think I should do? Should I get a job?" I was trying to figure out whether she thought of me as American. Dad always said that we were Americans and should act like them, especially after they became citizens in 1978.

"It's important to do something that gives you independence. A career of your own so you never have to rely on anyone else."

"Like what?"

"Well, you like to argue with your dad, I think you'd make a great lawyer."

"I guess I could." I didn't know what lawyers did but it sounded important. "Your Dad's family has a lot of lawyers and judges on his mom's side, for many generations back. It's in your blood." With that, she went back to the chicken in the sink.

I wondered how I could be a lawyer and a mom or what man would want to marry a girl with brown skin and if the other Indian parents came to America for the same reasons.

We didn't see other Bengali people much. It didn't matter anyway. They were different. Most of the Bengali families we knew lived in Monterey Park, twenty minutes east of us. The kids played musical instruments, not sports. The girls weren't allowed to wear shorts or bathing suits in public. They cared a lot about their grades and where they'd go to college, even though none of them were in high school yet. They spent all their time with other Bengali families.

Their fathers were far shorter and more awkward than Dad. They kept longer hair that they parted way on the side, combed into place with a lot of oil. They walked with rounded shoulders and their chins pointed to the ground. Dad cut his hair short and walked with ease. He held his neck long and head high, like Mom.

The Bengali moms wore saris and a bindi—the dot between the eyes which meant that a woman was married. Mom wore western clothes everyday, unless we visited other Bengali families. She never wore a bindi. Mom said, "They're gayan [Bengali word for village-like or unsophisticated]. It's no one's business whether I'm married or not."

The only time I saw the other Bengali kids was at large "functions." That's what I heard Mom call the gatherings when she spoke on the phone to other Indian moms, like Nandita Mashi, Shipra Mashi and Munju Mashi, who had sons and daughters the ages of Raj and me. The functions took place in other people's homes or in halls all over the San Gabriel Valley to celebrate birthdays or Hindu religious holidays.

My parents also invited their Bengali friends over to our house, but they argued a lot before the guests arrived. Mom glided around with a tense face, and Dad told her that she made too much food, got too "stressed," and it wasn't fun for him.

In the pool at practice, I searched the black tile line on the bottom of my lane for answers to all the things that didn't make sense to me. How Mom and Dad were married but didn't seem happy, how we were Bengali but didn't do what the other Indians did. Even though I felt different from the Bengali kids, I wondered why we didn't go to the functions every weekend like the other families. One evening after Mom picked me up, I was still thinking about it. "Why don't we see the other Bengalis as much as Uncle Stan and the girls? They get together every week."

"You have swim meets most weekends." I heard the click, click of the turn signal. Mom was scared to change lanes. She gripped the steering wheel with both hands, scooted up in her seat, turned her head far over her shoulder and moved with caution into the left lane. "Besides, we came here to be American, not Indian." She used a soft tone for American this time.

"Didn't they?"

"Bengalis don't want to change. They want to be here but act like they're there." Securely in the new lane, Mom continued. "They don't let their kids do American things, they stick together. They don't have American friends. What's the point of being here then?"

"Is that why you don't speak Bengali to us?" I'd learned some Bengali on my trip to India but hadn't used it since. I understood some still.

"Yeah, part of it, you don't need it here. It's better that your English is perfect. No accent, no problems with grammar." I felt embarrassed at the

Bengali parties. The other parents spoke in Bengali with their children. Except for Munju Mashi, they looked at me with a mix of pity and distaste at my failure to speak their mother tongue.

"Do you think the other kids speak with an accent?"

"No, but who knows how it'll affect them later, when they have to take tests to get into college. It's better to be safe."

On the night of our last Bengali function for a long while, Mom rushed into the kids' room, where the other kids were talking about what musical instruments they played and books they'd read. "Mala, come on. We've got to go. Now." Her full mouth smashed itself narrow.

I grabbed Raj's hand and followed Mom through the crowd of brown faces. A thick, yellowish haze met us as the outside air and cigarette smoke made the living room seem wet and dirty. At the front door, my father's familiar angry face yelled at a smaller man. Others held the arms of the smaller man who screamed back at Dad. I couldn't understand what either of them said. Their screams collided and sounded like dogs barking at one another.

Someone in the crowd shouted, "Ram, you're drunk. Go home."

Dad was acting how he did at home in front of other people. I put my head down, pulled Raj and hurried outside with my parents to find Dad's Volvo sedan, parked a few houses away on the street. Mom led Dad by his arm to her usual seat. "You're too upset. You've had a lot to drink." I cringed when she said it. I knew what was coming.

"You're just like them! You think I've had too much to drink?" Dad couldn't stand up straight, his speech was slurred and I saw drops of spit fly behind his words.

I'd never seen him so drunk. My stomach spun in my belly. Mom didn't drive at night or on the freeways. Her hands shook when she helped Dad into the car.

Raj and I climbed into the backseat and I wished I could disappear, like at school on a bad day.

"How could you do this to me?" Dad demanded. "You believe them!" He slammed his hand into the dashboard, and I jumped in my seat. "I never should've married you, spoiled girl from a rich family. What do you know about anything?" He yelled those same words in different ways the entire ride home.

The second Mom stopped the car in the garage, I rushed into my room and left Raj with her. I was too scared to go into the bathroom in the hallway to brush my teeth and held my pee until morning.

The next day, I feared what I'd find, but nothing was different. Mom and Dad sat at the kitchen table with their tea and read the Sunday newspaper. I couldn't look at Dad. Even though Mom appeared to have forgotten the prior night, I had not.

CHAPTER TWO
Survive

The safety of recesses out in the field with Cindy and Debbie didn't always protect me. By the third grade, I learned to defend myself against the hateful, relentless boys. I'd grown taller than all the boys in my grade and knew that two hours of a day of swimming made me stronger, as well. If any of them challenged me, I grabbed their arm and flipped them over my shoulder. Each landed on the grass with a thud.

I never got in trouble from the teachers. The boys were too embarrassed to tell on me, just like I was too embarrassed to tell on them.

The teasing wore on me. After school on bad days, I went outside to talk to Skippy. I told him how awful it was to be ugly. I told him that there was nothing I could do about it. I buried my face in his soft gray fur and cried where no one could see me. Skippy couldn't say anything, yet I knew he understood by the way he sat still until I stopped crying.

At school, I used my physical strength. At home, I used my voice. Dad's screaming grew louder and louder with each passing year. Many nights, he threw plates filled with Mom's delicious food from our dinner table.

A couple of times, he shoved her before I could throw myself between them. My fights with Dad trained me to use my mind to protect my family from his rage. If Dad got really angry, a gate in the back of my brain opened and a force bigger than me flew forward to back him into a corner with a twist of his own words. I didn't know how it worked, but it did.

One late summer Saturday dinner before fifth grade, Dad and I fought without restraint. "You forget the salt every night," he scolded Mom. Disgust drenched his voice. He had consumed most of his two, double scotches before dinner and sat with the sweaty glass of yellow-orange liquid in melting ice in his left hand.

My fist and stomach clenched in anticipation.

"I work. I make the money. All you do is make dinner." He made his sound of contempt: air pushed from his mouth like a "ch" sound. "Are you stupid or something?"

Mom got up and lightly placed the saltshaker in front of his plate. "I think I forgot," she said.

"How do you forget? Is it that hard?" he said and shook salt onto his food with hard sweeps of his arms. "Glad that I don't forget things like that. Where would you be then? Your rich dad can't help you here."

I rolled my eyes away from him, like I often did. However, that night, he challenged my silent protest. "You shouldn't do that." The table of food crackled with his fury.

"Do what?" I didn't meet his eyes. I hated how he looked when he drank. Tiny, red, puffy, squinting eyes filled with rage. Although people often commented on how handsome my father was, I never thought so. I saw him as he was that night and too many others: ruthless and out of control.

"You know what." He threw his fork onto his plate. "What kind of girl does that to her father?"

"I don't know. You tell me." He didn't scare me, even though frustrated tears watered my eyes.

"I'm not going to take it anymore! I make the money." His hand banged a few inches from my plate. "Do you hear me?" He only threw his plate if he was mad at Mom. "This is my house and, if you want to live here, you're going to respect me."

"Sure, I'll do that." My eyes rolled before I could stop them.

"Make her listen to me," Dad pointed his finger across the table at Mom.

She gave me her look that said "You're making it worse." I didn't want to listen to her either. I was sick of her giving in to him whenever he yelled. Raj sank lower into his chair and leaned his left elbow on the table to hide his face with his hand. I didn't want to hurt him, but I wouldn't let Dad win.

"Mala, stop it," Mom said. Her eyes pleaded with me.

"No, I won't. It's salt, Mom. That's it." She let him make a big deal out of everything. She looked away from me and at Dad to gauge how he would respond. "Don't talk to your Mom like that," Dad said.

"Why not? You do." My words flowed without my control. The bigger voice had arrived.

"Because I'm your Dad. I can do what I want, the way I want."

"That's not fair." I looked to my left and into his red eyes. I wanted to face the monster. He stood up, and so did I.

"You're going to respect me," he said, pointing his finger in my face.

"I don't have to."

He looked at Mom. "Do you see how you're raising her?"

"Calm down. She's little. She doesn't know what she's saying." Mom said to him in Bengali, which I still understood from that trip to India when I was three and a later one at age seven.

"You're making a mistake with her. No man would want this," Dad said back to her in slurred English. "She's too much, too smart for her own good. No one will ever marry her." His hand slapped the air near my face.

The larger voice flew forward to protect me. "Why should I respect you?"

"Because I give you everything you have."

"That's not enough. Don't you get it?" I shook my head and cursed the crying that failed my pride.

"No, you think you're so smart." He laughed at me. "Tell me."

I leaned toward him. "You have to give respect to get it, Dad. You'll never understand." I ran to my room, slammed the door and wept into my pillows without making a sound. I didn't want him to know how much he got to me. I wished Skippy were allowed inside with me.

Mom knocked on my door after the three of them had dinner and she had cleaned up. "Are you hungry?"

"No, I don't feel like eating." My stomach growled as I said it. "You should eat something. You can't skip dinner."

"I don't want to go out there."

"He's gone to bed." She touched the top of my head. "I don't know why you don't let it go."

"Because it's not fair."

"Life's not fair. You've got to grow up and stop thinking that it will be," she said and shut my door behind her.

Swimming allowed me to release my frustrations at a world in which the brown of my skin made me ugly and Dad ruled our home with rage. Every afternoon, I dreaded the shock of the cold pool water and stood on the deck staring it down, while, next to me, the other swimmers put on their swim caps and adjusted their goggles. I didn't wear a cap. I was convinced the chlorine could bleach my hair blond. Instead, it turned the top part fuzzy and reddish.

Mike, our coach, announced, "Two minutes."

At the base of each of the eight lanes, five or six swimmers fiddled with their gear. They rotated their arms to feign a freestyle stroke and shook out their legs to prepare for our workout. I wiggled my limbs without any intention of getting in the water.

Mike stood on the other end of the pool and rolled his handsome, tan head on his neck as if he were warming up to get in with us. The sound of each swimmer's effortless dives followed Mike's "Ready, Go."

Cursing the cold water, I ducked into the water many minutes later. Goose bumps erupted all over my body, but with each length of the pool, my body warmed. I relaxed and expanded into the familiar freedom and safety of the water. No one could touch me there. The rhythm of the water with my breath and movement suspended me in a cloud.

My ears filled with the sound of my arms entering the water. There was no screaming, no taunting and no rage, only Mike's shouts of encouragement in the distance of the pool deck.

I mostly tuned Mike out. Practice didn't interest me. I waited for our meets to give my everything.

Swim meets were the only fair place in my life. I was a sprinter. I liked to explode off the blocks and find a groove in the water that allowed my body to propel through it with little resistance. I didn't like the longer races where I had to pace myself and hold back in strategy.

I sacrificed all of me in every race, because the timers' watches that recorded me were unbiased. Their watches didn't care that I was brown or that no man would ever want me.

At swim meets, I couldn't be cheated out of what I earned. I wasn't always the fastest but I left my guts in the pool every race.

I had more friends on my swim team than at school, but met my best friend through both. A grade ahead of me, Cindy and Debbie graduated Badillo and were in junior high. Mid-way through fifth grade, my teacher, Mr. Nash introduced a new student, a girl with strawberry-blonde hair and lots of freckles.

Lisa looked at her feet and peered at our class from beneath her bowl haircut's long bangs. Like the other kids, I ignored her.

That afternoon at practice, I saw her again. She seemed more at ease on the pool deck. I introduced myself and discovered that her birthday was a day and a year before mine, that she'd just moved from Seattle to Covina for her dad's job and that her parents moved her around a lot so she was held back in second grade.

Swimmers shared an immediate trust with one another. Like a breed of dog that recognizes its own, we understood each other's unquestionable, unrelenting commitment to our sport, the fact that we spent hours a day in water. Land wasn't the same conduit.

The pool as our glue, Mr. Nash's class all day, Lisa and I were best friends within days. The only time we fought was when the Los Angeles Lakers played the Seattle Supersonics in the NBA playoffs. We didn't speak for a week.

Swimming, Lisa and Skippy helped cradle my days, but despair caught me at bedtime. I tried to concentrate on what to wear the next day, how I swam at practice or the romance novel that I found in Mom's bookcase. I went to Mom's novels, because the school library mostly had Nancy Drew books, which I didn't like, and the Judy Blume books that I'd read by second grade.

One day in the fifth grade too many things went wrong.

Following some standardized tests in second grade, the teachers let me read those novels under my desk.

Mom told them that if I didn't read, I'd get bored. Mr. Nash knew I finished our homework when he was teaching us how to do it and that I read books after that.

That day, he decided to change the rules. "Mala, what are you doing? Are you reading when I'm talking?"

"Um, yes." Full of Sidney Sheldon's suspense, I didn't notice his harsh tone. "Tell me what I just said?"

Even when I read, I kept one ear open to what was going on around me. I stung from his betrayal and scowled at his bearded face. "You said that even though we have calculators, it's important to learn how to do long division." I hesitated but wanted to acknowledge his attack. "And, I do." I waited for him to dare me, but he didn't.

After class, when Lisa and I walked together through the halls of Badillo's fifth grade building, she said, "You know what? You've got a big butt."

"No, I don't." I twisted my body to check behind me.

"Yeah, you do. You've got a bubble butt." Older than me, she acted like a big sister. Yet, she'd never been critical of my appearance, even about my skin color.

I hated the look of superiority in her eyes. "Yours is flat. Flat like that pole next to you," I retaliated.

"Everyone's is. It's supposed to be. Yours is just big." When I looked around, I saw that everyone's butt was flat. I relented and didn't say anything else. I assumed, like white skin, a flat butt was better than a big one.

At swim practice, I kept away from Lisa but felt jealous when I saw her hanging out with the other kids. My body didn't find the water's rhythm that afternoon. I struggled to make the intervals and felt like I didn't belong there. Even Mike's hearty laugh didn't lift my mood.

That evening, Dad pushed when I had nothing left. I bumped into the kitchen table with a loud thud that shook the plates Mom set for dinner. Disrupted from the enjoyment of his scotch and nightly news, Dad snorted his disgust. "No one will marry a girl who can't walk! Why can't you be more graceful?" He looked at Mom who stood in the kitchen. "Maybe we should send her to charm school."

"Don't say things like that," Mom said after Dad turned back to watch Peter Jennings.

I expected his taunts and rage. But those words, that night, stripped away my hope. My endless stream of romance novels filled me with a belief that one day a handsome, kind and generous man would love me.

Dad's words ripped more of the day's raw flesh. Who was I kidding? For the first time, I realized that I'd be alone forever. No one would want a girl like me.

After dinner, I skipped T.V. and went straight to my room. I sat at my desk with the unbearable weight of shame and defeat on my heart. My gaze fell to my open closet and at the attic door above it. The rats. Over the prior few months, the construction of several houses at the bottom of our hill had scattered rats through the neighborhood and into our attic.

Dad had tried traps with cheese and peanut butter as bait, but the sound of the snap and the rats' desperate scampering had been too sad for all of us. He decided to poison them instead.

That weekend, Dad had climbed a ladder through the attic door with a bright orange box of poison. A week later, he'd worn heavy gloves when he collected the dead rats in a paper bag. The orange box flashed through my head, a way out of the things I could never fix.

As if in a dream, I slipped into the garage while my parents watched T.V. in the family room on the other side of the house. I eased the heavy door to a hushed close. The garage scared me at night, yet I turned on the light and went to the tall metal rack where Dad kept the orange box, on the bottom shelf behind the car wash soap.

I read the back of the box. "DANGER" and a black skull beneath it caught my eye. The warning instructed someone to go to the hospital if the poison was "accidentally ingested." A few lines down, it said "Not for human consumption."

I wondered how long it would take to die. Dad had waited a week for the rats. I didn't know if I would die right away or have to take a little every night, like how the grandmother fed arsenic to the children in "Flowers in the Attic."

I didn't want it to hurt. When I had peeked into the brown bag filled with dead rats, their mouths hung open in agonized, futile screams and I imagined the poison felt like fire burning in their veins. In the garage, I found a plastic sandwich bag and filled it with the poison so Dad wouldn't notice the missing box. I snuck back to my room, turned out my light and sat at my desk.

I felt justified. I didn't ever have to feel ugly, useless or different again. I touched a grain of the poison to my tongue, which looked like Aunt Kathy's potpourri but didn't taste like anything. Not sour, sweet or bitter. I wanted it to taste like something.

The nothingness of the poison shook me. Something so bland could kill me. It was too easy. I dropped the baggy on my desk and sobbed, not from sadness but because I was trapped. That's when the larger voice found me. The voice folded itself into my own and became my clear thoughts and knowingness of what would happen if I killed myself.

If I ate the poison, I'd have to come back to a later but identical moment in time. I flew within myself to a life not yet born. I saw that one day I'd encounter the same type of night, with the same problems, but without the good things I had, like my mind, swimming, Skippy and Mom.

Somehow, Someone or God made it all clear to me. There was no other way for me to know the consequences of killing myself. No one had discussed reincarnation when I was in India, at home or at school, yet I knew the rules of suicide and didn't doubt them for a moment. I placed the baggy in the top drawer of my desk and cried myself to sleep.

Even with that knowledge, I visited that baggy most nights and gave myself the option to kill myself if things were too much for me. I didn't think about it during the day, but the choice barreled into my mind before I got into bed most nights. It became my secret and soothing ritual. Every time I made the decision to stay, no one controlled me, not even God's rules. I decided when I left my life.

Those murky, nighttime choices brought a lightness and power to my days. The secret tucked into my heart and, without my knowing it, replaced Lisa as my best friend. I acted the same on the outside but everything was different. I demanded that life show me a purpose and a reason to stay.

Late in the fifth grade, I discovered how dangerous the unyielding taunts of hatred like, brownie, ugly and smelly could be in the world. The fifth-grade teachers liked to plan special surprises on Friday mornings. We usually skipped class and played classroom against classroom in dodgeball, which I hated. Lisa wasn't afraid of the ball, so I stood close to her. She was stronger and faster than I was.

One such morning, the fifth-grade classes gathered in the hallway and were led to my old first-grade classroom. A small, older lady I'd never seen sat on a desk on the side of the room. Her face looked sad yet peaceful, her body as frail as a baby bird.

Mr. Nash said, "Everybody, listen carefully, this is Mrs. Rothberg. She's going to talk to you about what happened to her when she was a little girl."

Mrs. Rothberg didn't speak right away. Instead, she looked each one of us in the eye and half smiled. When her gaze met mine, I saw that her light blue eyes were gentle and deep. Not in color but a different way. I'd never seen anyone like her. She mesmerized me even before she spoke.

"Hello, everybody," she said and bowed her head to all of us. "I'm here to tell you about the Holocaust and what happened to many, many people only thirty years ago." Her voice was soft like her eyes.

She spoke for almost an hour. She told us that she had been sixteen years old when the Nazis invaded her home. She lived in Poland, and her family was Jewish. She told us how a man named Hitler built an army he commanded to kill Jews and anyone who was not white, with blond hair and blue eyes. Anyone different from what he believed ideal.

Her eyes watered when she recalled how she, her parents and little brother were taken from their home in the middle of the night to a dark train. I began to cry when she spoke of that night. I couldn't believe her family had been killed because they were different. Because they were considered dirty, too.

Mrs. Rothberg noticed that I was the only one crying and seemed to direct her words to me. She was the first person to let me know that people could be considered wrong and killed for reasons other than their skin color. I felt less alone, but more afraid.

My tears continued after she finished her story, and I bent my head so my hair hung over my face while the other kids left the room. Mr. Nash tapped me on the shoulder. "Why don't you stay here for a while and talk to Mrs. Rothberg." He led me to her and introduced us. We shook hands, and she patted the space on the table next to her.

She held my hand and said nothing, while I touched the blue numbers on her forearm. I didn't have any questions for her. She had told me the fullest story I'd ever heard. We sat together until my tears ran dry. When we stood to leave, she gave me a big hug with her tiny arms.

I thought about her story everyday. I thought of her parents and little brother and how they died because Hitler hated different people. I vowed that if any person spoke a word of hatred in my presence, I'd use my words to make them wish they hadn't. From her story, a seed of purpose birthed within me.

CHAPTER THREE
India

My parents arranged for us to visit India for the three summer months between fifth and sixth grade. They had saved money for a few years to pay for our tickets. It would be my third trip there. Mom planned what she wanted to bring back from India before we even left. "I can't wait to drink real tea." She held up a white Lipton tea bag. "This isn't the same," she said. She'd only recently run out of her stash from our last trip three and a half years prior.

Dad would join us for the last two weeks, because that's all the vacation time he got from his company. I couldn't wait to get a break from him and school, but was sad to leave Skippy.

Mike was concerned that such a long break from swimming would harm my training. I didn't care. Our whole family lived in India and I needed more than my fuzzy memories of their faces from our prior trips. I anticipated that world where I wasn't different because everyone was brown and where I was protected by aunts, uncles and cousins. It wouldn't be just me against Dad.

The long journey to India took a lot out of Raj, who was five at the time. A sensitive stomach, ear infections and sinus pain plagued his early years and worsened on the long plane ride. He later suffered in the extreme heat and humidity of Calcutta and its thick pollution. Mom tended to him for most of the flight, as I learned how to make paper cranes from the Singapore Airlines flight attendants. They were tiny women in kimono-like dresses, open sandals, white socks and perfect make-up. Even in turbulence, they moved up and down the plane's aisles like ballet dancers.

Toward the end of our flight, Mom took her carry-on bag into the restroom and changed from her pants and t-shirt into a sari. When she returned to the seat next to mine, her face shone with fresh make-up, she smelled of her perfume and toothpaste.

"Why'd you change?" I said.

"It's disrespectful for me to see my father in American clothes." I didn't understand why but didn't ask. I was too excited to see my favorite cousin Piu, who is one and a half years older and the youngest child of Mom's oldest sister. I remembered her more clearly than anyone else.

I hadn't seen or spoken to her in years yet didn't question my eagerness. I knew that Piu would come to the airport and hoped that the whole family did. I could already hear their laughter in my ears.

When we descended the rolling staircase onto the runway at Calcutta's Dum Dum Airport, the ferocious, thick, summer heat and the city's musty, distinct smell engulfed me. The damp air felt like a familiar hug that I'd waited years to receive. My nose remembered all of it.

I hurried Mom and Raj to the customs line where Piu's dad, my Boro Mesho, waited for us. His droopy jowls, thick eyebrows and small, neat mustache made him look like a basset hound.

Boro Mesho met us before we cleared customs, because he was a high-ranking officer in the Army and could usher us past the lines to avoid the standard rummage through our bags, which overflowed with make-up, electronic equipment and clothes to give to our family.

Boro Mesho pulled his impressive military credentials from his shirt pocket and said in a gruff, accented English to the customs officials, "It's okay." He held his credentials up for them to read. "They're with me."

The younger men saluted him. One said, "Of course, Colonel, take them through." Mom looked relieved, and I loved the special treatment.

After Boro Mesho shook each of the officers' hands and returned their salutes, he pushed our heavy cart of suitcases out the door toward the dense crowd of brown faces. Everybody was brown. No one was white.

People shouted unrecognizable names and a roar of Bengali enveloped me. Barefoot men in tattered clothing begged to carry our bags. Raj's eyes rounded in fear. I slowed down to shield him from the chaos, searching the rows of faces for the ones I knew.

Mom and Boro Mesho walked behind us and talked in rapid Bengali about the flight, Dad and the weather. When Mom spoke Bengali, her voice sparkled and floated through the hot air. She sounded like she was singing on her tiptoes.

When she spoke English, she halted in unusual places to find the right word, consider her impeccable grammar or for some reason I didn't know.

I first spotted Boro Mama (the oldest of Mom's brothers). He stood by himself with his large, serious eyes and contradicting wide smile. He looked a lot like Mom. Just behind him, my aunts and other two uncles waved in our direction. I pulled Raj with me to rush to them. Boro Mama barked orders at his nearby drivers to carry our luggage to the cars.

"Oh, look, you're so tall," Mejo Mashi (Mom's middle sister) said to me and reached up to pat the top of my head. I was a little over five feet tall and stood eye to eye with her.

"Your hair is shorter," Boro Mashi (Mom's oldest sister) said in Bengali. "Bachu, hey Bachu, why'd you let her cut her hair?" Mom's family nicknamed her Bachu because she was the baby of her two older sisters.

Piu pushed through all of them and pinched my arm, with a giggle. "You're the same," I said and soaked in her deer eyes, round nose and shiny, straight black hair. We stood in a silent bubble and realized, without words, that not one second had passed between our hearts. Despite all the years, we were the same to each other, two parts of one piece.

Everything in America disappeared from my mind. In India, I didn't think about the things that forced me to choose between life and death every night. I didn't need rat poison, a life purpose or a reason to stay. I only needed our family and their love. I left Raj with our mashis and skipped with Piu behind my uncles through the giant airport parking lot to the many cars they brought to take us home.

On the long, bumpy journey to their Jodhpur Park house in South Calcutta, Piu and I smashed together in the back seat holding hands. The car filled with the rustles of Mom's and her sisters' bright, flowered saris. I listened to the rhythm of Bengali spoken by everyone, all at once.

The fumes from the street were hot and dirty, and the city boomed with noise. People pushed and shoved all along the chaotic roads, but none of it felt dangerous from where I sat.

Most of Mom's family lived in a home built by Mom's dad, my Dadu. When we arrived, I counted six stories on the tall, pink concrete structure. The bottom floor housed Dadu's many cars and living areas for the male drivers and the women who worked in his house. Other people, who weren't our family and who I did not meet, rented the middle floors. Mom's brothers, their wives, and Dadu lived in the top two. Her sisters lived with their husbands and children a few minutes away.

Once we got to the house and up to their flats, Mom went to her mom's old room by herself. When I was eight, we had received a telegram informing us of Dida's (Mom's mom) sudden death at fifty-three. She'd been sick with diabetes for most of her life, but no one knew her heart had been so weakened by the illness. I didn't know what diabetes was but remembered being scared of Dida's frailty and of catching whatever illness it was that she had.

No one talked about why Mom went into Dida's room but my aunts and uncles gave each other knowing looks. Mom no longer had a mom, yet I couldn't imagine she needed one. She had left her mom for Dad long ago.

The rest of us sat in the living room where my aunts were enthralled with Raj. "Look at his long, long eyelashes," Boro Mashi said in Bengali that Raj didn't understand.

Boro Mashi was known as the beauty of the family. She had wide, chiseled cheekbones like Native Americans. Her skin was lighter than Mom's and Mejo Mashi's (Mom's middle sister) and her nose and cheeks were sprinkled with freckles. She wore her straight, dark brown hair in a low ponytail or bun. As the oldest of Mom's siblings, she bossed everyone around. I loved everything about her, the stuffy room, the fan turning with little effect overhead, my uncles' round, matching faces and even the pale green lizards that found their way in through the screen-less windows.

Raj looked at me with uncertainty. "She said you have long eyelashes," I said to him in rapid English, which I knew my mashis couldn't understand. "American English" they called it. "It's okay. They're just excited."

My aunts and uncles spoke at once and created a traffic jam of opinions. Although Mom's family spoke in loud voices filled with emotion, they didn't sound like Dad.

One morning, a week into that trip to India, Mom and both of her sisters sat in the living room while Dida slept and Dadu and Mom's brothers got ready to go to one of the movie theaters that they owned and ran. "We're going to your Dad's family's house today to pay our respects," Mom said to me and tapped my leg.

Boro Mashi laughed. "Oh, boy, wait until she sees this."

I'd never heard that said about Dad's family. "Why? What's wrong with them?" Mom made her disapproving clicking noise with her mouth. "Don't say that to her," Mom said to Boro Mashi.

Boro Mashi was unmoved by Mom's disapproval. "Why not? She should know what her daddy's family is like before she meets them again. She's old enough now to understand."

I wasn't that worried, because I figured it would be like Mom's family's house where anything I wanted to eat or drink would be brought to me within minutes, where everyone sat in the living room for hours filled with laughter, where Piu and I devoured movie magazines astounded by the beauty of Indian actresses.

Dad's family's house was a two-hour, hot, bumpy car ride away. His family lived in a town outside of Calcutta called "Barakpur." By the time the car stopped, I was tired and hungry. I looked up to see a gray narrow, fortress-like home and counted three stories, but had no memory of ever being there.

The driver opened the door and Mom got out first. "Watch out," she said and held her hand up. "The sewer's open." I looked down and saw brown, chunky water flowing down the street. Mosquitoes the size of quarters writhed on the surface of the putrid river, wings flailing in a vain attempt to escape their smelly death.

We walked up a few steps and the front door flung open. "Ah, esho, esho," a skinny, old woman said. "Come here, Come here," in Bengali. Her plain, lightcolored sari had yellow food stains along the front and was brown on the bottoms. Her hair hung to her shoulders, in gray, oily strings. Her crooked teeth made her look like a witch from a cartoon.

Mom bent down to touch each one of the old lady's feet and her own head and heart. I had seen her do that to Dadu and Dida, when she first saw them. The old lady touched the top of Mom's head when Mom touched her boney feet. I hoped that no one asked me to do the same thing.

The old lady took my face in her hands and told Mom in Bengali how pretty, tall and fair I was. I wanted to pull away but knew I shouldn't. "This is your Dad's mom, your Tacuma," Mom said. I was horrified.

"Ah, yes, I am your grandma. I am your Daddy's mom." She spoke English in a slow and thoughtful manner. I nodded at her and held onto Mom's green, festive sari.

Dad's mom turned her head and yelled in Bengali to the whole house, "Hey, Ram's daughter is here. Come quick, come quick." Dad was the eldest of the joint family and I, as his eldest, a sight to behold.

Many bare footsteps clomped down the concrete stairs in the center of the house. The bustle in the courtyard outside grew quiet. One by one, Dad's aunts, cousins and uncles, who lived in the same house and next-door, came toward me. They were much taller than Mom's family and none of the women wore the bright saris of my aunts and Mom, but plain, cotton saris like Dad's mom. The men dressed in wrapped cloths like Dadu wore to sleep or after he came home from the office.

Their voices were sharp and harsh, and they cackled at the same time in a Bengali that sounded rougher than Mom and her family. It didn't feel right. "I want to go home." I said and pulled at Mom's arm. "Let's go back to your house."

"We will. Be a big girl." She petted the top of my head. "You have to eat something. It's rude to not eat at their house."

I didn't want to eat anything. Everything looked filthy. "I can't, it's dirty here," I said. "I don't like it. They're too loud like Dad."

"Don't say that. You have to eat something or we can't go." She pushed my back toward the sofa. "Try."

When Dad's mom put a tray of sweets in front of me, I inspected them from afar. The rest of Dad's family stood around us and waited for me to eat.

"Why doesn't she eat?" Dad's mom said in Bengali to Mom. She sounded angry with Mom. I picked up a sweet and nibbled at it so Mom wouldn't get in trouble, but when I saw a long, black hair in my glass of cold, pre-boiled water, I cried and gagged. We left within an hour of our arrival.

Back with Mom's family, I pretended Dad's family's house didn't exist. We only had to see them one more time when Dad joined us. When we did, Dad pretended like he wanted to stay with them, but hurried back to Mom's family with us. Dad used the better food for the reason that we preferred Mom's family. The truth was that no one laughed at Dad's house. Dad didn't speak often of his family. When he did, duty not desire wove between his words.

Calcutta was typically close to 100 degrees and over 95% humidity everyday from May through September. Like most, Mom's family's home didn't have air conditioning. For hours every afternoon and sometimes evenings, the city was plagued by blackouts called "load shedding" due to the over use of electricity. Load shedding could last from one to several hours. Without fans, being indoors provided no relief from the wet, oppressive heat. I didn't mind the weather or the load shedding. In fact, I hardly noticed as the joyful rhythm of each day blended into the next.

Piu, Raj and I slept together in a large bed in our own room. Most of the time, I awoke first from the honks of the cars and the calls of the street vendors, which began at sunrise. I listened to Calcutta's morning music, as it seeped into my bones.

An hour or so later, Raj and Piu awoke, and we talked in bed until we heard the maids begin to make tea and ran into the living room to join them. After the grown-ups drank tea, they took turns in the puja room for their morning prayer and offerings. Since no one entered the puja room without bathing, halfway through morning tea, Boro Mashi shouted to the maids to boil the hot water for baths. There wasn't any running hot water, so we took baths by combining the right amount of boiling, hot water from the kitchen into the bucket of cold, which ran from the faucet in the bathroom. We dipped plastic cups into the buckets and rinsed ourselves.

The prayer offerings of flowers and fruit arrived each morning on the doorstep from a delivery service. The puja room looked like a tiny hallway with a ledge, upon which sat photos of our deceased family members, gurus and figurines and photos of Gods and Goddesses. Nothing else was in that room. I never went in it, because it kind of scared me, and kids didn't do puja.

"Ay, Burro, you go last." Mom said to my youngest uncle in Bengali. "We can't wait all day for your important prayers." He was the youngest of all six children. His nickname means "old man."

My youngest uncle gave a sleepy smile and sipped his tea. Mom's brothers and sisters teased each other constantly yet no one ever got upset.

"I don't know what he does all night, but he sure prays a lot in the morning," Boro Mashi said. Everyone laughed, except Raj who didn't understand. Sometimes I forgot to translate.

After lunch, the adults gave us their pan orders. Pan is a green leaf filled with lots of red, brown and gold flakes. It tastes like the most delicious mixture of candy and sweet spices. It's eaten after meals to help digestion. Raj, Piu and I walked the half a block to the panwala (the person who makes the pan). Raj came with us so that he could pick up his afternoon Cadbury chocolate bar. When I looked up to the balcony from the street, I saw Mom and Boro Mashi watching us.

Pans in their bellies, the adults and Raj napped. Piu and I went to the flat, algae-covered roof of the building. Dadu's building was far taller than most others around. From it, we could see much of south Calcutta. The sky was often heavy with rain clouds, which waited to burst in the thick, humid air. We followed the clouds as they moved over our heads and bathed in the light, which changed from gray to blue to an orangey red.

Tired of the clouds, we went downstairs to try on saris and jewelry. Piu loved to dress me in bright saris and heavy bangles and earrings.

One afternoon, our giggles woke up Boro Mashi, who had been napping next to Mom. "Hey, American Girl, do you know that Indian women are the most beautiful in the world?"

I must have given her a strange look because of my experiences at school. "Bachu, why don't you teach her?" She nudged Mom. "Growing up in America is ruining her."

Mom ignored her.

"Really, you let her do this swimming thing too? You've ruined her light skin." Boro Mashi raised her arched eyebrows in disapproval.

Mom rolled onto her side to face Boro Mashi, throwing her sari over her shoulder to cover her exposed stomach. "She likes it. It doesn't matter if her skin is light or not," Mom said. "No one cares about that there."

Mejo Mashi (Mom's middle sister) must have woken up from her nap in the next room. She stood in the doorway with her thin curly hair pointing in all directions. "Oh, yeah, Bachu, not like your in-laws," Mejo Mashi said to Mom.

Mom didn't speak of her in-laws. "What do you mean, Mashi?" I said to her, excited to get new information.

"Ask your mommy, she'll tell you." Her head bobbed with emphasis toward Mom.

"Oh, gosh, it's so long ago, I don't–" Mom said before I could ask.

"Your mommy fell in love with your daddy. Did you know that?" Mejo Mashi said. Her face grew animated, her words rattled like pellets from a BB gun.

I shook my head and turned to Piu. "Did you know?" She nodded.

"See, American Girl, in India, we have arranged marriages. Not like in America where boys and girls date and their parents think it's okay," Boro Mashi said. "Here, the family chooses the right guy and you marry him, without knowing him." She pointed to Mejo Mashi, who nodded her head in encouragement. "That's what your mashi and I did. But, not Bachu."

Mom had told me that she and Dad fell in love and got married but didn't tell me that it was unusual so I didn't know to ask for the details. The only difference I noticed in my mashis' relationships with their husbands is that they seemed happier than Mom with Dad.

Mejo Mashi held her hand up to Mom. "I'm telling her." Mom waved her hand in surrender.

"When she was sixteen and just about to start her college, she went with me to see the campus." She turned to Mom and they shared something unspoken. "Walking across, we saw Ram [Dad]. Tall, tall with very light skin. He was very handsome, you know?"

I nodded, tired of how many times I heard that Dad was handsome. "Yeah, I know," I said.

"He noticed your mommy and somehow without any of us knowing they started talking and meeting each other, like you would say," Mejo Mashi said. She nodded her head with pride in her ability to tell me a story in English.

"Right out there," Mom said and pointed to the balcony. "We'd plan to meet by Ballygunge Lake in the afternoons after I saw him walk by on the street below."

Her eyes shined with the excitement and mischief of those afternoons. "I'd tell everyone that I was going to get misti (Bengali for sweets) or something and walk with him for hours."

As Mom spoke, she didn't look like she did in America. Her face, mannerisms and voice lost their intensity, knowing authority and quiet worry. She was open and unguarded, like I was. India allowed us both our real selves.

"No one knew? Not even your sisters?" I asked. I couldn't believe she could keep such a big secret.

"No, until I caught her," Mejo Mashi said. "Your Boro Mashi just got married, and I was quite sad." She wrapped the dangling edge of her sari around her waist and used it to dab at the sweat on her upper lip. "It was much quieter in the house so I could notice that your mommy kept leaving in the afternoons."

"Busybody, always in everyone else's business," Mom said. "Nothing else to do."

Mejo Mashi sat on the bed next to her, pushed her and they giggled. "So, anyway, one day when she left, I searched through her things and found a pile of letters in her drawers."

"You looked through Mom's drawers?" I was impressed Mom's sisters ignored her wall of privacy.

"Oh, yeah, but she got in trouble for it," Mom said. The sisters laughed at the memory.

"I read all the letters and realized she'd been seeing your daddy for three years, even while he'd gone to Bombay for a job."

Piu jumped in. "No one does what your Mom did even back then," she said with pride. "She took a big chance. It can be quite shameful to the family."

"I was upset," Mejo Mashi said. "My marriage hadn't been arranged and I was older than her. So, I took the letters to your Dadu."

"What did he do?" I asked. Everyone was scared of Dadu and his temper. When Dida was alive, he bellowed more than he spoke. On this trip, with her gone, he was subdued and kept to himself.

"He said 'You're complaining about your sister, but you've gone through her things. Who's wrong here?'"

"Oh, yes, Bachu's Dadu's favorite," Boro Mashi said with a roll of her big, almond-shaped eyes. Everyone said I was like Boro Mashi, and I saw why. "Mom was his favorite?" I said.

"She's his good luck charm," Boro Mashi said. "See, when she was born, his business deals made lots of money. So, he said it was because of her." Mom never told me that either.

"Well, what happened?" I said.

"Your mommy came home from her walk with your daddy and Dadu called her into his room," Mejo Mashi said. "We waited by the door to hear him yell but nothing happened." She shook her head like she still couldn't believe it.

I looked to Mom to fill in the blanks. "Your Dadu asked me if it was serious, and I told him that it was," Mom said. "I loved your dad very much. It was love at first sight for both of us. Dadu told me that he wouldn't let me marry until I finished college, because I only had one more year left. Then, he said he would meet him."

"Ah, yes, and Ram came very soon after that. All nervous with that friend of his. What was his name?" Mejo Mashi paused, thought for a minute and waved her hand. "Oh, it doesn't matter. So, he came and Dida and Dadu liked him very much."

"What was the problem of the light skin?" I said. They'd forgotten why they started the story.

"Well, your tacuma, your daddy's mom, didn't like the fact that we're not Brahmin and that your mom is not fair-skinned like your dad," Boro Mashi said. I knew I didn't like Dad's mom for a good reason.

"What'd you do, Mom?"

"We got married."

"And? Did Dad's family come to your wedding?"

"No, we had 500 people, not one person from his family," Mom said. I was surprised at how much Dad went through to marry Mom, because he didn't act like it.

"Is that really why you went to America?" Not for better opportunities like she'd said before. Another layer to the story.

"Yeah, yeah, they went there to get away from your daddy's family," Boro Mashi said.

"No, not only, your dad was a very good student and had a chance to go to American graduate schools," Mom said. I didn't believe her.

Something clicked in me when I heard that story, and I understood why Mom didn't take my side against Dad when he yelled at me. She had abandoned everyone she loved for him.

Dad was coming the next week and I wanted to find the person they had described to me. This man that was tall and handsome and so smart that colleges halfway around the world wanted him to attend. A man who loved Mom so much that he would defy and abandon his family for her. He didn't seem anything like the person I knew.

When Dad arrived, he brought a "duty free" bag of scotch for himself and my mom's brothers. The scotch he brought with him told me he would not be the man I'd learned of, but the one I knew. He was less angry with Mom at her family's house, but still teased her. I avoided his attacks by staying connected to Piu at all times.

On Dad's second night in Calcutta, he took the Duty Free bag from his suitcase and got my uncles. Away from Dadu's strict and watchful eyes, they disappeared to the upstairs flat to drink before dinner. In India, no one drank in front of elders.

I liked that Dad had to hide his drinking and wished that Dadu could come live with us. I wished that they all could. When I asked them, they said they didn't want to come. They liked their home, their life and customs. I didn't blame them. I wouldn't have left it either, not even for love.

One afternoon a week before our departure, Piu dressed me up, as usual. I moved my head back and forth to feel a pair of thick, ornate hoop-like earrings in my ears hit my neck. The rain poured so hard it splashed water into the open windows. While Mom and Boro Mashi napped nearby, Mejo Mashi sat up and watched Piu put together my festive ensemble.

"Mala, come here." I sat next to her on the living room couch. "You like those earrings a lot, don't you?"

"We don't have them in America."

"Keep them. They were your Dida's and I know she'd want you to have them."

Her eyes watered with the mention of their mom. "Wear them and remember us here."

"I can't–"

Mom overheard us. "Let her give them to you. It's not nice to refuse a gift."

I wore the earrings all the time, even when I slept. They were heavier than I was used to so I fiddled with them to make sure they were securely planted in my ear. I felt loved and more Indian in them.

I ignored that we had to leave India until we loaded luggage into three of Dadu's cars. Mom's luggage bulged with many bags of loose tealeaves. My memories hung from my ears in gold.

In the backseat next to Piu, I played with my earrings. My stomach flipped as I remembered everything that awaited me. The long bumpy ride over too soon, we checked in our luggage and waited on cracked, plastic benches in the airport for our plane to board. No one said much.

I broke into hysterical cries when the loud PA system announced our flight number. I gripped Piu's hand. "I don't want to go. I hate it there." I never told her how hard it was in America.

"You're strong." She bent her head to look into my eyes. "You can do this. Go." With quiet sobs, I followed Mom onto the plane. I arranged myself away from Dad between Raj and Mom in the middle row of four seats and cried under the veil of my hair.

Mom leaned close to me. "It's okay. You get to go home to swimming and Skippy." The lilt and twinkle had already left her voice.

CHAPTER FOUR
Lessons

The many full-length, well-lit mirrors in our house reflected how much I'd changed over the summer. I hadn't noticed in India that the top of my hair was neither fuzzy nor red from hours a day in chlorine. Longer, it hung like David Cassidy's from "The Partridge Family".

My heavily muscled shoulders, arms and back from swimming had disappeared. My pants didn't fit, because I'd sprouted almost six inches, mostly in my legs. Away from the water, my body thinned and lengthened.

The day after we returned I overheard Dad ask Mom whether my teeth were a bit bucked and too big for my face. "We can't afford braces like rich people," he continued. "They better fix themselves."

Mom told him not to talk like that but sounded concerned, her voice again tight. Far from the rest of our family, we melted into our familiar roles in our American life.

I felt awkward in my weaker, gangly body and dreaded the start of junior high. I didn't know whom I'd hang around. Lisa, my constant companion by the end of the fifth grade, wouldn't be there. Her parents decided to put her in private school. Debbie and Cindy were in seventh grade at the same junior high, but the sixth grade was kept separate from the seventh and eighth. Although other girls were nice, I wasn't close to any of them.

I wanted to take India with me to school on the first day and decided to wear Dida's earrings. Mejo Mashi's teary and generous face flashed in my mind as I clicked the hoops behind my ears. Their thuds against my neck a reminder of love, certainty and safety.

At school, most everyone had on crisp, new Vans tennis shoes, shell necklaces and tight jeans. The girls wore tiny stud earrings of pearls or silver. I missed the flowing fabric of the bright saris of India, my family, the thick rain clouds and Piu's face. I wanted to see her roll her eyes at the Americans, while she mumbled something sarcastic in Bengali under her breath.

Out of place in the starkness of our classroom, I thrust my earrings into the pocket of my baggy Ditto jeans—baggy because tight jeans gave me a stomachache. Alone and unusual again, I wanted to hide.

The same bullies from grade school found me five minutes into the first recess. Ten feet away through the glare of the sun, a few of them turned in unison when one pointed at me. I shivered in anticipation of their aggression.

While I'd lost my physical strength, the bullies had grown bigger. I couldn't as easily flip them over my shoulder or win a hand-bending match. I hurried to the shade beneath the nearest building's eave, unprepared to defend myself.

After that, I inwardly curled into a quiet ball. Thoughts of Piu, the color of the sky and my mashis' laughter vanished. They weren't my reality; survival was.

At home that afternoon, I found the earrings in my pocket when I changed for swimming. The beauty of their engraving and the brightness of the gold glistened in the refuge of my room. I hid them in a drawer under my socks, because they had no place in America.

The mirror above my dresser reflected my disgust. When I looked at my reflection, fury flushed my cheeks. I hated everything and everyone who forced me and my earrings into hiding.

I thought of Mrs. Rothberg, the slaves I'd seen in the movie "Roots," which left me in shock and crying all night in my room. I thought of all the people who suffered because they were brown, black, like the slaves or Jewish, like the millions of people killed in the Holocaust. I imagined the faces of the bullies from that day, murderers from the Holocaust and the slave owners and glared at them in my mirror. Hate filled my eyes, overflowing with a force I'd not felt before. I found a new strength in my body. Not born from hours of swimming, my power was fueled by revenge.

The next morning, I walked onto the morning playground less afraid. I looked at everyone in the eye, instead of at the ground.

I scanned the playground and spotted the same group of boys from the day and years before by the tetherball courts. They paused when they saw me. Hostility oozed from their looks of disdain.

I didn't seek the darkness of the shade and felt the sun's late summer heat warm the top of my head. I willed my eyes to fill with the same power I'd seen in the mirror. Standing firm on a corner of the playground, my glare forced all but one to relent. I knew Steve Krall wouldn't let it go.

My stomach lurched, fearful of the imminent attack. Then, I relaxed a bit when I remembered how I survived at home, without physical strength but with my words. And, I didn't have to follow the same rules that I did with Dad.

After one of my many arguments with him, Mom came into my room. "I know I can't change you, but, just remember, he's your father." She emphasized her next words with a tap on my leg. "Never hit below the belt with family."

I knew what she meant without asking. Many times, I restrained myself from mentioning the unmentionable to Dad, like his drinking, how he treated Mom and his odd family in India. An invisible fence held my truest contempt in a harness. There were no such fences at school.

I watched the four boys approach me and gave myself permission to protect myself by any means. Steve, who hadn't learned to read until fourth grade, reached me first. There was a rumor that he took Ritalin, because the nurse got him from class at the same time every afternoon to give him his medicine.

"Hey, where're your weird earrings? You took 'em off yesterday," Steve stood no more than two feet from me. Up close, I noticed that he'd sprouted a few long hairs above his top lip.

I was surprised by the mention of my sacred jewelry and didn't answer. My blood boiled. My heart raced.

He put his hands on his hips and spread his feet wider. "Why do you go here?" He snorted his disgust. "You're not like us."

Phil, one of his friends, stepped toward me. "Yeah, your skin's gross," he said. His voice cracked mid-sentence. It had started to change.

Encouraged by Phil's participation, Steve took a small step toward me and sniffed the air between us. "You still smell."

My hands clenched, and I rose to my full height of 5'6", an inch or two taller than Steve.

"You're getting uglier too," Steve added. He was right. My body was gangly, and, like Dad said, my teeth were big and buck.

Despite the unwritten rule not to mention Steve's problems, I did. In a steady voice, which hid my shaking knees, I said, "How dare you even speak to me."

He wavered from the spite in my words. I stepped closer to him. "You can't even read correctly and we're in sixth grade." I laughed conceitedly in his face.

"The teacher won't call on you in class, because she's embarrassed for you." I waved my hand to the small crowd that had gathered around us. "We all are."

I couldn't be stopped. "It doesn't matter that you play football now. You're too small to ever play in the NFL and you can't ever go to college."

I noticed his eyes well up with tears and went in for the kill. "You're too stupid and you always will be. You're never going to become anything in your life, Steve. Nothing."

My breath shortened with the excitement of shaming him and the guilt from doing so. Although I'd protected myself, I felt horrible, like I'd doomed him to nothingness. Even though it worked and Steve didn't bother me again, revenge didn't feel good.

I'd never before spoken to Mom about what happened at school with the bullies and their teasing. I didn't want to worry her or embarrass myself. That afternoon, I needed to confess. I sat opposite to her on the sofa where she was reading. "Um, today at school, I kinda said some stuff to Steve Krall, because he was being mean." She lowered her Reader's Digest and peered over it at me. "I was pretty bad."

She didn't flinch or hesitate. "Mala, he's from nothing. Don't let him bother you."

"But, shouldn't I–"

"Shouldn't you what?" She waved her right hand toward the houses below ours. "Don't worry about him." Without an additional word, she lifted the Digest to read.

I was not only stunned but impressed. Her sisters said she didn't care what others thought, but I'd never seen it so clearly.

Different from her, I struggled to not care about what others thought. I walked with uncertainty, feeling ugly and inadequate, with deep marks on my heart from the daily taunting.

I wanted to be like Mom. Contained, quiet and non-reactive, not anxious, angry and fearful like me. I wanted to disregard the judgment of others with an easy wave of my hand.

After that, I spent hours every afternoon with Mom on the family room sofa or following her around before swim practice in anticipation of what she might share.

Her lessons began a couple days later. Her head lifted over the dishwasher, she arranged the dirty utensils, plates and glasses by size and type. "Don't ever need a man."

The clanks of the dishes threatened to drown out her words. I leaned in closer, careful to stay out of her way.

"Make sure you have something to fall back on, a career," she concluded. I accepted her instructions with open arms, even though Mom didn't have a career or job, because she spoke with such certainty, a certainty I didn't have.

More and more, while Raj played in his room or in the garage disassembling small electronic devices, Mom opened the door to her view of the world. Morsels of wisdom packaged in only a few lines spilled from her. With each bit, Mom grew into my teacher, my universe, my only trusted source for the things I didn't understand and my standard for humanity.

The lessons arose out of context, without connection to events in my life or even hers. Although Mom ignored my reality, I embraced what she shared.

Mom promoted a perfect exterior and presentation. No chipped nail polish, "yeah" responses or sleeveless shirts for women. Young girls shouldn't wear dark colors, especially black.

I used Mom's lessons as a sword. I believed I was superior to anyone inarticulate, with a sloppy, outdated appearance. I held my head high with arrogance at school, which felt better than fear and shame.

In the mornings while Dad showered and shaved, Mom laid out his suit, shirt and tie on their bed, placing his shoes and socks on the floor beneath them. His suits were of luxurious fabrics custom-made in India, his shirts pressed and his ties distinct but appropriate. Men needed to be pressed and polished and Mom made certain Dad was.

She coached him, as well. I often overheard her at breakfast giving him pointers for his day, how to speak to his boss with a respect he didn't feel, how to behave with colleagues, how to maneuver through the corporate structure. Dad listened, while he slurped at the milk she'd warmed for him and nodded between bites of his toast with orange marmalade jelly.

Mom made sure Dad was prepared for the outside world, like me. Neither of us questioned how she knew so much.

Despite my learned sense of superiority, the daily tormenting about my ugly, odd appearance created an obsession with beauty. I subscribed to *Vogue* from the fourth grade. Photos of Iman cut out of the magazine papered my bedroom walls. I studied her face in wonderment.

Iman was dark-skinned, different, yet astounding in her beauty. I analyzed the shape of her nose, width of her lips and distance between her eyes to figure out why her features worked and mine didn't. I'd read that the eyes of the most beautiful women were spaced one eye length apart. I studied my face in the mirror, feature by feature, certain my eyes were too close together, my cheekbones undefined.

I sought Mom's opinion on physical beauty one afternoon when I was home early enough from school to watch soap operas with her. Mom watched "All My Children" and "One Life to Live" but not "General Hospital," which she deemed stupid.

I thought the character Cassie on "One Life to Live" was pretty. She was one of very few ethnic-looking women on television. With no Indians on American television, my exaggerated features didn't exist in mainstream culture.

Cassie wasn't white, black or Asian but something unrecognizable. Her hair wasn't straight or curly. Her eyes were slanted but not Asian.

That afternoon, I pointed at Cassie. "Do you think she's pretty?"

"No, no, not really. Her nose is chapta." Bengali for flat.

"I think she is." I was too embarrassed to admit that I wished I looked like her. "She has itty, bitty eyes," Mom said. Certain ugliness to an Indian.

Over our years of afternoons, I questioned her about other women. She only found Jane Kennedy in the Tab commercials beautiful. Mom listed many reasons to find the other women unattractive: thin hair, fat ankles, "no waist" (meaning no curvy shape), thick thighs, skinny lips.

She made only one direct comment about my appearance. I stood next to her in the garage one afternoon, while she folded the hot laundry from the dryer into a square, plastic basket. Without warning, she said to the dryer, not me, "You can't try to be sexy. You either are or you're not." She placed her delicate, elegant hands on the washing machine. "It's in the face, in the eyes."

She leveled her gaze on me and proclaimed, "You are. It's in your face." Her long nails clicked on the metal machine. "It's not something you ever need to worry about."

Stunned by her mention of sex in relation to me, I didn't respond. She closed the subject by looking at the clock in the garage above her head. "Did you have your snack yet? We're leaving in a few minutes for swimming."

It was unlike Mom to mention sex or sexiness in a positive way. She'd said many times that "American girls look cheap, in their low-cut shirts and short shorts with their butts hanging out." She'd shake her head. "Disgusting, their moms should say something to them."

She sometimes pointed her comments at Rosalie, the youngest of Uncle Stan's four daughters. "I can't believe no one says anything. I don't want to see her butt when she walks away." Although I liked Rosalie, I nodded in agreement. I rarely disagreed with Mom.

At eleven, I hadn't begun to think about sex outside of my Danielle Steele, Jackie Collins and Sidney Sheldon novels. Despite that, her odd words of encouragement bolted themselves to me. Mom was the toughest critic I've ever known. If she said so, then so it was.

Puberty prompted change in my body the summer before seventh grade. I realized that one day I'd be a woman, not a girl stuck in a small town of homogenous faces, that I could have a bold and glamorous life. A life that would show the bullying boys that somebody wanted me. In the hours in the pool and in the privacy of my room, I created a picture of how my life would unfold.

The novels I read and Mom's observations weaved together to form my secret, fantastical future. I created a pretend life of wonder, fulfillment and love. I revised the fantasy with each book I read, at least a few every week.

Sometimes, I was a doctor, a mother, a lawyer, a politician or even an actress. What I did didn't matter. The fantasy revolved around that one man who would love me. He looked like Prince Charming from any fairytale, tall, broad-shouldered, with dark hair and greenish, kind eyes.

I lived more in my fantasy than in my reality. I floated through my school days engrossed in my possible future, which ran through my head over and over. I hung on to the happiness I would one day feel.

I needed my fantasy the most at the holiday season. The rest of the year, Dad's presence had diminished. In the advanced group in my swim team, practice was from 5:00 to 7:30 p.m. every weekday and swim meets most weekends. I was rarely home when Dad was. I thought of him more as a burden than a parent.

At the Christmas holidays, school, swimming and Dad's work were abandoned for time with family, which, in our case, felt fake and forced. Even Mom didn't act like herself for those two weeks. She seemed confused by American traditions, uncertain in her role and let Dad take the lead.

We went as a family in the second week of December to choose a tree from a small, urban farm close to Dad's office. Dad budgeted $40 for a tree so it was never over six feet tall and rarely full. Sadness filled my heart as I watched the tree cut from its roots. Its fate to end up forgotten, dry and left as trash on our curb after New Year's Day. I imagined the trees that grew next to it missed it.

Dad hauled the tree from the top of Mom's station wagon into our living room. With no ornaments passed down through generations of our family, we emptied Styrofoam boxes from Sav-On Drug Store filled with plastic balls and tiny lights to decorate the tree, topping it with an angel of no sentiment. Mom looked miserable creating the American picture. Her normally confident face was droopy, distant and disoriented. Her certainty my compass, I was lost.

At that time of year, Mom didn't mention that we weren't American or Christian, that we didn't have numerous family members gathering in celebration. Mom and Dad didn't teach us about the Bengali traditions. Instead, we did as the Americans did.

Mom's birthday was December 24th. I knew she didn't like it associated with Christmas Eve by the downturn of her mouth when it was mentioned. Mom and Dad took us to the Burks every Christmas Eve and Christmas, until the Burks divorced when I was in high school. Christmas Eve dinner was spent at Grandma Margaret's house, who was Aunt Kathy's mom, Christmas day with Uncle Stan and the girls at their house.

Before we left to join the Burks at Grandma Margaret's, Dad, Raj and I gave Mom her birthday gifts. Dad presented Mom his sloppily wrapped box with the eagerness of a child. Mom hid her disappointment over Dad's gift to her. Slippers, a nightgown, a robe or some other object he associated with her that she didn't associate with herself.

Her face changed from hopeful to blank when she opened it, although she said nothing but "Thank you," as if Dad were a child whose efforts she didn't want to stifle. I envied her self-discipline. I tried, but Mom wouldn't make eye contact with me.

Later, when I earned my own money, I gave her long, draping cashmere sweaters with pockets for the tissue she perpetually crumpled in her hands. Each year, her face lit up. "You shouldn't have spent this much money," she said while she slipped into the sweater. It became our tradition.

Uncle Stan, Aunt Kathy, Grandma Margaret and all the girls embraced us with a sliver of pity in their eyes. They graciously amended their holiday to include us, but while copious gifts were exchanged between their family members, Raj, Mom, Dad and I each received a token for which we exclaimed authentic gratitude. Beggars in a foreign land.

There could be no banter and teasing as in India. We needed to remain grateful to be included lest one of us would admit that it was a mistake and a falsity for us to be there.

By the time we left Uncle Stan's house on Christmas evening, I was exhausted from pretending to ignore that we were the brown spots on their white Christmas.

CHAPTER FIVE
Freedom

Despite my disappointment over Mom's annual holiday charade, I revolved around her. She was the fire that kept me warm, the only place I felt at home other than the pool. I spent as much time with her as possible, but that time grew less in high school when swimming and then tennis took up many hours of my day.

I didn't care much about anyone other than Mom, even Lisa, who'd returned to public school in 8th grade. I'd long forgiven Lisa for her comments about my bubble butt, needing her too much. Her friendship insured others' acceptance.

Lisa came from a white, freckled family with the type of mom that other kids called by her first name. Our swim team gathered at Lisa's house. She was the star of the team, the person everyone wanted to be near. I felt lucky to be her closest friend.

Most of the boys on the team had crushes on Lisa, and it was Lisa, not Mom, who taught me how to get boys to approach me. She shared her secret method with me our junior year in high school. "All you have to do is smile," she said at lunch one day.

"Come on, that works for you but wouldn't for me," I said without mention of why. We never mentioned my brown skin and that I remained the only Indian anyone in my high school had ever seen, let alone knew. Though my buckteeth had straightened, I remained unusual. Our tennis team picture provided undeniable evidence. Several shades darker than any other, my un-sunscreened face peered out from the back row in hesitancy and obvious embarrassment.

I flinched when I saw the picture and wished it wouldn't be included in the yearbook.

"Look, try it," Lisa said. "The next time you think a guy's cute, smile like someone said 'cheese.'"

Doubtful, I tried it for the first time at our swim meet a week later. I smiled at the tennis pro who stood overlooking the pool. I was shocked when he came down to the pool and asked me out on a date for that Friday night.

I didn't worry about whether Mom would let me go. I never asked her for permission to do much. Instead, I'd inform her of what the next stage in American life was. "So, go ahead," she'd say.

I was sixteen, and Mom knew that Lisa had been dating since before she turned sixteen. I only saw the tennis pro once, because he was twenty-three years old and, without me knowing it then, Mom told him she would report him to the police, because dating me was not only inappropriate but illegal. I thought he hadn't liked me and learned the truth ten years later.

I didn't date anyone in particular until my senior year of high school. Yaser was Egyptian and had transferred to our high school our sophomore year. He and his two cousins were the only other brown people in our high school. Yaser was a football and track star. He came to my swim meets and found me between classes to pursue me, although I couldn't understand why. I didn't love Yaser. He wasn't the guy in my fantasy, The One. But, with Yaser in my life, the bullies, who grew up to be cops and drug addicts, didn't bother me.

More than Lisa, Yaser validated me to the outside world. Different but paired up gave me my first invisible acceptance certificate.

A few weeks after I started seeing Yaser, Mom began to give me her rules on relationships in short, disconnected bursts. "Do you need gas money?" she asked as I left for swimming one afternoon. "Oh, make sure a man doesn't need your money to pay the mortgage." The absurdity of her delivery made me laugh. It was like she wanted to stuff me full with anything she thought I needed to know.

Dad didn't offer insight. Thrilled any guy wanted me, he tripped over himself to welcome Yaser into our home when he'd come to pick me up for a date, Mom didn't move from her spot on the sofa and allowed Yaser to come to her. She greeted him with a tight smile, a nod and a handshake.

"I don't think your mom likes me," Yaser said one such night.

"Why'd you say that?"

Yaser thought for a minute. "I don't know, it's like she looks right through me, like I'm hiding something."

"Huh, she hasn't said anything to me." It was true. Mom seemed to sense that I wasn't serious about Yaser and hadn't wasted her words on him, only on the general topic.

Yaser and I dated for most of our senior year, which changed my relationship with Lisa. Either I wasn't the same or she didn't like that I had a boyfriend or maybe even something else that I didn't know. We ignored that before practice and in class we didn't laugh until our sides hurt or give each other knowing looks about our inside jokes dozens of times a day and went through the empty motions of friendship. Though we went to lunch together everyday, we barely made eye contact and often sat in a cold silence that I wasn't brave enough to address.

Our relationship disappeared into the place of things unspoken. The distance between us devastated me, which is why I was relieved when early in the spring of my senior year, my French teacher arranged for an exchange program with a high school in Le Mans, France.

I told my parents about it at dinner that Saturday. "I can't pay for it. It sounds expensive," Dad said without knowing the cost.

"I will," Mom said. "With my own money." Mom had started working in customer service at a savings and loan a few months after I got my driver's license and could take myself to swimming. She decided at twelve Raj was old enough to walk home from school with his friends or get a ride with me if I didn't have practice.

"Oh, yeah, you have so much money now," Dad said.

"No, but she should go. It's important," Mom said. I was happy to hear the strength in her voice on the issue of money. Prior to getting a job, she accepted Dad's stringent guidelines about the difference between necessities and luxuries.

"I'll think about it. I just don't know if it's spoiling her," Dad said, but the next day he told me he would pay for it with the stipulation that the $1,500 cost was my graduation present.

I wanted a break from everything. I liked Yaser but hated the tension between Lisa and me. I needed relief from my routine: swim practice by 5:30 a.m., school by 8:00 a.m., tennis practice after school, time with Yaser and a second swim practice from 5:00 p.m. to 7:30 p.m.

Because of swimming, my life had been regimented since I was four years old, but for our trips to India. Everyday, I collapsed into bed by 8:30 p.m., unless I forced myself to stay awake for "Dynasty" on Wednesdays or "Dallas" on Fridays. I rarely went out with Yaser to parties or the movies on the weekends. I was too tired.

I loved France from the moment our plane landed. The clothing, art and architecture awakened a dormant part of me. Art was a luxurious pursuit with no place in our immigrant home. I had no idea how much it fed me.

After a few days in Paris as a group, each student stayed with a French family for two weeks. I went to a small cottage outside of town to live with Sabine and her chic mother, who'd divorced her second husband a few months before I arrived. Sabine was petite, with an easy style of baggy jeans, boxy sweaters and clunky shoes. Her bright blond bob and small blue eyes twinkled in mischief when she lit one of her many cigarettes throughout the day and mentioned her boyfriend's name, Christophe.

The first night in their home, Sabine gathered her friends for a dinner. Her mom sat with us, an abundance of wine and cigarettes consumed. Halfway through her first glass of wine, Sabine asked the table, pointing her cigarette at me, "She's quite beautiful, non?"

My face heated in embarrassment, then astonishment when each of them agreed with sincerity.

For the first time in my life, people outside of my aunts and Piu found me attractive. Even Yaser hadn't said so. I soaked their kind words into my core. My protective shields lowered, I glowed. I unilaterally placed my relationship with Yaser on hiatus and welcomed Jacques as my French boyfriend. He looked like Robert Downey Jr., with big brown doe eyes and thick dark brown hair.

Sabine's friends used my short stay as a reason not to attend class. We hung out at cafes and shopped all day. While everyone else smoked, I remembered my upcoming regional high school championships in both swimming and tennis. Yet, for once, the smell of the smoke didn't bother me.

Like everyone else, Jacques and I made out in the cafes. There were neither the hang-ups as in America nor the level of social propriety required by Mom. Smoking, drinking wine during the day and making out in public were embraced. France felt more like home than even India.

A few nights before I was to return home, Sabine said, "You can't leave France without trying a Martini Rouge. It wouldn't be right." In a small, empty bar, we talked about clothes, her boyfriend and Jacques. When our martinis arrived, Sabine lit another cigarette. She smoked Marlboro Reds, like Dad had until my pestering provoked him to quit years earlier.

"May I?" I held out my left hand, fingers pointed without a thought.

"Bien sur, take one." She offered her pack with its open paper lid. "You don't smoke, non?"

"No, I don't, I think, but I want one, only with my martini." I took a cigarette from the red and white cardboard box and held it like it had always been between the tips of my middle and forefingers. Its delicacy enticed me. So light, it felt like air in a stick.

As Sabine leaned forward with a lit match, I inhaled as I'd watched so many times in the prior two weeks, my eyes closed in concentration. The fire met the tobacco with soft pops. Smoke entered my windpipe in a warm, smooth wave. A gentle heat filled my lungs, like an embrace.

I didn't cough or choke on the hot, foreign air. Instead, an unknown dark hole inside me soothed itself. I loved each inhale of every cigarette I smoked that night, the next day and every day but few since.

I envisioned smoking at the breakfast table with Mom and Dad over the morning paper. When Mom called the night before I left, I shared my newfound love.

She slammed the door on my vision. "If you're still smoking, don't bother coming home," she said and hung up. Her harshness surprised me, especially over something that seemed small. I couldn't recall a time she'd been as mean. I smoked what I thought to be my last cigarette after we spoke.

I fell apart more leaving France than I did leaving Piu. I always knew that I would see Piu again. When I left France, I knew that I would never again experience such a perfect few weeks but promised myself to go back as soon as I could.

I started smoking again a few days after I returned. I hid my packs of Marlboro Reds in my purse and sneaked home between classes to smoke in our backyard, burying the butts in the bushes. Shrouded again, I wanted to escape.

France changed me. I found parts of me, unformed and unwelcome in Covina or under Mom's watchful eye. I liked cigarettes, vodka, the absence of hours in the pool. I was done with Covina, the people there, my schedule, swimming, Lisa's distance and Yaser, who broke up with me right before graduation. I couldn't wait to get to UCLA to which I had gained early admission.

On the first day of freshman orientation, a 6'4" boy with cupid-like, curly brown hair, puffy lips and sea foam green eyes spotted me through an open door to a dorm room where a group of us had gathered. Without a word to anyone or an invitation, he came in and grabbed my hands, flipping them over and back again. "You have the most beautiful hands I've ever seen," he said.

I still hated my dark, long hands and jerked them away. "Very funny," I retorted in defense. My stomach sank in fear that UCLA would bring the same ridicule as Covina.

He kneeled down, still without a glance at anyone else. "You don't know, do you?"

I gave him a puzzled look.

"They really are beautiful." He left the room without another word. The few people in the room looked at me, but I shrugged my shoulders to dismiss the whole episode.

After a proper introduction a few hours later, Chris and I spent the couple days of orientation together in a big group of new friends. I liked that even though he was Jewish his father named him Christopher to spite his mother-in-law. Chris made me laugh with his stories of his boarding school, his ski team and his warring parents.

I didn't feel giddy with him, like I imagined I would with the guy in my fantasy. Yet, after the thin swimmers I'd been around my whole life, I loved his enormity. His legs were as big as trees from skiing his whole life. I liked the way his thick eyelashes curled almost to his eyebrows. His East Coast, blue-blood schooling resulted in gentle manners with snotty critiques of others, so much like Mom's. I was comfortable with Chris.

We pledged our respective sorority and fraternity and spent most afternoons together on one of his friend's motorcycles. Chris drove us around Los Angeles, east on Sunset Boulevard, through the hills of Bel Air, down the streets of Beverly Hills. Snuggled into his back, I rejoiced in the city of Los Angeles, the motorcycle, the freedom from Mom and swimming and having enough energy to stay awake until early morning. I was no longer in a constant state of exhaustion.

A month or so later, Chris and I became lovers. Because the first time he entered me felt like my insides caught fire, I considered the second time my first.

The night after the painful one, we kissed, touched and giggled in our familiar way in his dorm room bed.

When Chris placed himself above me, I froze, fearing the pain. "Are you going to do it again?" I wanted him to.

His bear paw of a hand smoothed the hair off my forehead. "If it's okay with you."

"Yeah, it's okay, but wait." I pushed him a little to see his face, comforted by the familiar curl of his lashes. "I just hope it doesn't hurt again."

"It won't. I promise." I believed him, because I knew he'd been having sex since he turned fourteen. His first lover was a friend of his mother's.

I braced myself a little. But, it was different. When he entered my body and moved against me, my body filled with the sensation I had only felt upon my first inhale of a cigarette, except it was more intense and ran from my toes to the top of my head.

"Is this what it feels like?" My voice caught from pleasure. He kissed me with his soft lips. "Yes."

I closed my eyes again and found the harmony between our bodies. The physicality of our expression, the wordless communication of our two beings felt like a sacred ritual or worship of a God I'd not known.

I enjoyed sex with Chris so much that I tried it with a few more guys. I gravitated toward athletes but also found comfort in the kindness of Jewish boys. I no longer felt awkward and ugly as I had most of my life but powerful, desired and alive.

I hadn't discussed my new sexual experiences with anyone and didn't realize that any protocol existed. Like the cigarettes and vodka, I didn't want to disappoint Mom or hear her harsh disapproval. She was raised in a puritanical, Indian, old world where a momentary kiss with closed mouths was considered provocative. If she didn't like the suggestive way in which Rosalie wore short shorts, she would be repulsed by the fact that I was naked with a boy I wouldn't marry. Without Mom's input, I made my own rules.

Sex replaced swimming in my life. In the water, I'd felt a type of wholeness that I felt during sex. I quit swimming when I arrived at UCLA, because I could never make the Olympics and would have to fight to earn and keep a spot on UCLA's team. I didn't want to fight for anything. I wanted to enjoy my life without regiment. Sex, but not my lovers, filled the void of the spiritual and physical satisfaction I got from swimming.

I didn't want a boyfriend. After a lifetime of feeling separate and different, I wanted to enjoy myself while I waited for the man in my fantasy to find me. I ignored academics, figuring school had always worked itself out. I was uninterested in anything other than the awakening of the undisciplined, hedonistic me I'd never known.

I talked to Mom many times everyday about everything other than sex, cigarettes and vodka. I talked to my sorority friends a little about sex and everything else we shared as we took our fledgling independent life steps. Even on a long leash away from her, Mom was still my anchor. I could try anything, be anywhere, live freely, because she was there, a phone call away.

I could call her from any place, because she got an "800" number when I went away to college. I spent a lot of time talking to her at Lu Valle, an on-campus café, which hid many private, pay phones by the restrooms in the back. Surrounded by roommates, privacy was sacred.

A few weeks after my first quarter at UCLA, I discovered that college wasn't like high school, that I couldn't skip class and ignore the books. I held back tears behind dark sunglasses and focused on the row of pay phones a block away from where I stood.

I dialed Mom's number with one jittering hand and held a lit cigarette in the other. "Hey, Mom." I started to cry when she answered.

"What's wrong? What happened?" She was used to me calling her with anxious worry but not full-blown tears as an introduction.

"I just found out that I'm on academic probation, I can't initiate into the sorority until I'm not." I dropped my backpack on the ground.

"What do you mean academic probation?"

I turned my head away from the girl on the phone next to me. "My G.P.A. first quarter was a 1.8"

"Are you kidding?" This went far beyond a disappointing surprise to her.

"No, I'm not kidding." Angry in the face of her disappointment, I lashed out. "Why would I joke about that?"

"Did you know it was going to be so low? How could you let that happen?"

"I don't know." I dropped my cigarette and crushed it into the ground with my black cowboy boot. "I told you that I'm not as smart as everyone thinks."

"That's not true. You are." It was confusing, because I didn't feel smart. I felt like there was so much I didn't understand.

"Then why am I on academic probation?" Since I got to UCLA, I blamed her when things went wrong, even as I asked her for help.

"You're going to try harder next quarter, get off of this probation, do better."

"You think I can?" My anger waned with her encouragement.

"I'm not telling your dad about this." Having gotten me under quick control, she worried about Dad. "He'd be so upset."

"What do I do?"

"You study." She stated her words like an edict, too late for an instruction. "You know I don't know how." I never had to study. I didn't know how to feign interest in what I found useless. I felt lazy and stupid for not knowing how.

"You'll figure it out. You have to."

"I guess. But, it's embarrassing." I didn't mean just the probation but not knowing how to function like everyone else.

"I bet. It should be." She sighed. "Are there other girls who are on it from your sorority too?" She measured the amount of shame I should feel.

"Yeah, some, I think." The pay phones had emptied around me.

"Well, you have to fix it. How are you going to get into law school like this?"

"I'm not worried about that. I just want to stay in my sorority. I like it." She didn't know how much I liked my life, Thursday night parties, weekends of folly.

"You will. I have faith in you. You can do anything when you try."

"You really think so, Mom? Or, do you just say that?" Every part of my life seemed in conflict with the other.

"No, haven't I told you that your whole life?"

"Yeah, you have."

"Well, I'm not a liar and I've never been wrong with you."

"No, you haven't."

"Okay, then. Stay calm, take it a day at a time."

"I will." I pulled my grades up by next quarter by attending more classes and skipping "All My Children" a couple of times a week. I wasn't a straight-A student like the other girls in my sorority but I'd figured out how to get decent grades despite my complete inability to read and comprehend textbooks.

I assumed that Chris understood that we weren't in a committed relationship. One cold morning in January, he saw me leave another guy's apartment and looked away, but not before I saw his surprise and hurt.

I ran to the scooter Mom and Dad bought me for my eighteenth birthday, after Mom had said, "I have to trust I've raised you well enough not to be stupid." Back to my apartment in less than a few minutes, I called Chris. "What's up? I know you just saw me. You didn't wave or say anything."

"Why'd you think?" The growl in his voice was unfamiliar. "Come on, don't be dumb, we've been together for months, since school started."

"Yeah, but, you know we weren't together, together." A rush of nervousness flooded my body. "You talked about other girls all the time."

"That's because you talked about guys." He was mad.

"Please, don't be upset with me." I liked him a lot, as a person, my friend and lover. "You know I wouldn't want to hurt you. I just–"

"Hey, let's forget this. Let's not talk for a while and stop whatever it is that we do when you're not doing it with someone else."

Tears stung my eyes. "Wow, that's kinda mean, don't you think? We're friends."

I paced my apartment, stretching the phone cord to the front door so I could smoke. "You never said you wanted a commitment."

He lost his temper. "That's it. I'm hanging up and, when I see you on campus, I'm ignoring you, okay?" The phone went dead in my hand.

I was confused and hurt. I wished that I could ask Mom if I handled it correctly but couldn't. I missed him already and thought he'd come around in a few days. He didn't.

Prior to the start of my senior year, I realized I had to do well on the LSAT. I wanted to go to law school, because I didn't want to get a job and needed to keep to the plan, Mom's and, thus, mine. My grades were higher but not good enough to gain entrance to a decent law school without a boost from a high LSAT score. I signed up for a class in preparation for it.

The class met a couple evenings a week at a prep school in Beverly Hills. At the first class, I felt intimidated by the haughty stares of a Japanese woman with a thick, swinging bob of hair. I had just cut my waist-length curls in a similar style. I sat up straight and scowled back at her.

The class took a break mid-way. I went outside to smoke. Cigarette in hand, Tiffany followed and said, "You smoke?" She lit hers with a tiny pink lighter and held it to my cigarette. "I'm surprised."

She was no taller than 5'2" but seemed 6'. "Why's that surprising?" I held my ground.

She flipped her bob and lit her own cigarette. "You don't look like you would." She stood next to me for a few moments, looking me up and down. I didn't want to fold under her scrutiny by talking first.

"So, what do you do?" she finally said.

"I go to UCLA," I said maintaining our staring contest. "Sorority?" she asked in a challenging tone.

I nodded. "Which one?"

"D.G."

A giant, bright smile of approval erupted on her face. "They're good there. I was a Kappa at 'SC." Her whole body relaxed.

Because I met her standards, she opened up and told me she was thinking of changing careers from advertising to law. She was three years older than me, had recently moved out of her boyfriend's and lived with her parents, a short distance from my sorority house.

I liked her, her bratty attitude, sharp mind and directness. Like Mom, she oozed her ancient culture by a slight tilt of her head. I trusted her by the end of our first cigarette together.

CHAPTER SIX
Love

I'd worked through college in various jobs, from nanny to a newborn, holiday sweater-folder at Bullock's in Westwood to a personal assistant for an attorney, which I started the last quarter of my junior year and continued through the end of college. My parents paid for college, but I liked extra money to do what I wanted.

The first months of Tiff's and my new friendship were spent in parts of Los Angeles I'd not seen. Hip restaurants and off-campus bars weren't accessible by my scooter.

One night, we ventured to Le Dome, a new restaurant on Sunset Boulevard in West Hollywood. I was intimidated by the glamour of it as soon as we pulled into the valet. Actors I recognized but could not name crowded the entrance. Women in tall, skinny heels and tiny black dresses vied for their attention. Nights out around UCLA were very different. No one wore anything but jeans.

Tiff pushed through the front door to the bar without hesitation. I followed behind her like a football running back.

Somehow, Tiff found two seats in the bar area and surveyed the scene. "Hm, it's alright," she said. "I would've thought there'd be a lot more cute guys." Her red-lipsticked mouth turned downward. "I mean, these old ones are gross."

I noticed that more than a few gray-haired men sat beside Barbie-like younger women, who looked bored, if not lost. Outside the bubble of UCLA, it was my first introduction to the underbelly of life in Los Angeles.

"Dude, let's not waste our mascara," Tiff said. "I'm gonna find someone interesting in this place." Looking around again, Tiff saw a passable guy and invited him over with a toss of her shiny hair. He was at her side in less than ten seconds.

Upon his arrival, I understood that life off the UCLA campus might be more glamorous, but it would never be filled with as many handsome, athletic, sexy guys gathered together in one place again. I sighed in sadness and watched Tiff flirt.

Less than an hour later when the guy left to get more drinks, Tiff whispered, "Dude, we gotta get out here. He's weird." She looked to the back of the restaurant and furtively pointed. "There, let's sneak out the back door." She grabbed our purses off our chairs before I understood what she meant. "Come on!"

Tiff pulled my arm. I crouched down behind her, and we scooted out the back door, giggling into our hands. Although an unnecessarily dramatic exit, Tiff made it more fun than a simple night out.

Despite glimpses of life outside of UCLA, I was uneasy about the end of my college years. I enjoyed a good life in the sorority house, where the cook provided meals at specific times, tons of friends were available any time to share whimsical stories, watch soap operas or "Beverly Hills 90210," Mom an 800 number away and Tiff to shuttle me to unknown places and return me to my cocoon.

Santa Ana winds blew for weeks that October, bringing a sensual heat that illuminated the already-red glow of our campus. In the renewed summer, I rode my scooter in shorts and a t-shirt into the office one morning to get my day's errands from my boss.

I waited in the hallway for her to conclude a meeting and saw Ben at his desk in his office. My boss told me he'd been recently hired as an associate pending his bar passage. Ben stared at me with a big, warm face.

I felt self-conscious in my inappropriate office wear but gave a slight wave of my hand. He responded with a beautiful, wide smile filled with perfect teeth and looked back down at his desk. It was as if the warm wind from outside filled the hallway.

Over the next two months, every time I went to the office, I paused by his office door and waved with a smile. Without reason, I felt we'd be together for a long time, though he wasn't the man I'd clung to in my fantasy.

I mentioned Ben to Mom in one of our calls, unsure if I should initiate more than just the exchange of waves and smiles. "No, no, let him make the first move," she said.

He did at the firm's afternoon holiday party. I stood by an assortment of cookies, waiting for him to approach me. He leaned against a doorframe and introduced himself with a firm shake of my hand. When he spoke, I notice that dimples dented his full cheeks. His delicate sage green eyes seemed out of place in his bulk. I'd always liked bigger guys and didn't notice that he was over 250 pounds until my roommate told me weeks later. I didn't care once she did.

I learned he was four years and one day older than me. Like Lisa, his birthday fell the day before mine. We were both left-handed.

"I'm skiing out of town for New Year's, but I'd love to have dinner or something after that," he said without nervousness.

I accepted with poorly hidden excitement. I'd never waited months for a guy to ask me on a date.

We saw each other several times in the first week following our Monday night dinner and movie date. After which, we kissed passionately for hours on the sofa in the living room of my sorority house. We made love a few dates later, which is why after only our first week of dating, I asked him for exclusivity.

That Saturday after breakfast next to an ATM machine in Brentwood, I said, "We're not dating anyone else, right?"

He laughed in nervousness. "We just started dating a week ago. I'm not sure." His words contrasted the excitement in his face and failed to deter my feelings.

"Come on, you know we're gonna be together." I threw my arms around him. "So, let's just say it now."

Ben huddled me into his broad body, our relationship sealed.

Ben was my first love. Physical affection and warmth our greatest strength, we shared laughter, Saturday hikes and weekends away. During our first months together, I found out that my LSAT score had been high enough to gain admission to Pepperdine Law School, which was my first choice because of its location.

Mom had few comments about my new relationship, no doubt sensing I was happy by how much less I called her. She encouraged me to see him. Everybody else felt differently.

I planned a dinner for Tiff to meet Ben only a few weeks into our relationship. Strained conversation and Ben's comment that he had to pay the bill "or Mala will be upset" led Tiff to proclaim en route to the valet within Ben's earshot, "He's crass, a loser. Dump him." Ben didn't mention Tiff's comment on the way back to his house, where I slept every night.

He said nothing because, unbeknownst to me, his world didn't approve of me either. Over the first few months, when we met his friends for drinks or dinner, they were cordial but distant, rarely asking me questions and not looking me in the eye if they did.

I felt his family's dislike of me before I understood why. I couldn't have predicted how protective his family was of being Jewish. My family didn't close the same doors.

I endured several odd encounters with his family in the first year we dated. At a party his parents threw for Ben for passing the bar and a few of the dinners at his sister's house, his mom and sister watched me with smirks and knowing glances to each other. I tried to engage both of them in conversation but was met by walls of one-word answers and nervous twitches of their faces or bodies, like they didn't want to be near me.

Their disdain was subtle but stinging.

At his apartment after a strained Sunday family dinner, I'd had enough. "Why are your parents so mean to me? Your sister too."

"It's weird for them." Ben looked more uncomfortable than I'd ever seen him. His discomfort made my stomach drop. When he released my hand that he was holding, I panicked. "You know they expect me to marry a Jewish girl."

"No, I don't know." I felt spun around by a hard slap. "What're you saying?"

"Look, I love you a lot." His eyes welled with tears. "But, I can't. . . I'm not sure. . . "

"Not sure of what?" Unhidden rage laced my words. I hadn't felt that way since Covina. "We've been together for almost a year, everyday, every night and now you're telling me that the weird vibe I pick up from your friends and family is discrimination?" I'd rationalized his family's odd behavior as social awkwardness and his friends' as unfounded arrogance. I shook from his words. It wasn't fair.

He changed from uncomfortable to indignant. "It's not that simple, it's not discrimination to them."

"That doesn't make sense," I said, not wanting to accept his truth.

"Look, you're far from what they want for me. You're even Indian, not white." His eyes turned a darker green. "So different from what's right to them."

His words hit an unhealed wound. I burst into tears. Unpracticed in self-defense, I found my footing quickly. I noticed his multiple chins and stomach hanging over his pants for the first time and pointedly stared at each of them with pause for effect. "Yeah, I'm sure my parents are fucking thrilled I found you." That meanness made my stomach sink deeper.

My unkind jab at him didn't trigger more of his anger. "Look, don't cry. I love you. I just owe my parents a lot." He put his arm around me. "It'll work out somehow."

But, it didn't.

A week prior to my first set of law school finals and two days after Dadu (Mom's dad) passed away, Ben broke up with me. "I need some time to think, just a little time. I don't know a month or—"

"What do you mean you need some time?" I hadn't yet begun studying for my first final and looked up from a pile of other people's outlines of our Contracts class.

"I'm just confused." The heap of his shoulders slumped with a weight I couldn't know. "My family's not close like you and your mom. We share being Jewish. You and your mom share each other."

"What're you talking about?"

"In the way she babies you yet treats you like an adult at the same time, like she gets that she's the mom, but that you're her equal. There's respect between you before obligation. You finish each other's sentences." He crumpled some more. "My parents aren't like that, the way we are isn't like that."

He shook his head. As he did, his heart closed to me. "They've given me everything I could ever want. I owe it to them to give them what's important to them."

Ben didn't call me for three weeks, not even to wish me luck on my first set of finals, which counted for 100% of my grades. During those weeks, I wandered around shivering cold no matter the temperature, with a pack of cigarettes clutched in my hand. I passed my classes with marginal scores but didn't care.

I hadn't slept without Ben in almost a year. I felt sick. I drove to Mom's house by 6:30 Saturday mornings to get a hug and hang out with her. She let me cry with my head in her soft lap. "I know he loves you. You've just got to give him time to figure this out," she said, patting my back like she did Raj's when he was little.

Tiff didn't agree with Mom. For moral support, she met me for a late-night French onion soup at the Hamburger Hamlet in Brentwood, where we could smoke indoors on the couches in the back. "He's a pussy. You can do so much better than him," she said, exhaling smoke in disgust.

"But, I don't want better." I howled. "I love him." Even though he wasn't anything like the man in my fantasies, I had grown to love him with my whole heart. I didn't need my fantasy; I needed Ben.

By the end of the third week without a word from him, I knocked on his door. "I can't be without you," I said.

He opened his arms to me. I nestled into him without the courage to ask if he was still confused.

After our third breakup during my winter finals of my last year in law school, Mom lost her patience with Ben. "Why do you let him do this to you every year? Is he trying to sabotage you? Doing this during finals all the time." I heard her bracelets over the phone line. She must've been waving her arm. "You've got to make him stop," Mom said.

"I don't let him do anything. He just does it," I said in defense. "You think I like this?" I felt weak, because I stayed with him, but my life didn't feel right when he wasn't in it.

In that call, Mom suggested we consult a rabbi. I passed her idea on to Ben in an unsolicited visit to him after two weeks of silence from him. "It can't hurt," he said.

Raw from all the ups and downs, filled with resentment from the seesaw of acceptance and rejection and tired of his confusion, I wasn't as certain and joyous as I had been about us.

Ben picked me up the following Sunday afternoon to take us to the Stephen S. Wise Temple. I waited outside my apartment with a teaspoon of found hope. Maybe the rabbi could help us.

"You ready to do this?" he said when I got in his car.

"Yeah, I want to hear what he says." I looked for some enthusiasm from him. Instead, his dimples were missing, his full, wide lips were tight and thin. "You nervous or what?" I asked.

"No, I mean, it's kinda weird, but–"

"Why's it weird?" The hope in my heart evaporated from his reticence. "God, Ben, I–"

"Let's not fight on the way there."

"I don't want to fight at all. You're the one who can't stop breaking up with me every year." I stared out the window to my right but saw nothing. Tears burned behind my eyelids but didn't fall.

"What more do you want from me?" I said without expecting an answer. He knew that I didn't mind if our kids were raised Jewish. Proud of my Hindu heritage, I wouldn't convert.

Even though strained, we held hands when we walked into the rabbi's office at the imposing temple on the hill between the Westside and the Valley. The rabbi spoke to us about the difficulty of inter-faith marriages. He informed me that children were only Jewish if born from a Jewish mother.

He lectured us on the importance of Jews creating Jewish children, because so many Jews were murdered in the Holocaust. He recited the percentage of the already small Jewish population lost fifty years prior.

I nodded but said nothing. I couldn't challenge the Holocaust.

"But, with enough love and commitment, inter-faith marriage can work," the rabbi concluded.

The whole experience was grim and didn't ease Ben's confusion, which continued. He alternately acted passionately in love then distant, cold and closed. It changed by the hour. A short time after our visit with the rabbi, his confusion destroyed the purity of love I'd felt for him.

A few months away from graduation, I panicked about the impending California Bar Exam. Although I was getting through law school, like UCLA with mostly Bs and a few Cs, I never learned to study. The bar was different. More than half the people that took it failed. It scared me. The anxiety I'd been able to manage most of my life grew. More days than not, when I thought about the bar, I couldn't breathe and would freeze in place.

I cut my hair short, one inch in length at its longest point. Mom pursed her lips when she saw it. "Why do you do things like that?" she asked. In Bengali, Dad told Mom in front of me that I looked like an Indian widow.

It was my way of feeling some control over the vast expanse of unknown ahead of me. I knew Ben and I would be over soon. I had to take the bar but couldn't fathom how I'd pass it.

One Saturday morning around that time, I called Mom but Dad answered. "Before I give the phone to your Mom, how're you doing?" he said.

"Um, I'm okay." Sometimes Dad wanted to feel like a dad. "Just freaked out about the bar."

"What do you mean 'freaked out'?"

I fiddled with the unlit cigarette between my fingers and wondered whether to tell him the truth. "Well, I've got a lot of anxiety."

"How? When?" He was genuinely concerned.

"Most of the time." I didn't want to admit to him or myself how often. "No, I mean, mostly when I think about the bar. I'm not good at—"

"Do you have panic attacks?"

I was surprised that Dad knew what one was, that he and I were talking about it. "No, not really." Hiding the truth wouldn't help. "Um, maybe, I think so."

"Okay, listen, I do too. I've been seeing a therapist to help me with it." Neither hesitation nor shame shadowed his voice. "Let me ask him for the name of someone you can see, close by you."

"Sure, I'd like, I mean, I need some help." Silent tears slid down my face with my admission.

"Good, that's why your Mom and I are here. To help. And, if we can't we'll find someone who can." Dad had never said that to me.

"I appreciate it." I didn't want him to know that I was shaking from relief. "I'll pay for it until you take the bar."

Stunned, I said good-bye without talking to Mom. It was almost harder when Dad was nice.

I was curious about therapy and knew that I sat on a large mound of experience that caused me to cry disproportionate tears to mundane life events. Ben and Mom coddled me through many of my breakdowns, but neither of them could sit with me while I took the bar.

Around that same time, my changed feelings for Ben began to show. His dream was to buy a big house in the Pacific Palisades or Rustic Canyon, make partner at his law firm and have children. It was a beautiful dream, but every time he mentioned looking for homes at Sunday open houses, sobs choked me, forcing my head between my knees to breathe.

He stopped the car one night after a movie. "You don't love me anymore, do you?" Giant tears that left his eyes red around the sage green. He had recently resolved his Jewish dilemma by accepting that our children would be raised Jewish.

"Start the car, Ben. Let's just go to sleep." I wasn't ready to end it with him and still thought I may even marry him. Although I didn't love or trust him anymore, I couldn't imagine life without him.

The morning I broke up with Ben started with me trying to connect with him. "You know, I'm getting kinda nervous about the bar. I talked to my Dad about it, he's going to find a therapist for me to talk to."

"You don't study. It's that simple." He turned up the volume of the Irish alternative rock he loved, because he knew I hated it and loud music in the morning. "You'll never pass the bar the first time if you don't study," he said over the music.

"Will you please turn it down?" Ben wanted me to doubt myself about the bar. Maybe Mom was right that he did want to sabotage me.

"I'll play it as loud as I want. It's my car." He turned the volume higher. Although angry, I said nothing for the remainder of the drive to my apartment.

I'd never been so angry at him that I didn't want to yell or scream. I was quiet angry.

When I got out of his car, I finally spoke. "You know what, Ben?" His indignant eyes met mine. "It's your fucking life and I suggest you do whatever you want with it. I'm done." I slammed the door. That was it. For me.

Ben believed my declaration resulted from my moods or over-sensitivity but learned over the next several months, when he showed up on my doorstep with various gifts, morning and night, that I meant it. I didn't want to go back to us.

The week after our official breakup, I got a bulldog puppy and no longer needed Ben for safety or cuddling. But, Ben decided he needed me forever.

One afternoon at my parents' house, I was home doing laundry, while Dad played with Boo, my bulldog in the backyard. "Do you know that Ben called your Dad and me, separately?" Mom said to me in the garage.

"Really? Why?" I didn't even know Ben had their phone number.

Mom put down my towels, pushing the bag of laundry away from us. "He wants to marry you."

I laughed. "Oh, God. Sure he does." I remembered the breakups, his confusion, his mood swings. "What about his parents?"

"What do you want us to tell him the next time he calls?" Her tone told me she was serious.

"What do you really think about him, Mom? You've never totally said."

She took a deep breath. "He'll never have the guts to stand up to his family." We didn't reference the fact that she knew a similar story, because Dad left his family for her.

She continued despite my silence. "You can't trust a man who can't stand up to his family. Trust makes a marriage. Without trust, there's no real love." This time, I only half-listened to Mom. Not because I didn't respect her or couldn't understand her relationship with Dad and how she could trust a man who diminished her.

My relationship with Ben taught me a lesson opposite to Mom's view: Love wasn't enough to hold a relationship together. Love was a fantasy.

I had trusted and loved Ben, but life's complexities outweighed and destroyed that love. I missed Ben over the next several months and years. Although many nights I wanted to sleep on his front step just to be near him, I never again knocked on his door and begged him to take me back.

PART TWO

Cremation

CHAPTER SEVEN
Divergence

Life without Ben, beyond my complacent box invigorated me with hope. I felt purposeful, alive and, despite my short elf-like haircut, more feminine than ever. After graduation from law school, I studied for the bar a couple hours a day throughout the summer. Boo sat on my lap as I did one or two practice multiple choice tests every afternoon. I'd heard that fish was brain food and made plans most nights to meet a friend for sushi.

The practice tests, Mom's and my prayers and the fish created a miracle. I passed the bar on the first try. Relief was short-lived; I needed a job fast. My bar study student loans were spent and all of my loans were due for payment, rent needed to be paid, food eaten.

An acquaintance in law school told me that a sole practitioner in Century City was hiring an associate and sent him my resume. Jerry called the day he received it. We met for my interview at a restaurant in the bottom of his office building. Naïve and hopeful, I waited for him by the hostess.

Awkward on the phone, I recognized Jerry by the sideways tilt of his walk and rumpled suit. He shook my hand with his soft, sweaty one, waving us to a booth. Before ordering lunch or any other pleasantries, Jerry admitted that in his sixteen-year career he'd only handled transactions, never litigating a case.

"My biggest client wants to give me a chance at a large litigation matter," he said. His left eye winked continuously in an exaggerated twitch as he spoke. At first, it distracted me.

"That's great," I said, though I didn't wholly understand what litigation was. "Look, I bill 80% of my time to this client. They take care of my family."

The pupils in his light blue eyes shrank to pinpoints. "If they want me to handle this case for them, I will. But, I need help, someone that can learn how to litigate." My head nodded in understanding. I needed to feed Boo and me, too.

He took a closer look at me. "You seem bright," he said. "Are you up to handling something this important right away?"

Without hesitation, I said, "It's why I became a lawyer, to practice law. Not to read cases in law school and sit in a back room researching for the rest of my life." Desperation made me confident and accepting. My hope of practicing civil rights law had long faded as my student loans mounted to over $100,000. Those jobs and the public defender's office didn't pay much.

"Well, then, let's not waste either of our time, the job's yours if you want it."

I accepted, agreeing to start the next day. It would be the first time in my life that I supported myself without the help of my parents or student loans. Even though the pay was about $15,000 less than other first-year associates made, I was thrilled.

New lawyers had glutted the legal market the prior few years. Jobs were scarce, especially for someone with poor grades from a mediocre law school. Pepperdine was no Yale, Stanford or Harvard. It wasn't even USC. Worse yet, I graduated thirteenth from the bottom of my class.

The reduced pay seemed a fair exchange for comfort. The office was ten minutes from my house. I wouldn't have a 2000-hour yearly billable minimum or the stifling corporate environment of larger law firms.

Billable hours dominate the existence of most lawyers, especially young lawyers. They dominated mine to a lesser extent than my peers in bigger law firms. The amount I recorded and reported at month's end mattered to Jerry, but he gave me more encouragement for the quality of my work rather than the quantity. That was rare along with the amount of responsibility I had from my first day.

Learning the deadlines and procedures of litigation engaged every moment of many long days and too many nights and weekends. I was terrified of making a mistake.

I continued in therapy even after Dad stopped paying for it. Although a huge additional expense, I needed Sharon, my therapist. I racked up thousands of dollars in credit card debt to pay for food, gasoline and a few nights out, because her observations revolutionized my world. Early into the therapeutic process, I found little relief. It was confusing, like a crossword puzzle with no clues.

Her office a short distance from mine, I left to see her every Wednesday at 11:45 a.m. Jerry never discouraged it or asked me to cancel an appointment for a deadline. Less than a month after I started working with Jerry, I sat on the sofa opposite Sharon's chair in anxious fear about my first document to be filed as a lawyer by 2:00 p.m. that day.

Overwhelmed by Jerry's trust in me, I said, "If one tiny step in this whole filing isn't right, it's malpractice." My foot jiggled in nervousness, while Sharon sat perfectly still. "And, Jerry'll look bad in front of his huge clients."

I watched Sharon for any subtle reaction to my words. I noticed again that she resembled a blond Maria Shriver, with a less angular jaw. It was her abundance of hair and aquiline nose. When I asked her in our first session, she'd told me she was in her later 30s.

Sharon considered my words, leaned to the left, placing her elbow on the arm of her chair for support. "Why do you think you took a job with so much stress? One in which you're left to figure it out by yourself." She paused for a breath. "Why are you worried about the well-being of the person who should know but doesn't?"

"I guess I've always had to figure this kinda stuff out by myself." A small bell rang in my right ear. "My parents didn't know what was going on when I was little. I felt bad that they were so lost. . . ."

She batted her thick lashes with exaggerated pause. "Exactly, you were their cultural ambassador and, now, you're Jerry's."

I never would've linked my present to my past without her help, her insightful, leading questions. That day and most others, I left her office battle-weary with only the memory of a sentence or two of what was spoken. I didn't feel better or understand how each session fit together but kept going, compelled by the mystery of myself.

A few weeks following that appointment, my body fell apart. I couldn't tell if it was the stress of learning law, missing the safety of my relationship with

Ben, the beginning awareness of the connection between my childhood and my current life or the combination of all of them.

I developed acne, which covered both my cheeks. With my hair only an inch or two long, the angry, the cystic mounds were exposed and acted as signs of my confusion and failure. A sudden, debilitating reflux ailment made it difficult to eat. My 5'7" body shrank to 100 pounds within weeks. I wore baggy clothes and layers to hide it. Anxiety rang through me, shrill and constant.

I tried to talk to Mom about some of it. We spoke every morning around 7:30 a.m. and several times throughout the day. I complained to her about the stress of law practice, about Jerry not being able to help, but didn't mention my health. She hadn't seen me in weeks, because I was busy working on the weekends. She had no idea that I was a wreck. I hid it from her, like I hid the racist taunting at school.

"Mom, it sucks. Law's so stupid even though it's hard. It's the rules, the procedures are like landmines." Although in natural development a child begins to individuate at three, I began to distinguish myself from Mom in my mid-twenties.

"I don't know why you say that. You should be so proud of yourself. Most women don't get the chance to create a life for themselves."

I baited her some more. "They're lucky. I wish I didn't have to." I stared out my office window at the centered view of downtown. It was beautiful, especially at night under a full moon.

"You could've married Ben."

"Because I didn't know how awful this would be. Maybe I should've even if he never would've stood up to his family, right?" I'd grown more easily frustrated with her since I'd started therapy. "You know what, you don't understand." Mom was too attached to my status as a lawyer to hear me.

"If I don't understand, then why do you tell me?"

"Fine. I won't tell you then." She didn't want to hear behind my words, like Sharon did. Sharon searched for, even celebrated, parts of me that weren't obvious. "You're not listening anyway."

"Oh, that's what your therapist says?" It was the first time Mom seemed threatened by my therapy, uncertain of her role as I found a different type of wisdom from another source.

"No, it's what you're saying right now, in this conversation." Mom was right. Since I'd started therapy, I didn't find simple solace in our calls like I had in college and law school.

"Look, do this for a while then think about other things you want to do." Mom wanted to placate me, ease my pain with words that no longer helped. "A law degree can never hurt you."

"Yeah, I know."

"What do you want me to say?" She sounded more defeated than angry. "I don't understand you anymore."

"I don't know, Mom. I'm just stressed or tired." I didn't want to blame her. I just did.

Although broken down, I didn't miss a day of work or deadline, even as I visited my doctor once a week. First borns of immigrants don't easily drop responsibilities. My doctor prescribed me Prilosec, ran many tests, but I didn't feel better.

Several visits later, I pleaded for something else. A pill to make it better.

"Why don't you try to meditate? You're stressed, your body is breaking down," he said.

I laughed at him. "Come on, that's hippy stuff. I'm in therapy. It's just not working yet."

He eventually got tired of me and prescribed Xanax. It changed my life.

After work, I went home, walked Boo, poured myself two vodka and cranberry juice cocktails, ate what I could ingest, which for many months was broth and mashed potatoes and took half a Xanax an hour before bed.

I hugged Boo against me and cried until the Xanax knocked me out. Each night, I killed the pain but didn't cure the illness.

I began to see Sharon twice a week, Wednesdays and Fridays. My credit card debt grew, but it didn't matter compared to how much I received from therapy. I trusted Sharon and the process more with each visit. The pain I'd stored in my being poured out. Instead of an hour of intellectual discussion about the connection between my current and early life, I cried through most sessions, allowing Sharon to witness my pain.

In one vivid session, the fear of racists I'd buried to function barreled forth.

"It was scary. I mean, I was scared all the time. At school, I had to figure out who was going to get in my face, and, at home, Dad was a time bomb, especially when I was little." I shook my head. "No, that's not true. Not just when I was little, it was the whole time I lived there."

She listened with deep empathy in her eyes, not interrupting my release.

"I'm still scared if I'm by myself and big, white men are walking toward me. It's like these men are the same boys from school grown up. Even though they aren't, my heart beats fast. I can't breathe."

I clutched at the pillow on the sofa, wanting to hide beneath it. "No one knows that if I'm out and that happens, I leave. I run to my car, looking over my shoulder. I know it doesn't make sense, but I do it anyway."

It kept coming in non-linear spurts. "Still when I go home, if Dad pours a cocktail in the late afternoon, I get nervous. I want to make an excuse and leave before dinner, because I'm too afraid to sit next to him. It comes back like I'm little all over again, except I feel weaker now."

When I settled down, Sharon watched me for a few moments. "Of course you're more scared now. You're not in survival mode anymore. There are times in your life that you do feel safe, so that when you don't, you're unprepared."

"I thought I'd lost my courage. . . ."

"Where was your Mom? Why didn't she say something?"

I didn't want to ask myself those questions, but also didn't want to stay sick and drugged.

"I don't know. I'll ask her." I didn't know when I'd hold Mom accountable for some of Dad's actions, but I trusted I would.

"Until you do ask, learn to visualize that little girl in you. Hug her, listen to her, give her what you never got."

The "little girl" in me stuff felt as silly to me as her suggestion that I journal. I resisted both until I realized I would do anything to feel better. I trusted the therapeutic process, the release, the buckets of emotion once locked in my body finding their way out through my tears.

My health improved within the year. I threw out my Xanax, swearing never to take a pill again. I wasn't happy but more accepting of myself and my reality.

As I got well, Mom was hit with some difficult news. She called at work one afternoon with a dark cloud over her voice. "I have diabetes," she said.

"Oh, God, Mom." Her mother and all of her aunts died of the same disease in their early fifties. Despite the fact that her aunts were doctors, they ignored treatment, placing teaspoons of sugar in their tea, eating Indian sweets in abundance. Dida (Mom's mom) was allergic to insulin and searched her whole, short life for other ways to control her blood sugar but failed.

"I know you don't want this," I said. Dozens of times, I'd heard her say that she didn't want this disease. "You're going to be okay." She remained silent. "Has anyone called Raj?"

"No, no, there's no need to worry him," she said. "I'll tell him when I feel better about it." I never understood why my parents spared Raj the turmoil and uncertainties of life.

To my surprise, Mom adjusted to diabetes with her quiet grace. She didn't falter or rebel, she ate what and how instructed, took her medicine and poked her finger several times a day to check her blood.

I still talked to Mom many times throughout the day but struggled to bring her with me into my new way of viewing the world, to communicate with her about what was real to me. She didn't understand that I needed Sharon and therapy to fill in the blanks of my life during my transition from girl to woman.

One afternoon after a session with Sharon, I called Mom from my office. I was ready for those answers only she could give me.

"Um, I was just at Sharon's and wanted to ask you about some stuff from when I was little."

"I don't know why you still go to her. It always upsets you." Angry heat filled my body from her judgment and closed mind. "That stuff happened a long time ago. You just need to let it go," Mom said.

"God, Mom, no, it doesn't upset me, and, no, I can't let it go. A lot of shit happened."

"Like what?"

I willed myself not to scream. "What were you thinking when dad yelled at me every night at dinner?"

"I don't know, it was so long ago and I–"

"No, Mom, it wasn't that long ago." She was still protecting herself instead of me. "Come on, this is important." I wanted the truth so I could heal and then move on.

"I wanted him to stop yelling at you, but you yelled back." She blamed me, not Dad.

"Right, do you know why I did? Because I didn't want to let him get away with it." She hadn't answered my question. "Why'd you let him scream at me when I was too little to defend myself?"

"I know you and Sharon think I was a terrible mother, but I did the best I could." I hated when she got defensive and used stupid arguments. "God,–"

"No, you'll see when you have kids. No one teaches you how to do it. My mom was too sick to wash our hair, Dadu did it for us." Her voice cracked.

I sat still with the new information that gave me more insight into her.

"I was young when I had you. None of my family was here." She started to cry. "It's different in India. Parents are different here. We didn't know how to do it the American way, all the hugging and touching."

"It's not about that." I stared out my window shaking my head at my reflection in the glass. The America Excuse. "And, it's not my fault that you were young. Why have kids that young then?"

"Everybody did at that time. It's different now." The universal "everbody did" excuse.

"No, it's not that different. You think it is, but I'm working hard not to repeat what you did." Anger rose in my chest.

"Yeah, I know, you're better than me. Everybody knows it." She sounded nuts. "That's not what I'm saying. I–"

"That's exactly what you're saying. I don't want to talk about this right now." She gave up.

"When do you want to talk about it? Never?"

"I have to go." She hung up.

I called her right back.

"You know what, Mom? That's bullshit. You can't hang up on me, because you don't want to talk about something."

"It's too upsetting." She sighed for emphasis. "I don't feel well today."

I wouldn't feel guilty. "Right, why do you think you don't feel well?"

"What do you mean?"

"Well, you just said that your mom never felt well enough to wash your guys' hair, that your dad did everything, right?"

"Right. So, what are you trying to say?"

"That you never felt nurtured by your mom." The charge of an epiphany buzzed in my head.

"Are you saying that I didn't nurture you?"

"No, Mom, I'm saying that you picked Dad who doesn't give a shit about anyone but himself, because you never got over the stuff with your mom. Now, I've got to deal with it."

She didn't say anything. "Do you get it?"

"Yeah, I get it. I'm not stupid."

"I know you're not, that's why I want to talk to you about it."

"What am I supposed to do now?"

"Help me talk this through and understand that you loved me but didn't stop Dad. I need to know why you let a grown man yell at a child."

"I didn't know what to do. We had a lot of stress on us." I'd heard it so many times. "You were strong, so smart. I didn't worry about you. You took care of yourself better than I did." I remembered her eyes so many times pleading me to behave. She was frightened and didn't know what to do for either of us.

That's why I stepped forward every time. "I was a child."

She was crying harder. "I'm sorry you were hurt. I don't know what else I can do now."

"Nothing other than what you're doing. It's enough. It has to be." I hoped it was.

I cried with her for a few minutes. After we hung up, I cried more tears. I cried for the girl who was too little to defend herself, her brother and her mom against a grown man. I cried for all the times I defended myself at school. I cried from the pain of the truth.

I was fully engaged with work during the day, self-discovery at night and Friday and Saturday night dinners with Tiff or Daria, who was an old friend of Ben's and mine. Errands took up most of Saturday, cleaning and reading astrology books on Sundays. My routine cradled me so I could dig deeper into myself through therapy, my journal, thoughts and prayers.

I no longer fantasized about The One, until I saw him.

On my way to see Sharon, a man in my building caused me to stop and stare. "If I ever fall in love again, I want him to have eyes like this guy in my building." I started our session.

"What do you see in them?"

"They're soft. There's something familiar in them." I recalled his eyes, probing and almost distant. "I like how he looks at me."

For months, Mark trampled over anyone in between us to open a door for me, yet only said "Hello" and, on rare occasion, "How are you?"

I talked to Mom about him countless times over that time. In a way, Mark helped Mom and I connect again. We shared an uncontroversial topic, too mundane for me to share with Sharon. "Why doesn't he talk to me?" I asked her over and over.

"I don't know, but he will in a little while. Just be patient." Mom could read the future and people without knowing them. I relied on her like a psychic.

"I'm trying, but it's hard. There's something special about him."

Growing my hair out from the shearing I gave it in law school, I lightened it to a dark, honey blond. I had never dyed it and wanted sexy, dark roots like everyone else in L.A. Four weeks after I dyed it, I realized that roots were not sexy but tedious and expensive.

With inch-long black roots, I hurried back to the office after a morning meeting in downtown. I stopped in the cafeteria to order my daily grilled cheese, fries and side of mayonnaise to dip both. Mark stood inches away, staring at my right profile. I was nervous.

I looked at him after I ordered. "I'm waiting for my food too. I'm not just standing here," Mark said, shifting his feet.

"Congratulations." I smiled. "For saying something other than 'hello, how are you?' to me." I delivered it with innocent confidence. As with Ben,

I had that feeling that we'd be together for a long time, except this time, I knew he was The One I'd seen in my visions. God had answered my childhood prayers.

His green eyes danced in play. "I like how you dyed your hair."

"Thanks, but that's like saying 'Nice facelift' to someone." We both giggled at that.

"You want to sit down with me?" He motioned with his head to the tray of food in his hands.

"Oh, God, I can't. I've got a filing that I have to get to the service by 2:00 p.m."

"Oh." Embarrassment sent a pink flush up his tan neck.

"No, no, look, I really do have a filing, which I'm now hating." I made sure I looked him in the eyes. "I'd rather have lunch with you. We could do it another time."

"I'd like that." He recovered with my forthrightness. "Do you have a card?"

"I actually do." I grabbed a crumpled card from the bottom of my giant purse, handed it to him and floated upstairs with my food. I called Mom before the first bite of it and left her a message about my thrilling encounter. She called me back within minutes. We giggled at the beauty and surprise of life. I swelled with hope that Mark would rescue me from law, validate my inner knowing of our entwined fate, and protect me from the harshness of life.

After all of the months of "hellos," I thought Mark would call right away, but he didn't for two days. I called Mom several times a day to ask why.

Each time, she said, "Be patient, he will."

On the third day without a call, I saw him in the lobby a couple steps in front of me. "Hey, Mark." I quickened my steps to meet him.

He turned around, recognizing me, his smile warm and sincere. "Hey," he said, his face softened. "I wanted to call you, but I must've been nervous, I missed my pocket."

I shook my head at him not understanding. "I think your card fell on the ground."

I laughed at the image and appreciated his admission of nerves.

We agreed to meet the next day at the same place and time and synchronized our watches for effect.

I raced up to my office before ordering lunch to ring Mom. "I saw him! We're going to lunch tomorrow." No need for explanation or introduction.

"I told you so. I knew he wanted to call." She was right, again.

I couldn't stop smiling, grateful for my lunch date and Mom's endless patience and infallible intuition.

The next morning, I billed hours, ran downstairs three times for a cigarette, called Mom and popped breath mints. At ten after 1:00 p.m., I went down to meet Mark in the lobby.

He chose a restaurant near our office with a quiet back room in which we sat. "It's nice to see you like this," he said.

"I'm glad that we could do this, finally."

"I know that was strange how I didn't ask sooner." He fiddled with the basket of bread between us. "There was a reason."

"Okay."

"I was getting out of a three-year relationship." His admission removed my cloud of hesitation. I relaxed a little. "I didn't want to complicate anything."

"Now, it's–"

"Over, yeah, no, it's done." I knew it: He was The One. The embodiment of what I had prayed for.

The background information he shared at lunch fit into my fantasy. His father was a professor of law in northern California where he grew up. Seven and a half years older than me, he graduated UCLA when I entered high school. His older brother lived in Covina with his family, though I didn't know them.

His parents divorced when he was young after his father had an affair. I concluded that the early strife gave him the depth I saw in his eyes. He had been a golden glove-boxing champion at 18, liked sports, travel and his family.

From the mailroom, he worked his way into his position as a stockbroker and built a stable business, a "machine" as he called it, which required him to work only from 10:30 a.m. to 4:00 p.m. His hazel-green eyes made me believe in love again.

I told Mom what I'd learned at lunch. "I knew there was a good reason he didn't talk to you before. See, he's a good guy," she said. High praise from Mom. She sensed how special my connection was with Mark.

A storm of confusion hit me when our courtship didn't follow my fantasy or what I felt for or from Mark. He cancelled many of our dates at the last minute. "I haven't had time with my friends for three years. My ex was really possessive." He rarely saw me on the weekends, because he traveled to see his mom in northern California or to local bars.

I wanted to be understanding and patient. A month later, he called on Sunday morning to cancel our afternoon plans. He said he was sick from his trip up north. I listened in a panic of familiar disappointment.

"You know, I didn't think I'd meet you so soon," he said. My ears perked. "What'd you mean?"

"We're soul mates. I know it," he said, though my anxiety continued. "It's just that I got out of this other relationship," he reasoned. "I need a little more time."

I wanted us to work so much, but something didn't feel right.

Mark's reticence destabilized me. I cried to Mom day and night for those few months. "Be patient," she said. "I know he cares."

Although Mom told me to be patient, I couldn't. I was distracted, moody and devastated. My stomach revolted, like it had been when I was sick and on Xanax.

At work, I was handling a large arbitration with complicated business valuation evidence and expert witness testimony. Our client was a small-business woman who'd been defrauded by her much wealthier, more experienced male business partner. It was important to me to win. I resented that my focus was distracted by the rollercoaster of Mark's actions and inactions. I felt weak and stupid.

Mark left for a ten-day trip to Cuba with his best friend. The morning of his flight, he said, "Don't expect me to call. I just need to get away." He hugged me, kissing my cheeks, hair and lips. "Besides, it's hard to make a call from there." I wiggled away from him. If I could call out from India, he could figure out a way to call me from Cuba.

He called when he got back. The day he returned we met for lunch. Though excited to see him, distrust infected my feelings for him. "Hey, listen, I'm probably not gonna be able to get together for a couple nights. I need to keep taking it slow," he said.

His words didn't bother me as much as his tone and presumption. I had an appointment with Sharon the next day. "Well, he did it again. He didn't want to get together this week, because he wants to take it slow." I cried from frustration when I said it.

Sharon leaned forward in her chair, elbows on the knees of her long, thin legs. "Are you the type of girl that waits around for someone?"

"No, gosh, well, I hope not. I don't know." Was I like Mom who could love a man who gave her so little?

I thought about the answer on the short drive back to my office, picked up the phone at my desk before putting down my purse to dial Mark's office.

His secretary announced my call. He answered with his usual "Hey, sweetie,–"

"Listen, I think you know why I'm calling." If he meant even half of what he'd said over the months, he should've known.

"No, why–"

"I don't want to see you anymore. You're not ready or whatever. I can't do this."

"Mala, it's me." He was referring to his declaration of "soul mate" status. "You can't do that." Too many times, his words didn't match his actions. With each inconsistency, I lost a bit of the precious self-esteem that I was trying to develop.

"Look, this isn't working." I hung up devastated but had to protect my fledgling sense of self. It couldn't take another week of his partial rejections and baby steps towards and away from me. I'd worked too hard and spent most of my resources figuring out who I was to allow any relationship to break me. Not even if Mom said to be patient.

With that phone call, I chose a path different from Mom's insight. I chose to find my own way.

I still believed Mark was the only One for me. He just didn't want me in the way that I wanted him. That truth sank me into a chasm of despair in which nothing made sense.

I joked to Tiff that "Prince Charming rode into my life and left nothing but a hoof print on my forehead," yet didn't feel the same levity on the inside.

I couldn't bear to see Mark in our building. My heart broke a little more every time we waved at each other downstairs. When we did, his steps slowed and mine quickened away from him.

I hated law with its tedious technicalities. We won the arbitration for our underdog female client, but my nerves were shot. I was exhausted from the long hours I'd worked over the prior weeks in preparation for it.

Cracked open in the pain, I wrote poetry and sketched not ever having done either. The depth of therapy I'd undertaken the prior three years, the acrimonious litigation, the loss of my fantasy and the void of any promise of relief caused my stomach to rage in violent protest. No matter how many times I hugged the little one within me, I cried from hopelessness and despair.

My doctor placed me on temporary disability at my request. A few weeks into my leave, I told my boss I wouldn't be coming back to work for him. That Saturday, I packed my office into one large duffle bag, leaving my keys and parking card on my cleared desk.

I had no idea what I was doing and there was nowhere outside of myself to find the answer. I wanted peace.

For it, I stopped my world to rest and, beneath my collapsed fairytale, I clung to my prayers.

CHAPTER EIGHT
Discovery

After Mark and quitting my job with Jerry, I headed down a road from which I could never turn back. I'd surrendered the way I'd been taught to live, my planned life purpose and the dreams that held my hope.

I'd hoped I'd marry The One and his face would smile at me from a picture on my law desk. I fantasized that with his help, I could afford to practice civil rights law or work in the public defender's office. Life would be simple, meaningful and complete. The failure of Mark and me proved that The One didn't exist. The truth of law practice left me no way to survive.

Reality shattered my understanding of life. I needed time to recover before I could search for something other than that dream to keep me alive. Suicide lingered in my mind as an option.

With only the small disability check for income, I darkened my hair to its natural color. Time, not my appearance, was my new luxury.

Dad supported my decision to quit law; Mom did not. On a trip to the Cabazon outlet mall near Palm Springs, Mom drove while I sat in the passenger seat. Raj was in the back in his usual spot behind the driver, the same as when we were kids.

"So, when do you think you're going back?" Mom stared at the freeway in front of us.

"Back where?" I played dumb, not wanting to make it easy for her. "You know."

"I think I do, but tell me."

"You're making a mistake." Mom used my captured attention to give me her opinion about my recent choices.

"Dad doesn't think so." I turned sideways in my seat, leaning against the door, as we'd been taught not to do. "He said he didn't care if I dug ditches as long as I was happy and could pay my bills." Again, Dad had supported me when I didn't expect it. Like finding Sharon.

"Why are you doing this?" Her fingers gripped the steering wheel at ten and two.

"Doing what, Mom?" I'd never realized how important it was to her that I practice law.

"Quitting law, you worked so hard to become an attorney."

"No, I didn't and you know it." Mom betrayed my truth. "You know more than anyone how much I hate it. How could you want that for my life?"

"I just never thought of you as a quitter. I—"

"A what?" A glance at Raj revealed a familiar look of dread on his face. I was ruining his day to stand up for my beliefs, again. "Do you sit at a desk all day billing your life six minutes at a time?"

"I don't want to talk if you're going to be like this."

"Like what? It's my life, and I hate law." Out of control, my voice grew shrill. "It's killing me and the fact that you don't care about that freaks me out." Tears spurted from my eyes. I wiped them on my sleeve like a child.

She ignored me as if I hadn't spoken. I waited her out as long as I could. "Mom, really you don't want me to find out what makes me happy?"

She clucked her tongue against the roof of her mouth. "Of course, I do."

She waved her hand to dismiss the conversation and never mentioned it, again.

For five months I didn't do much in the outside world. I spent my days painting, writing, smoking and watching the light change. I'd taught myself to paint with the encouragement of my neighbor, Sophia, a disheveled girl, who painted like a combination of Rembrandt and Matisse and had an encyclopedic knowledge of philosophy and psychology.

Painting frustrated me more than my early years in therapy. It forced me to accept that I wasn't good at something I loved to do. I was mediocre. My hands didn't have the gift, yet my eye was decent enough to know the difference.

Most afternoons, Sophia came by for coffee and endless cigarettes. She often quoted a long-deceased Indian man named Yogananda who started the Self Realization Fellowship. My face pinched when I heard his name because of my irritation in Americans giving praise to Indian gurus. Sophia ignored my reaction and invited me to join her and her husband for the Sunday service at a grand temple in the Pacific Palisades. After several invitations, I joined them.

Service began with a meditation. A charismatic, strangely sexy monk offered instruction to those, like me, who had never meditated. "Gently close your eyes, keeping your inner gaze directed toward the space between your eyebrows and ask God to reveal himself to you."

I still associated meditation with hippies but did what he said. To my astonishment behind my shut eyelids, I saw gold dust rising from the head of each person in the temple. The dust floated up through the ceiling, back into hands that I saw as God's.

It was glorious. I was awestruck.

The monk ended the meditation with a soft chant of "Om." Sophia seemed to know what I'd seen. "Amazing, isn't it?" she said and squeezed my hand.

Afraid I'd burst from bliss, I nodded at her. My body flooded with a boundless joy that a world beyond the mundane existed. I wanted more.

I told Mom about my experience later that day. "Does this mean you're running away to the Himalayas like all those other crazy holy people?" Mom seemed afraid that God would take me further away than therapy. Again, her comments didn't dissuade me.

I felt at home in Yogananda's temple. He also came from Calcutta and it filled me with pride. Our shared origins helped me feel welcome in his temple and embrace my heritage for the first time.

I devoted myself to meditation and Yogananda's teachings. I read his books and signed up for the weekly lessons. Consciousness became the truth I'd searched for my whole life. Marriage and law felt like what I was supposed to do. Awareness of self and God felt like my truth.

Learning about the unseen world, I recalled my fifth birthday party at Farrell's Ice Cream Parlour. Time stopped for a moment that day. I was suspended in quiet amidst the ringing of the birthday bell on the wall and the other kids blowing horns.

As I separated from everyone there, like I was visiting from another place, a clear understanding passed through me like a cool breeze in my blood: Our parents weren't our parents but just people that we knew from other lives that we called "mom" and "dad." A strange sensation enveloped me from this awareness and returned many times over my life. It was similar to what I felt in temple that day. An awareness that life wasn't what and as it seemed. There was more.

In my younger years, that feeling comforted me. As I got older, I mistook the sensation for anxiety, not recognizing it as my intuition or knowing. Yogananda's teachings provided tools like meditation to reclaim the knowing of my youth. Its restoration left me feeling like a cat stretching after a long nap in the sun.

I meditated every morning, yet, after that first experience in temple, I felt nothing but the clutter of my mind. Like painting, I did it even though I wasn't any good at it. I cemented myself to the foot of my chaise with Boo for back support. As Yogananda instructed, I sat upright, my feet flat on the ground and focused my attention on the space between my eyebrows, which grew uncomfortable within seconds. It took many months not to feel uncomfortably cross-eyed.

Through my efforts at meditation, my dreams grew more intense. Most of them took place on the glowing cliffs above the Malibu sea. Nightly tidal waves swept me from those cliffs and into the ocean, within which I could breathe, overwhelmed but not scared. I clutched at Mom's hands in most of the dreams.

In another repetitive dream, throngs of people walked along the Pacific Coast Highway while I swam next to them. I kept pace without strain, taking easy strokes. I dreamed the same dreams every night.

Sharon was unavailable on maternity leave and couldn't help me understand the messages from my subconscious mind. Not wanting to wait months to hear my inner self, I studied any book I could find on dream interpretation. Exhausting myself but not the available material, I concluded that the symbols and themes in my dreams could only be defined by the associations I made to them.

I learned the language of my subconscious mind in tiny, endless steps. My single apartment became a library of books. Scattered in no order over my table and the surrounding chairs in the kitchen, I sat for endless hours after my meditation, searching for answers. A highlighter in my hand marked what seemed important.

I immersed myself into the symbols, themes, colors, elements and messages of my dreams. I devoured books on numerology, psychology, philosophy, religion and astrology and learned to study.

My wooden folding chair with a thin blue-striped pillow on it never grew uncomfortable, no matter how many hours I sat in it. I opened the window beside me to blow my cigarette smoke onto the trees. Within my pages and pages of dream logs, I looked for patterns. I lived in a different world, spoke a different language.

I cooked at home, not wanting to break my focus by going to dinner or having conversations about mundane life. My limited resources forced me to prioritize my inner world versus the outer. Although obsessed, I had no idea what I was doing. More than once, I thought I was sailing a flat world in futility. Had Boo not needed to be walked three times a day, I would've floated away.

The clues to the messages of my dreams couldn't be rushed. In time, I realized that instead of walking like others in my dreams, I swam, because I associated swimming with strength and safety, even if I was different.

The tidal waves were years of emotion meeting my conscious mind, the shore. I could breathe within them, because I was ready to heal and my true emotions were no longer buried. I held Mom's hand, because I wanted to take her with me wherever I went.

My interpretation of my astrological chart wove into my dreams, as I searched deeper into the repeating elements of water and earth. I learned that water endured through the ages as a symbol of spirit, that the rhythm of breath in swimming most closely resembled meditation. Pieces of my life fell into place. I had been searching for peace and God my whole life, in the pool and through my prayers.

My tiny tree house apartment became my womb. I wrote on the white walls of that womb. Messages from fortune cookies written in bright pastel chalks became art, reminders to continue the search within my soul, encouragement to trust that I'd find my lost pieces.

Consumed with what mattered to me, I didn't care about money and sustained my life by supplementing the disability income with my Los Angeles County Bar Association MBNA credit card.

My mind indulged from time to time on Mark. With no urge to contact him, I wondered why he didn't come find me. Yet, when my Friday evening dirty martini warmed my blood and loosened my mind, I replayed my memory tapes of our few months together and rummaged for the reason of our failure.

I'd heard someone say "God is a fantasy for the weak." Perhaps they were right, because I found my most authentic self in my weakest point.

While I'd hurled myself into my inner world, Mom had kept a secret: For over a year, blood filled her stool up to twenty times a day. A long overdue doctor's appointment revealed that she had a severe case of ulcerated colitis. I was relieved she hadn't shared her difficulties with me. They would've distracted me from my studies.

The day after her diagnosis, I visited her. She looked drawn, almost helpless under her make-up, worse than after her diabetes diagnosis.

We assumed our positions on the sofa in the family room. I waited for Dad to go outside to water his rose bushes before I said, "Do you feel okay? I mean, is the medicine working?"

"It's working, but they have me on steroids." She averted her eyes, which flashed in pain. "They're awful."

"How?"

"They have a lot of side effects." I wanted to ask a hundred questions but could see how scared she was.

"Like what?"

"I can't sleep, I'm bloated. I just feel weird."

"Is there anything they can do?"

"No, I don't want you to worry about this right now. You're not here that much." I'd avoided her during my inner journey, because I didn't know how to put words to it and was too fragile to withstand her critical eye.

"Okay, but–"

"What's going on with you? How are you feeling?" She didn't want to talk about it. A part of me was grateful.

After that, I went home to see Mom most Sundays after Self-Realization Fellowship service. She wasn't the same. Distracted, in pain and moody, the colitis diagnosis and the steroids changed her.

Those days we often went to a South Indian snack shop in Diamond Bar that served our favorite food, dosa, a thin, crispy crepe served with different chutneys. Mom ate hers filled with potatoes. I liked mine plain.

A hot, smoggy August Sunday, we enjoyed our dosas in silence for a few bites until Mom put hers down. "I wish He'd go pick on someone else," she said. "What did I do to Him?"

I knew she meant God. "You could look for a connection between the mind and body, why you created the colitis," I said.

"You're blaming me for this?"

"It's not about blame. Maybe we create our realities, which means our health too."

"It's too much." She gave up when I knocked on the door to her closet of stuffed emotions. "I don't care why it's here. I want it gone."

"It won't just go away. You've got to figure out why it's here. Why it came to teach you something."

"I don't want to talk to you about this right now." Mom grasped at her dignity while she searched for the nearest bathroom every half-hour or forty-five minutes.

That afternoon, we stopped twice on the way home for her to relieve her body of blood and stool. The restaurant was twenty minutes away.

A month prior to the end of my six months of disability income, Ben called to tell me he had a lawyer friend who needed a part-time associate. I rarely heard from him. Ben had recently become engaged to the Jewish girl of his parents' dreams, who I'd met at Daria's recent engagement party.

"By the way, what're you doing? Your fiancée looks like Phyllis Diller in drag. She has fake hair, teeth, and whatever else. This isn't like you," I said.

He laughed but didn't agree or disagree with me.

"Seriously, I hate to see you do this. She's a total mess, I can tell."

"Why do you say that?" Again, he didn't admit or deny.

"Really? How. . . ." I remembered his mother's hard black eyes and stopped myself. "You know what? Do what you've gotta do. It's none of my business anymore." I thanked him for the job tip but shook my head at his mistake as I hung up the phone.

I met with Ben's friend in his office. Like my job with Jerry, I got the job in my interview.

I was happy to make money again, even happier that Kevin paid me as an independent contractor. I worked about twenty to twenty-five hours a week as opposed to the fifty to sixty with Jerry with more net income. To me, my new job evidenced some unspecific inner progress. My life could change.

The work itself was remedial, nothing like what I did with Jerry. Minor real estate issues and small bits of litigation filled his files. Not needing to prove myself in law, I didn't mind.

Soon after I started work with Kevin, I was served sixty-day notice of the landlord's intent to demolish our apartments. The little paradise tree house in which I'd learned so much was doomed to be torn down for new condos. I'd found myself and God within those walls and was afraid He wouldn't go with me.

I couldn't imagine where Boo and I would live. I only paid $675 per month in rent. Although I made a little more money with Kevin, I didn't have much extra. I never thought about money with any precision, but an exponential increase in my rent seemed impossible. With no money saved for a down payment, I couldn't buy.

I scoured the rental listings, looking at a few places. Each place was more hideous than the next. One-bedroom apartments in ugly, Seventies-style buildings, with hallways, elevators and carpet. I needed the impossible, a place that inspired me.

Armed with the desperation of the soon-to-be-homeless, Boo and I jumped in my car. "Mom says you're the lucky dog. Let's find a place to live." I said to her.

I drove west into Santa Monica from Brentwood and discovered the sweetest building I had ever seen. A teal and white sign in front of it stated, "For Sale."

"Well, I'll just take a look at it and see how it feels," I said to Boo. It was everything I wanted, a one bedroom with a big balcony, bougainvillea wrapped around its façade and endless charm.

I ran to the car, kissed my lucky dog and raced home to ring my parents. For the entirety of my life, if Dad answered, all I said was "Hi, Dad. Is Mom there?" Especially, if I needed money.

This time when Dad answered, I said "Boo and I found a place, but it's for sale, not rent."

Without a moment's hesitation, he said "Great. Call the agent and we'll meet you there tomorrow."

"But, Dad, I don't–"

"Your mom and I'll give you the down payment."

He didn't ask how much it was. Where it was. Nothing. "You don't have to, I'll pay you back some day."

"No, you know my rule: Never loan money to a family member. It's always a gift."

Tears of relief stung my eyes and took my voice.

My parents gave me a down payment large enough to keep my mortgage payment close to the rent I paid for my tree house apartment. Unpacking, I read through some old journals. I flipped to a random page from prior months and froze. I'd asked God to help me buy a place of my own. I'd forgotten, but He had not.

The environment of my new home allowed me to see myself in new clarity. I considered all parts of my life and thought about what I needed to further my spiritual studies. I continued the weekly Self-Realization Fellowship lessons but wanted God to send me a teacher in the flesh. I had many questions that I wanted to ask but had nowhere to go with them. Neither Sharon nor Mom could fill that spot.

Back from maternity leave, I resumed work with Sharon, still sometimes twice a week. I tried to integrate my spiritual studies into our work. "You know, my meditations have been opening my mind a lot, really changing my dream time over the past several months."

"I have a cousin who teaches Transcendental Meditation," Sharon responded. I didn't know what that was but wished she'd admit that I was growing in an area in which she wasn't familiar. I left many of our sessions frustrated by our inability to connect the way we had. I continued to see her, because it was still the only place I found objectivity.

I put myself on a strict plan in accordance with Yogananda's teachings and observed my every thought and action to make certain that my thinking was right and that my action followed. Somehow, this practice mixed with my years of therapy and Sharon's consistent presence in my life created self-esteem.

Awareness of my intentions and thoughts destroyed doubt in myself.

My truth poured out in poetry. Poetry I wrote from a flash of inspiration, read over once and, depending on the hour, read to Mom. I called her late one night following a flash of writing. "What're you doing?" I asked.

"Watching something stupid on TV." I heard her turn it off. "Your dad's asleep. Why?"

"I just wrote a bunch. Can I read you some?"

She agreed, and I read her the following poem, skipping the other three I wrote that night:

lost glory

there she sits

in forgotten glory

no one remained to tell

her story

the soul erupted

to consume her form

the fall's cool breeze

to a winter storm

foot after foot

she continued to travel

as her fairytale life

slowly unraveled

all she had known

was blown to bits

she babbled endlessly

without her wit

so lively and twinkling
she used to be
her laughter now
drowned at sea
the child that
lost her mother
desperately searched
to find another
pieces she assembled
to gather maternal
her hope to create it
burned eternal
trembling and scared
she is afraid to move
too aware
of all she did lose

Mom didn't say anything when I finished. "Well?"

"Oh." She sounded deep in thought. "It's good. It's just, well, I worry about you."

"Why? I'm fine."

"It's so dark. Could you be, are you depressed?" I rolled my eyes on my side of the phone. "Isn't Sharon helping that?"

"God, Mom. It's—"

"I didn't mean to upset you. It's really good. I always like what you write. I wish other people could hear it."

My poetry high depleted, I wished for the millionth time in my life that I wasn't so "dark" and sensitive. I'd tried to get rid of it, but couldn't.

Around then, I began inwardly repeating, "When the student is ready, the teacher will come." A few months later in January of 1999, she did. I met Susanna through, Rita, my esthetician of many years.

Rita said in her light voice laced with a slight Hungarian accent, "Honey, I know you don't like psychic readings, but my friend's coming to town again." Rita arranged Susanna's schedule when she came into Los Angeles from New York.

I'd sworn off of psychic readings when I immersed myself in spiritual studies. It made no sense to embrace the moment and wonder about the future. This time, I heard or felt Yogananda's voice in my mind. "Go. Try it."

I wanted to trust his voice, because I'd never heard it with such clarity.

The following Friday evening, I left work early to walk Boo and grabbed my gym bag to take my ritual Friday evening swim. Most Friday nights, I swam, picked up a bean and cheese burrito and ate it in front of the Laker game with Boo at my feet. I loved my life.

I found the little house attached to the address Rita gave me and walked toward the front door. The cigarettes on the front stairs put me at ease. I usually liked fellow smokers. Susanna answered my knock, but was rushed and intimidating.

"Have a seat, I'll be with you in a few minutes." I sat where she'd pointed and played with a cat that appeared from beneath the sofa.

Several minutes later, Susanna walked through the living room to show out her prior client who left in tears. She narrowed her eyes at the cat and me. "That cat doesn't like anyone," she said, motioned for me to follow her to a dining room table.

At the table, a photo of Yogananda topped the tiny altar to the right of where Susanna sat.

"He told me to come here." I pointed to the small picture. "Yeah?" Her eyes lit up. "He told me to come to L.A., too."

I don't recall much of the reading other than she said, "You're not alone. Others feel the way you do. It's a gift." My eyes welled with tears from her words.

"Just keep doing what you're doing. It'll come together in time."

In Susanna, God answered my prayers for a teacher. My life was about to change.

CHAPTER NINE
Surgeries

Colitis consumed Mom. The side effects of steroids brought insomnia, which created moodiness and exhaustion. Without steroids, Mom's stomach cramped at least every hour, forcing her to rush to the bathroom. With them, she wasn't the mom I knew.

In early 1999, Mom decided to undergo a two-step surgical process to remedy her colitis. Her research found that Dr. Bird from the USC Norris Center was the best in the United States at removing a colon and creating a substitute pouch from a portion of the small intestine. After consulting with Dr. Bird in April, Mom scheduled her surgery for early June. Uninvited into their decision-making, I watched from a distance.

I was frustrated that Mom didn't want to explore the psychological reasons for her physical disease. Her decision contradicted my five years of introspective effort. The surgery proved to me that I had failed to inspire her to look within herself.

Instead of talking to Mom or Sharon about it, I got a reading from Susanna over the phone a few weeks before the first surgery.

"How will the surgeries go?" I asked and heard the flipping of the tarot cards. "They'll go well, but your Mom will have to decide how she heals. It will be in her hands how she takes care of herself."

I found her answer obvious and obtuse but felt relief.

Checked into her hospital room at 10:30 p.m. the night before her surgery, Mom still didn't know what time her surgery would take place. Dr. Bird was concerned her blood sugar would be too high if her surgery wasn't his first of the day.

Dad, who was asleep by 8:30 p.m. most nights, called at 11:00 p.m. to let me know the surgery would be at 9:00 a.m. Because neither Mom nor Dad had ever had surgery, I didn't know what to expect and set my alarm for 6:00 a.m. to insure that I had time to prepare.

I slept until 5:00 a.m., when Yogananda's calm, deep voice woke me. "Get up. She's having surgery earlier than planned."

Less shocked than I should've been by the wake-up call received by my inner ear, I rushed east on the 10 Freeway to my undefined deadline. Mom's hospital room was empty, except for the blue photo box of Yogananda I had given her for support. I hurried through the hospital, discovering Mom by herself in pre-op.

"How'd you find me?" She gave me a relieved but quizzical look. "The surgery just changed."

"Because you're my Mom, and I could find you anywhere." I pulled up a nearby chair and sat next to her. "Plus, the coolest thing happened. Yogananda woke me up and told me it would be earlier."

She tilted her head on the pillow, unable to challenge how I knew to get to the hospital early.

Despite the fact that we'd never been touchy, I held Mom's hand. Her eyes sat larger than usual in her round, soft face. Their uncertainty scared me.

Her eyebrows scrunched together in disgust.

She'd noticed my face, which was burned raw. Giant flaps of skin flew from my face as I walked. The coolness of the air stung when it hit the raw skin beneath the burned. "I got an acid peel a few days ago, because I've been breaking out. It's supposed to look better in a few days." It was a mistake that I wouldn't admit.

"Why do you do this stuff to yourself?" she said.

"Look who's talking," I said with a wave at the cold pre-op area. We both laughed without a mention to the fact that the whole conversation started with only a look from her.

Mom grimaced when the anesthesiologist inserted the I.V. needle into her veins. "I'll be right here until they take you in." I held tightly to her fingers just below the needles and tubes. "I'll be the first face you see when you wake up."

"Promise?" I nodded.

I walked along side her until they wheeled her into the operating room and peeked in through a tiny window in the door. It was oddly barren except for the tiny lump of Mom's body on the table. I watched until the surgeon leaned in close and spoke to her.

I sat in the waiting room by myself until Dad arrived an hour later. His small eyes widened when he saw me. "How're you here?"

For our points of contention, we spoke the same language of short phrases.

I told him how and said, "Don't worry I was with Mom when they wheeled her in to the operating room. She wasn't alone." Neither Mom nor Dad was outwardly spiritual or religious, but neither questioned my supernatural wake-up call. It was a benefit of having Indian parents. They were raised in an environment in which people regularly discussed visitations by long-deceased saints, gurus and relatives.

"Where's Raj?" I said. He was always late, never in a hurry.

"You know your brother." He shrugged his shoulders. "I left him a message that it was changed, that he should get here, but who knows if he got it yet."

"So, he'll be here soon."

"Do you think he's lost?" Dad said.

Dad always thought that Raj must be lost because otherwise he'd be on time. "No, he's just late," I said.

Raj arrived an hour later.

Three hours after he promised, Dr. Bird walked into the waiting room. My father recognized him and stood.

"The surgery went really well." He took off his light blue, paper surgical hat and his tone darkened. "Her colon was more severed than we had realized. It was torn forty of its eighty centimeters."

Dad started to cry, maybe from guilt from all the years of his demands, tantrums and anger or maybe because he really did love her. I left him with his tears to smoke outside.

As promised, I was there when Mom opened her eyes.

Mom didn't have any of the usual post-surgery symptoms, except her speech slurred slightly when the morphine dripped into her veins.

Mom stayed in the hospital for several days. Dr. Bird released her with a colostomy bag to hold her waste until the pouch created by him healed enough for use. He said it usually took six weeks.

My law work blurred those weeks between surgeries. When I reviewed the files from that summer, I had no memory of them. Letters I'd written and documents I'd filed were unrecognizable. That summer, I alternated between my hatred of law practice and appreciation of its banal distraction, a place to escape that took no real effort or thought.

I began dating Scott, a neighbor of mine, who I'd seen near my condo for a year. He was a contractor, who rented a single apartment in the building next door to me. Unbeknownst to both of us, his window looked into my kitchen.

On our first date, he played "Jessie's Girl" by Rick Springfield. It reminded me of high school, like our relationship. We had light fun, went to dinner, the beach and had everything but sex.

I had a nice weekend routine. I saw Mom on Saturdays and went to the beach with Scott on Sundays. Even though we lived next door to each other, Scott and I spent many late weeknights on the phone sharing thoughts on philosophy, politics and family. His slow, sensual voice warmed my ear.

Our time together was simple, as was he. He didn't eat onions or garlic, had never touched coffee, alcohol, cigarettes or drugs. A strange, unintentional, mystical beauty who could slow his heart rate to thirty beats per minute on command. Raised on a farm in Michigan, he was pure Midwestern goodness.

I checked in with Mom throughout the day and tried to talk less about me, listening more for any thoughts she wanted to share.

Mom was obsessed with the six-week mark for her second surgery. Because of her diabetes, she wasn't sure if it would take longer for her to heal. She would've yanked the colostomy bag out of her body if she could.

A couple of weeks before the six-week mark, she was more restless than usual. "We don't know now if you're healing fast enough, we can't see inside your body. But, we can pray you are," I said.

"There's no point. I don't think God hears my prayers, otherwise I wouldn't be stuck in the house with this bag." It was God's fault again.

"Okay, I'll pray then." Mom didn't need a lecture on spirituality.

I changed the subject to Scott. "It's weird that he doesn't drink or even eat garlic."

"It's a good thing." Mom loved that Martha Stewart phrase. I'd given her a white T-shirt with that phrase written across the front in turquoise. "I'm not sure–"

"You know, I never told you this, but I've prayed you'd end up with someone who doesn't drink or do drugs."

"Why? It's so boring."

"Trust me, it's better than what I've lived with." She had never said anything about the effect on her of Dad's drinking.

I froze.

"Can I ask you something?" she said. "What?"

"Can you come stay with me for a week after my next surgery?"

"Of course, why? What's going on?"

"Your Dad has to start traveling again for Enron." After a short retirement, Dad got a job with Enron that required him to travel to Houston ten days out of the month.

"When?"

"He said right after I get out of the hospital, he can't not go to Houston any longer."

"Why can't he handle anything by phone?" I couldn't believe he'd leave Mom right now.

"I don't know, but tell me how much you'd make if you worked, I'll pay you."

"Come on, you don't have to pay me to stay with you."

"Yes, I do." More than anyone, she knew how I stretched my finances. "You don't make any money if you are not billing hours. God knows, that boss of yours is too cheap to give you paid vacation."

She was angry, hiding something. "What's going on?"

I called Betty to ask her, she couldn't." Betty, Mom's best friend lived in Connecticut. They met while Dad and Betty's ex-husband were at USC getting their graduate degrees.

"Why couldn't she?" I knew Betty struggled with money after her divorce having raised her two girls alone.

"She made up some excuse about work even though I told her I would cover what she would make and pay her plane fare."

Mom didn't ask for much from anyone. For her to have asked Betty for anything and for Betty to refuse wasn't good.

"I'm sure it had to do with Mick. I don't know why she's still with him. He's really an idiot." Mick was Betty's long-time boyfriend.

"Maybe she really loves him." Mom couldn't see that Betty's love for Mick mirrored her own for Dad in that it seemed unearned.

"Why would she?" She was angry.

Mom had a low tolerance for anyone she thought was an "idiot." Once she determined someone was weak or selfish, they vanished from her mind, like they never even existed. She was most often right to do so.

She eliminated the parents of a Bengali family we'd known for many years when a tragic secret surfaced through the resurrected memory of their daughter. The father had molested two of their three daughters. When Mom heard, she told the other mom, Nandita Mashi, "If you allow him back in your life, you and he are not welcome in my home and I'll never speak to you again."

She kept her word. When other Indian families considered the children pariahs, Mom threw them birthday parties and invited them over regularly.

I hoped Betty wasn't heading down a similar road. Mom was on edge those days. I knew that any perceived slight from Betty could kill their long friendship.

I turned the conversation from Betty. "Of course I'll stay with you, just give me the dates so that I can tell Kevin." I looked out my office window at the cars on Canoga Avenue.

"Okay, I'll let you know." I wondered if she knew that it had not been Betty but Dad who failed her with his mention of his possible travel.

"Who does he think he's kidding?" Her words spurted with fire. "What're you talking about?"

"I hear him go into the cabinet and pour more scotch when I'm in the bathroom." I wanted her to purge, though a little afraid of what she would say next.

"I'm just so sick of this." She was confessing to herself.

"What are you saying, Mom?" She protected Dad, especially from the glare of my eyes.

"Oh, come on. I'm not stupid. I might not be as smart as you or your Dad but I know what goes on."

"No one thinks you're stupid." I hated when she said that but let it go. "You're obviously smarter than Dad and me. We ask your advice on everything."

"I'm just saying I don't know how much longer I can take it."

"What'd you want to do?"

"Leave him, I think I want to leave him."

"Really? You mean it?"

"It's never going to get any better, right? All these years the same thing." She spat out a breath of revulsion, while I remained silent and still.

"He wants to buy a beach house. I can't even think about having another place where he sneaks around drinking."

I pressed the phone into my left ear.

"Do you know what it's like? After 8:00 p.m. if something happens to me, there's no one to take care of it. You're too far away."

I didn't mention that Raj was down the street and let her continue.

"After two scotches, he might as well be somewhere else. I live alone after 8:00 p.m. He's not available to talk to or do anything. I'm sick of it."

"Come live with me."

"You can't live with your mother. You have your own life."

"No, I don't." I laughed at the truth of it. "We'll sell my place, get money from Dad and buy a bigger place in Santa Monica so we can live together. That would be my dream." I saw it in my head. A large townhouse, no, a small house for mom, Boo and me.

"You'll have a husband one day who wouldn't want to live with his mother-in-law."

"Mom, he'd be so lucky. You're so not the mother-in-law type." I paused to listen to see if she'd say anything. "Anyway, I'm not married and there is not even the remotest possibility that I will be." I felt like I did when I was three and had told her to let Dad go when he was screaming one night. I promised that I'd take care of her. I meant it then and I meant it twenty-six years later. "Think about it."

I was too excited to let her back out of her confession.

"If you won't stay with me, go to India to be with your sisters. I know how much you miss them." Each time I mentioned them over the years, yearning filled her eyes.

"I can't leave you and Raj."

"We're fine."

"No, you're not fine. You and I talk a hundred times a day."

"Good, it'll make me grow up and stop leaning on you for everything."

"You're supposed to lean on me, I'm your Mom."

That was Mom's big thing. Whenever I thanked her for something, she said, "Don't thank me. I'm your Mom."

"You'll see when you're a mom, you can't leave your children."

"Mom, you're the bravest person I have ever met. I can't believe you have the guts to just put this out there."

"Well, they say 'the truth shall set you free.' Maybe it will. What else do I have to lose?"

My tears didn't allow me to speak.

"I think that I'll wait until I recover from the second surgery, then tell your Dad that I'm going to India for six months, and, if by the time I get back he hasn't quit drinking, I'm leaving him."

I couldn't think of anything else to say. Although her colon ripped in half from stuffing her truth, she never let on that it had crawled so close to her surface. She'd seen a therapist a few times named "Grace" to help deal with her chronic illnesses. I guess she'd done more introspection then I'd thought.

"Oh, before you hang up, don't tell anyone about this, especially Raj. I don't want him to worry." My brother planned to leave for Europe with his friend, Kent, a few days after her surgery. She had slipped him a couple thousand dollars so that he could have a little extra fun.

After our good-bye, I sat in my office, stunned. The show's over, everyone. We could stop pretending. I wasn't crazy. Mom had noticed all of it.

A few days after our call, Mom found that she had healed and could proceed with the second surgery. She would leave the hospital in two or three days without a colostomy bag, ready to institute her plan to go to India.

On a hot mid-July Friday, I took the day off from work to be at the hospital for her surgery. Mom and Dad were already in pre-op when I got there. Mom looked like a queen in full make-up. Her curtained area smelled of her gentle perfume.

"Gosh, Mom, you look more beautiful every time I see you." She looked younger everyday.

"Thank you." She smirked, which was all she'd allow of a smile if she received a compliment. I couldn't wait to get Mom back when she came home from India, after implementing her plan. I figured she'd be forced to leave Dad, because I couldn't imagine him without scotch.

Mom went through the second, less complicated surgery with ease. For the first few days, she progressed as hoped and Raj left on his trip to Europe.

The next day, everything fell apart. I called her room in the morning around 8:00, and Dad answered. I was surprised that he was in her room so early in the morning.

"She's not good. I've been here since 7:00 a.m." His voice shook. "She called me late last night and early this morning in a lot of pain."

"What do you mean? She was fine yesterday."

"Last night her stomach started swelling and they don't know why."

"Oh, my God—"

"Mala, she's in a lot of pain." His solemn tone told me how serious it was. "What did Dr. Bird say?"

"He left on vacation, but Jonathan, his apprentice said that the morphine might've stopped her intestinal track. So, he took her off it." I couldn't believe Dr. Bird left town. "He said it happens."

"I'll leave work now and be right there."

"Hold on." He moved the phone away from his face. "Do you want her to come now?" he said in Bengali to Mom.

"No, no tell her there isn't anything she can do. Tell her to stay at work, come later," Mom said to him in a strained voice.

That afternoon, Dad called me at work in hysterics. "Dad, I can't understand you. What's going on?"

"Your Mom's pain's been getting worse and worse. I can't take seeing her like this." He was sobbing.

"Okay, what are they doing for her?"

"Nothing. There's nothing they can do."

"I'm going to get there as soon as I can." It sounded like torture. The whole point of Mom's surgery was to get rid of the pain.

I got to the hospital around 7:30 p.m. after I stopped at home to walk and feed Boo. The nurse told me that Dad left at 7:00, after Mom sent him home. He'd cried the whole day while he watched her writhe in pain.

For once, I didn't blame him. It was hideous.

I poked my head through her hospital door and saw that the room was dark, except for the lights on the I.V. machine, which fed Mom nutrients.

"I'm in so much pain," she said in a cracked voice. Her eyes held despair and exhaustion.

I felt helpless. None of the lessons of God and spirit mattered if I couldn't alleviate Mom's suffering.

"Can you rub my forehead? My mom used to do it for me when I was little if I didn't feel good."

I had never seen or heard her so vulnerable. I sat on the edge of her bed and stroked her forehead, praying with everything I was that she would feel some relief.

She opened her eyes. "Please do something." She grabbed my hand on her forehead. "I can't take this pain."

"Okay, I will."

"Can you meditate or something to get rid of it?"

I closed my eyes and laid my hands on her abdomen. It was swollen almost as big as when she was pregnant with Raj. Within my mind, I begged God to take her pain away, to start her intestinal track or to alleviate her suffering in some way.

After some time, she said, "I can make it. Go home. You don't need to see me like this."

"I can't leave you."

"No, go but rub my forehead again for a little while first." I did until her breathing calmed.

When I left, I sobbed through the hallways, to my car, the whole way home.

Dad answered when I called the hospital room the next morning and told me she was still in a lot of pain.

Half dozen calls to him throughout the day informed me that her condition had worsened, but no one knew why.

That night, Dad told me that the doctors finally gave her morphine, because they figured out that the pain was coming from something else.

"Well, what's it coming from?"

"They don't know."

"How can they not know?"

"I don't know. I can't answer you." Fear flooded his voice. "I don't understand what's happening." I pictured him as a young man alone in America with no one to ask for help.

"Okay, don't worry. Mom's not in pain now?" He paused to peek at her. "No, she's sleeping."

The next day, a Saturday, she wasn't in her room when I went to see her. Dad and I planned that I would go in the morning and he, in the afternoon. We tried not to be there at the same time, because Mom hated the tension between us.

The nurse on duty told me that Mom was getting a CAT scan. The scan found that her stomach had abscessed. They drained more than a quart of pus from her abdomen, while I waited in the hallway.

They'd let her sit like that for days. I swore then that no one I loved would ever go to the hospital again. Mom herself had said a few days prior to both Dad and me that if she ever had to have surgery again she'd "go buy a gun and shoot" herself.

Back in her room, as Mom slept, I laid my head on the foot of her bed. My poor little mom. She was only 5'2" though she claimed 5'3". Her small body had been through hell. The reality of her pain, the infection in her body, the drainage bags attached to her sides pushed nails in my heart.

Dad poked his head in the room a while later, fresh from a shower after his Saturday morning tennis. I waved him into the hallway and told him what Mom went through that morning.

"I'm gonna go," I said to him. I looked back at Mom to watch her sleep for a few seconds.

For the next couple of days, she rested in the hospital, while the two new bags drained the unwanted pus from her body.

On Tuesday morning, she said, "I'm leaving tomorrow. I don't want to stay here anymore. So, don't come after work."

"But, I want to."

"I know how tough this has been on you coming by after work and taking care of Boo Boo. Take the week off. I'm fine."

I was relieved. I worked in Woodland Hills, and the extra drive from Santa Monica to East Los Angeles after work each night had wiped me out. The traffic and filth of the roads took their toll on me.

CHAPTER TEN
Choice

Mom slept most of Wednesday after she got home.

When I called Thursday morning, something was different.

"How'd you sleep not being in the hospital?" I asked, excited for her to be in her own bed.

"Not great. It's not easy with these bags." She sounded like a gray, stormy sky, thick with gloom.

"But, these ones are coming out really soon." Unlike her colostomy bag, the bags draining the pus in her abdomen, these would be removed within the week. "Yeah, that's what they say, but they don't know how they're going to fix it."

The doctors had no idea whether Mom would need another surgery to repair the damage done by the infection in her abdomen. "You're getting better, Mom."

"I guess so."

"Soon this will be behind you." I tried to shift her perspective. "We'll be looking back at it while we're out shopping."

"I don't know why I'd want to bother getting better. What for? Who cares?" I wished she'd go back to blaming God. This was eerie.

"What do you mean?" I said in a gentle voice. She was like a rabbit that I didn't want to scare away.

"Nothing. I don't know." It didn't make sense. She wasn't in pain, she was getting better.

"Tell me, what's up? Have you talked to Grace?" I asked. She needed to talk to her therapist, who I knew she saw intermittently. I couldn't help her.

"No. What does she know? She doesn't know me."

"Sure she does. You two have been working together for a while."

"No one really knows another person." She was distancing herself from me.

Red bells rang in my body. "That's not true."

"You know, I'm not feeling well. I'll talk to you later." She hung up without waiting for my good-bye.

I didn't put my phone down and dialed my father's home office.

"Dad, don't leave Mom by herself today." My words echoed in my ears, as if in a surreal dream.

"What're you talking about? She's doing great." Dad thought she was "doing great," because she was home with him. He wasn't alone.

"Dad, listen to me." His exaggerated sigh told me he would listen. "Something's wrong with her. I think she's going to try to kill herself." I said it, I put words to what I felt, a feeling so strange and out of context to anything I'd experienced.

"What? Why are you so dramatic?"

"Dad, Dad, listen–"

"She's not going to kill herself. What's wrong with you?"

"Don't leave her alone today. Promise me."

"Mala, I've got to go to the grocery store to get us food, then, I'll be home, then, we're going to her appointment at 3:00 p.m."

He wasn't going to be any help. "What's her therapist's number?" I looked around my kitchen for a piece of paper. "I'm calling her. Something's not right."

Reality blurred. I ignored reason and trusted my gut.

On the therapist voicemail, I left the following message: "Hi, Grace, my name is Mala Mukherji, I'm Dipta Mukherji's daughter. I don't know if you know, but she's experienced some difficulty from her surgeries. I'm calling because, when I spoke to her this morning, she sounded suicidal." My own words shocked me.

"I've never heard her like this. Will you please give her a call and call me back if you think it's appropriate to do so." I left all of the numbers where she could reach me.

Although I took definite action, I doubted myself. How could I have heard what I heard in her voice? Maybe I was wrong, maybe I was creating a giant mess. Was I being dramatic or over-sensitive?

I got ready to go into the office in a shaky, uncertain fog. At my desk, I billed a couple of hours, called Dad a few times and waited for Grace to ring me back. I went to my pre-arranged therapy appointment. Although I told Sharon that I thought Mom was going to kill herself, she didn't appear alarmed or suggest any courses of action that stuck with me.

Back to my office around 2:30 p.m., I found that Grace left a message. She answered when I called her back.

"I spoke to your Mom, you were right. She's intending to take her own life and has a plan." She was smooth, unwavering and authoritative.

I stared out the window of my office, wishing for anything else.

Grace continued. "She's going to overdose on insulin. That's why she wanted to leave the hospital."

Her confirmation brought me no validation. "What're we going to do to stop her?"

"I'm calling the Norris Center so that I can speak to her doctors and get them to hold her there. Not a psychiatric hold but just to keep an eye on her physical health. Your Mom should go along with that."

"Go along?"

"Yes, I don't want your mom to become alarmed, because I think she'll try to run."

"Run? You do?" My mind coughed and sputtered.

"Yeah. I also don't want her knowing that we spoke because it'll break her trust in me."

"Fine, yes, I understand."

I sat paralyzed at my desk and tried to understand what was happening but couldn't. I felt three feet away from myself. I wished I could call Susanna, but she was in Europe visiting a living saint named Mother Meera.

I left Sharon a message and called Dad to tell him what Grace had said. I hoped he'd believe a professional since he couldn't believe me.

"She doesn't want to stay in the hospital. She hates it there," Dad said.

"Jesus, Dad, I know that. She doesn't want to stay in the hospital, because she wants to kill herself tonight." Chaos settled into my being. "Don't you get it? She doesn't want to live anymore." I started to cry from frustration. "You have to make sure they hold her there. She has a plan and everything. She's going to overdose on insulin."

"Okay, okay, I'll get Norris to hold her."

I knew he wouldn't do a thing to help. He'd ignore what Grace had said and what I was screaming.

Maybe it was because she was sitting right there in front of him and looking like her normal self. After thirty-three years of marriage, he should've realized that Mom was the master of hiding her inner world.

I wanted to tell him the truth. She hates that you're an alcoholic, that you sneak extra scotches when you think she can't hear you. She hates that you are checked out, caring only about whether you have food to eat and tea and scotch to drink. I said nothing because it wouldn't have helped Mom.

I stared at the piles of paper on my desk. I spoke with Sharon, who returned my call. "What do you want to do?" she asked.

"What I'm doing." Without hesitation, I admitted my best effort was in effect. I waited at my desk to figure out my next move.

Grace called no more than a half-hour later. "I spoke to Jonathan and alerted him to the situation." Jonathan was Dr. Bird's stand-in while he was on a holiday.

"What'd he say?" I relaxed for a second knowing that Grace and Mom's doctors were in contact. They'd handle it. They had a legal duty to do so.

"He said that he'd have therapists from his staff talk to Dipta, your Mom." Mom had taught me to never think that anyone other than your family cares about your well-being. I wondered if she was right again as I chewed on the inside of my mouth in thought.

Grace sounded too calm. If she'd spoken to Jonathan in the same tone as she spoke to me, he might not understand how serious it was. I had to make sure the hospital would hold her, to get her help. I'd wait until my parents got there and call Jonathan myself.

I watched the digital clock on my desk phone. I didn't do anything else. At 3:10, I dialed the number I'd gotten from Grace and spoke to the receptionist. "I'm looking for a doctor named Jonathan who's filling in for Dr. Bird. My Mom's one of his patients." I pointed my next words. "It's imperative that I speak with him right away, while she's still there."

"Please hold."

"I'm sorry he's with a patient right now. Can I take a message?" Her routine response unhinged me.

"I know he's with a patient. He's with my Mom. I need to speak to him right now. It's a matter of life and death, and if you do not let me speak to him right now, I'll make sure I find you."

I was out of my mind. My gut screamed too loudly to hear anything else. Mom was going to kill herself unless I could get someone to hold her at the hospital.

"Hold on, let me get him," the nurse said to preserve her own safety. I gripped the phone, like a lifeline.

"Yes?" Jonathan said in an arrogant, annoyed tone.

"Yes, hi, this is Mala Mukherji, Dipta Mukherji's daughter. I understand that Grace, her therapist, spoke to you today." I calmed my voice in hopes that he wouldn't dismiss me as a hysterical female.

"Yes, she did and we've had some people from our staff speak with your Mom." He was even more sedate than Grace, almost comatose.

"What'd they say?"

"They've determined that she's fine." The coldness of his vacant heart made me shiver.

"You've got to be kidding me."

"Look, you're clearly not seeing this correctly." Sadistic surgeon prick. "Your Mom's here now. I'm telling you she's fine."

"How can you believe that?"

"We asked her if she was planning on harming herself, she said that she wasn't."

Was I crazy or was he? "Do you think she'd admit it so that you'd keep her in the hospital?" I threw the pen in my hand across my office.

"Look, Jonathan, I promise you, as smart as you think you are, my mother's brilliant. She's tricking you and your whole staff." I slowed my words to a vicious hiss. "She's going to kill herself if you let her go. I'm her daughter, I know her."

"We're not going to hold her. She wants to go home and short of putting her in a psychiatric hospital, which would be dangerous because of her delicate health, there's nothing I can do." His small mind slammed shut.

"Fine. I want to speak to my father. Put him on the phone." I waited for a minute or two on hold.

"Hello? Mala?" Dad said, sounding out of sorts, overwhelmed and exhausted. "Dad, what is going on over there?" I was hysterical.

"I don't know why you're so upset. She's fine. She's not going to do anything."

"Dad, please don't leave the hospital. Please make sure she stays."

"Okay, if you really believe it's that dangerous. I'll make sure she stays somehow."

"Okay, Dad, it's really important."

"I know." His patience broke. "I'm doing the best that I can!"

"I know, I'm sorry, I appreciate it." It was absurd to thank Dad for helping me save Mom.

I concocted my own plan. I'd leave work, walk Boo, get to the hospital and talk to her myself, face to face.

I walked into Kevin's office around 5:00 p.m. "I've got to go. My Mom's dying." His head jerked from the papers on his desk in surprise. "I thought she was doing better, that she didn't have anything life-threatening."

"She's going to take her own life," I said as I closed the door to his office. I drove home with an odd humming in my skull.

Home by 6:00 p.m., I listened to my messages. It was Dad at 4:45 p.m., in a chipper, cheery voice, "Hi, honey, we're in the car on the way home from the hospital and everything's fine. She's doing great. We'll talk to you later." He'd avoided me by not calling me at work or on my cell.

Nothing I'd said the whole day mattered to him. It's like I'd been screaming into a hurricane, my words drowned out by a larger force.

They would've already gotten to the house. I walked Boo and gave her some dinner. Then, huddled on my kitchen floor in the corner by the back door, I dialed Mom's number.

"Hey, what's up?" I hadn't spoken to her since morning, which was odd for us. "Nothing," she said.

I pretended not to hear the anger in her voice and that I hadn't been talking about her behind her back all day. I'd never done that outside of Sharon's office. "Really?"

"Have you been telling people that I'm going to kill myself?"

"Why do you ask?" I played it off because I wanted to assess where she was with her plan. Maybe she'd turned the corner. Maybe I'd fucking fabricated the whole thing.

"I can't believe you've been telling people that. How could you embarrass me that way?" I was stunned by her venom.

"Calm down. I'm not trying to embarrass you. I don't know what you're talking about." I wasn't a good liar.

"Oh, come on. Yes, you do," Mom spat at me.

"No. What happened?"

"The people at the Norris Center were asking if I was thinking about harming myself. It was ridiculous."

"What'd you tell them?" I kept my voice even.

"That I wasn't." That's all the doctors needed to give up. No need to inconvenience themselves.

"Do you want me to come home and hang out?"

"No. You're such a spoiled brat. Don't you have tickets to the tennis tournament tonight?" My parents had tickets to a Los Angeles tournament, which they gave me. "Why don't you go to that?"

Again, I thought I'd lost my mind. Should I have gone to the tournament, ignoring my every instinct? My eyes burned from too many tears. "I don't feel like going to the tournament. I'd rather see you."

"Stay away from me. Leave me alone! I don't want to see you." This person wasn't my Mom.

"Why are you speaking to me like this?"

"It's been a long day, I'm tired," she said more cold than angry.

"Okay. I'll leave you alone, if you promise you won't do something to hurt yourself." No longer calm, I sobbed and gulped for air. "Mom, I could never make it here without you."

"I won't. I promise," she said, sounding unmoved by my truth or tears. "Here, talk to your Dad."

I didn't hear them say anything to one another when she handed him the phone. My heart beat so hard the walls of my house seemed to shake. Boo stared at me, because I was on the floor curled up as small as I could get. I wished I couldn't see what others didn't and that my truth wasn't so toxic to them.

The phone rustled when it changed hands on their end.

"Mala? I don't know why you're so upset. We're just going to eat some dinner and go to bed." He didn't mention his scotch.

"Dad, please keep an eye on her." I was crying.

"YOU KNOW WHAT. I CAN ONLY TAKE SO MUCH. IF YOU'RE SO WORRIED COME HOME AND WATCH HER YOURSELF!"

His screams quieted me. Something in me conceded. This was between their souls and God. I was done. My years of therapy and studying philosophy, psychology and religion collided in that moment. I hung up my superhero outfit. I was just their kid, not their savior. I was just a person.

I understood that my usual response would be to rush home, sit by Mom's side, talk to her, direct Dad to call Grace and Mom's brothers and sisters. Tired of cleaning up their messes, it was time to see what they were made of, what they meant to one another.

I couldn't will Mom to live or teach Dad how to wake up. I had to accept Mom's choice instead of propping her up to be who I needed. I loved Mom enough to let her find her way.

I would no longer act as a cushion to soften reality's blow, a confidante to supplement my father's narcissism, an ambassador to American culture, a stylist for special occasions or fill in for her missing family in India. I knew if she did it, I'd feel like I failed in my quest to protect her. Everything in me told me to let her choose.

The simple proverb flashed through my mind: "If you love someone, set them free and, if they come back, it was meant to be."

That night, by not going to Mom, I knew I would learn about love. "I'm not coming home," I finally said to Dad.

"Well, do whatever you want, but stop telling me what to do," he said.

"You're right. She's your responsibility tonight. Just make sure you take all the insulin away from her, all the knives, too. I'll talk to you in the morning."

I still hoped that I made up the whole thing in my mind. I even fantasized about the shame I'd feel in the morning.

I paged Sharon. Again, she rang right back, which surprised me.

I answered her call on the first ring. "Are you going to go home?"

"No, it's between them. I can't take care of her anymore. I can't buffer them from their reality." Hearing my truth out loud, I shuddered from my toes up.

"Then, you just take good care of yourself and call me if you need to." She had said those words to me after every session for five and a half years "Take good care of yourself."

I knew that I was taking "good care" of myself by not going home. I was applying the things I'd learned at the risk of ultimate consequences.

I trusted that it would unravel by God's plan. I knew that my father was a child, that he would not be able to stop himself from his two, large, double scotches and that he would pass out before Mom would fall asleep. I knew that she knew that, as well.

Even though she promised me she wouldn't harm herself, I didn't trust her. I couldn't move from my kitchen floor where I watched a nightmare that I refused to stop.

At 5:25 a.m. on my bedroom clock, I jumped awake with a sick feeling in my stomach that pulled the air out of my lungs. The center of my body sucked itself into a bottomless vacuum. I sat straight up, coughing to breathe and waited in my bed until the phone rang at 6:30. I answered it without surprise, on the first ring.

"Mala, your mom's in the hospital." I recognized the voice of Mom's friend,

Kuntula Mashi who lived five minutes away. "You need to come home."

"Where's my dad? I want to talk to him." She gave him the phone.

"Mala, the ambulance came. She's in the hospital. I don't know what's happening," he said between sobs.

"Dad, listen to me." He continued to howl. "I'm coming home right now. Go to the hospital. Don't drive yourself, I'll meet you there."

An hour to prepare for the call, I was calm. I made a cup of coffee and got dressed. I wore a gray-blue cotton sweater, leggings and ballet flats, which

I never wore again. I didn't think about the fact that it would be 100 degrees in the July heat in Covina.

I walked Boo on the way to the car. From the freeway, I called Grace and paged Sharon. Sharon called me back right away. "No matter what's happened, we'll have a lot to deal with."

I knew Mom was gone. I prayed I was wrong. I told God over and over that I wasn't ready to lose her.

Several police cars were parked in front of my parents' house when I arrived to leave Boo in the yard. Boo and I walked to the house through the front door passed several policemen poking around in the closets and drawers.

"I'm putting her outside." I said to one of them, pointing at Boo. Six inches from him, I stared him in the face. "If anything happens to her and my mom in the same day, I'll kill someone." He held my gaze with compassion. "Please do not let her out of the yard."

I raised my voice to address all of the policemen. "Does anyone here know anything about my mom?"

One of them approached me, shook my hand and gave me his card, which sat in my car for over a year. "She was taken to the San Dimas Hospital. They're still trying to resuscitate her."

I nodded wordless thanks to him.

At the hospital, Kuntula Mashi and her husband stood around Dad, who sat in a plastic chair outside the Emergency Room.

Hope flashed for a split second. Maybe Mom was in surgery, maybe they were waiting for her outside. Why else would they be sitting there?

Dad stood up and hugged me.

"I'm so sorry, I'm so sorry," he sobbed.

I squirmed from his wet hug. "Okay, where is she?"

"Through those doors," Kuntula Mashi said. "Do you want me to come?"

I shook my head and walked to a glass door with a red sign to its right, which read "Emergency Room." I pushed a button on the brick wall under the sign. The door opened with a swishing noise.

A policewoman sat in a chair in the first draped-off room. "Um, I'm looking for my. . . ." Then, I noticed Mom who was on a table face up with a tube dangling from her open mouth. Her eyes were closed.

Concerned I'd wake her, I said in a soft whisper, "Is she in a coma?"

The policewoman's eyes widened. She took a deep breath. "No, I'm sorry, she's gone." I stared at her. "Your father didn't tell you?"

I walked up to Mom's body, placing my hands on the softness of her legs beneath the sheet. I couldn't believe I'd never see her eyes open again.

Time froze and I with it. The finality of her still body stopped everything. This was real.

It was all happening. This was it.

This was our life.

Her beautiful hands, her manicured nails, her perfect lips pried open by the giant tube shoved down her throat. She had chosen. She hadn't let the tube bring her back to me, to us, to life.

I confirmed with the policewoman that Mom wouldn't be moved for a while. Then, I rushed outside in a white rage. "I TOLD YOU SO!!" I clenched my fists, wanting to hit him. "Now, what are you going to do? She's dead!"

"I'm sorry. I'm so sorry," Dad said.

"Give me your phone. I need Raj back from Europe." I needed him. I needed to see his face.

We had no idea where he was. He and his friend, Kent, intended to pick up a friend's new BMW at the factory, follow the wind around Europe and then come home. I called his best friend who said he'd work on getting him home. I didn't break the news in a gentle way. He'd known Mom for half his life, and I failed to consider his shock and sadness.

Two police officers approached where we stood, guns in the holsters at their sides.

"Mr. Mukherji?" one of them asked Dad. Dad nodded, his eyes unsteady.

"We need to talk to you, sir."

I stepped forward. "About what? This isn't the best time."

"Well, ma'am, there was a death at his home, we found a note. So, we need to speak to him now."

A note? "I'm an attorney. You can talk to him with me there."

The officers led us through the Emergency Room, passed Mom's still warm body to a supply closet. "Like we said outside, we found a note which we believe is in your mom's handwriting?"

"What does it say?" I said.

"'No heroic measures. My husband and I agreed.'" The officer turned to Dad. "Sir, did you help your wife do this?"

Dad couldn't answer through his sobs. "Dad, tell them." I nudged his arm. "No, no I didn't," he gurgled and lifted a shredded tissue to wipe his nose.

I tilted my chin with false authority. "Gentlemen, obviously he didn't. He's a wreck." I waved over my head to the hospital floors above. "I'm actually hoping we can hospitalize him to help him through this." I walked toward the closet door. "So, if there are no more questions, we're finished."

I settled Dad outside with Kuntula Mashi and went back in to see Mom. I needed something from her, though I didn't know what.

The policewoman excused herself to give me time alone.

When she closed the curtains behind her, I collapsed on the ground. Primal pain erupted from my core. "Mommy, please don't go. Mommy, please come back." I couldn't stop screaming. I rocked on the floor for a long time, holding my knees to my chin, sobbing and shuddering until I leapt to her side.

"MOM, WAKE UP! COME ON, MOM, WAKE UP!" I thought that if I could focus all of my will, all of my energy and force on her, her body would come back to life and she would wake up.

I wanted to see her eyes open one more time. Her big, soft, round eyes that loved me.

I wanted her to say good-bye to me. I couldn't believe that she would leave me without saying good-bye.

Something moved. I saw it out of the corner of my eye. I thought it was her. "Mom?" I froze to listen. I waited for a breath, a click from her sarcastic smirk, the heat of a loud look. Nothing happened.

It had been me jerking her body with my heaves. I couldn't accept it. "MOM, PLEASE, PLEASE DON'T LEAVE ME. I can't do this without you. PLEASE, MOM, PLEASE WAKE UP."

I tugged on her heavy hand. "You promised, Mom, you promised me."

I laid my head on her lap next to her drainage bag poking through the thin hospital gown. Her forehead was thick without expression, her skin void of moisture. Clusters of gray hair framed her face. She hadn't been well enough to color her hair.

How had we gotten here? How was she laying here like this?

In that instant, I understood that I was experiencing the most painful thing I'd ever know. I was certain of it.

It was as if God himself whispered, "This is as bad as it will get."

I stood away from Mom's body, exact and steady to soak the truth into my being. This dead body was Mom's. I stayed with her for a while, memorizing where her cheeks met her chin, the arch of her thin eyebrows, the straightness of her lashes.

Her face burned into the memory of my soul, I opened the curtain and nodded the policewoman back into the room.

Tears streamed down her face. She had heard me.

CHAPTER ELEVEN
Consequence

I stormed outside to find Dad, my murderous rage weighted down by my crushed heart. I pulled my keys from my purse. "I'm going home. I have to see Boo." Dad told Kuntula Mashi that he'd ride home with me. We didn't speak for the ten minutes alone in the car.

As if on invisible rails, I led myself to my childhood bedroom. I wanted to lie where she had lain down to die. My room had been my sanctuary from harm for twenty-four years. That morning, I was scared of it. The mirror into which I had prayed to God to make me pretty stood in the same place. Remnants of the tape from Mom's "no heroic measures" note remained in the upper-left corner. I took it off and scratched at the sticky stuff left over.

I looked in the drawer where I'd hidden my rat poison. The poison gone, unused, full vials of insulin were in its place. In the trashcan under my desk, three empty insulin vials and three used syringes laid on a pile of paper scraps. The policemen hadn't taken any of it as evidence.

I sat down on the corner of my bed in which Mom had taken her last breath. Above her pillow on the ledge of the window, the blue photo box of Yogananda had watched over her. I needed to know what he'd seen, what had happened.

I found Dad on the sofa where Mom and I converged thousands of afternoons. "What happened last night?" I asked without kindness.

Dad told me that, home from the hospital, he and Mom talked for hours. Mom had dismissed my panic about her suicide by calling me "precocious" and telling Dad that I thought I knew everything. His words hurt, but I asked him to continue.

She told him to put the insulin he'd hidden back in the fridge because she might need it in the morning, even though she hadn't in a few days.

She told him that, if he didn't put it back, she'd take the car and drive it off a cliff. She told him that if he put her in the hospital, she'd hang herself by the sheets.

She told him everything he needed to know to stop her.

Dad chose to place the insulin back in the fridge.

They went to bed around 11:00 p.m. Mom had slept in my room since the first surgery, because the discomfort of the colostomy bag made it difficult for her to sleep. "I don't want to bother your Dad," she'd said to me weeks prior.

Dad woke up several times during the night to look in on her.

Around 2:00 a.m., he noticed that the door to the kitchen was slightly open. They shut it every night so that Heidi, their German Shepherd, couldn't wake them too early in the morning. He didn't think anything of it.

He noticed that the light from the full moon illuminated Mom, who seemed in a deep sleep. "She looked peaceful," he said.

Around 4:00 a.m., Dad laid next to Mom for a while. "I didn't want her to get mad at me if I woke her, so I went back to bed."

A little before 5:30 a.m., he checked on her, again. That time, her arm hung over the edge of the bed, her head bent to her left. She was lifeless. He called Kuntula Mashi and then 911.

Dad bowed his head at the end of his story. "No matter how smart we are, we can't change this. It's done, it's all gone."

Contempt overrode compassion. "You don't get it, do you? She was sick of your drinking. She wanted to get away from you. She told me." I wanted to demolish him. To wound him as badly as his failure to listen had destroyed me. "Now, we're in hell because she's dead and you're still here. I wish it were you. I wish you were dead and not her!"

I ran to my room and cried like I always did after I fought with Dad. This time, Mom wouldn't come to talk to me.

I came out of my room to call Tiff. We cried together. Of all my friends, she was most like Mom. Each time Tiff and I went to the spa in the desert, we dropped Boo off for Mom to watch and Mom and Tiff would take a few minutes to themselves, embrace and whisper things to one another.

Within an hour, the phone started to ring and things began to move quickly. I let Dad answer all the calls.

He found me curled up with Boo in the living room between calls. "Your mom didn't want another surgery."

"Yeah, so?" I couldn't look at him.

"They're taking her to the morgue. We can't let them cut her open for the autopsy." He contacted a judge he knew who found Mom's body en route to the morgue and stopped the process.

Grace rang me on Mom's line and Dad handed me the phone. "I thought you would go home," she said.

I didn't take it as an accusation, although it might've been. "I wanted them to deal with it. I didn't want to get involved anymore."

"Oh, well–"

"Why didn't you do anything else? Wait, it doesn't matter." She was gone no matter what Grace did or didn't do.

"Your mom was such a proud woman. I didn't want to humiliate her." Was Mom proud of her suicide?

I couldn't believe she did it and felt the smallest bit of humiliation well up inside of me imagining the rest of my life. Nice to meet you, I'd say, my mom committed suicide on July 30, 1999 and I knew she would but didn't stop her.

I only wanted Raj to come home from Europe. She was his mom, too.

I went outside, away from the ring of the telephone, Mom's things and Dad's hysteria. I clutched Yogananda's picture in one hand, my yellow cigarette box in the other. On the patio off the kitchen, I sat in one of their blue, plastic chairs where my gaze drifted beyond the rows of houses to the bare mountains. Mom would never again see the snow on them through her kitchen window.

I shook my head against the finality of my thought and lit a cigarette. It tasted the same, but I felt different. I wanted to see if I looked different so I put out my cigarette and went inside to my childhood bathroom.

That mirror held my life's changes in its memory. Every time I came to the house, the first thing I did was look in it to see how the time away had impacted me, whether the circles under my eyes were deeper, my hair longer or frizzier, my skin broken out, my blemish scars faded.

I held my breath as I locked the door behind me and turned on the light. Over the years, my face hid nothing from that mirror.

I walked away from it to get the full-view from the step in front of the bathtub. My body looked the same but deflated. I walked up to the right sink, leaned in close to look into my eyes. Then, I bent back to see my whole face. I looked younger.

The fragility and fear in my eyes drained the life experience from my face. The new, hard-fought sheen of womanly strength dulled. The invisible, arrogant safety from Mom's presence vanished like the ground beneath me. I looked alone, feeble and unprotected.

I rushed out of the bathroom, grabbed a bottle of water from the garage and went back outside to my chair, blue photograph box and cigarettes. I thought about the look in my eyes. I didn't stop her. Forget what Sharon had said, "You can't stop someone from killing themselves." I could've but chose not to drive home.

I imagined how different that day would've been if I'd come home and sat next to her for however long it took for her to get well. Days or months, it wouldn't have mattered.

I remembered the certainty in my gut from the night prior but questioned the outcome. She couldn't come back. I couldn't re-create July 29th and choose an alternate ending no matter how hard I meditated, prayed or begged God. I'd lost that chance forever.

I lost her, because Dad was who I always knew he was. I didn't protect her from his weakness. She was gone and I was lost without her.

I worked so hard for four years to follow my gut. I'd done the right thing, but expected that when I did the right thing, everything worked out. My trust in the universe ruptured. My breath grew shallow and hollow. I tried to smoke a cigarette but started to cry so the smoke escaped from my lungs in jagged puffs, leaving a rancid taste on my tongue.

I went inside to her kitchen. Everything was where she left it. I opened the dishwasher. No one was allowed to load it, and, if we did in helpfulness, she rearranged it her way, the dishes facing the same way, the forks, knives and spoons separated in the utensil baskets.

I opened the fridge. There were no Tupperware containers filled with her leftovers. She'd been so sick she hadn't cooked in weeks. I couldn't remember what her food tasted like.

I opened the cupboard to the dishes. Her favorite mugs were lined up on the first shelf, more haphazardly than the dishwasher. One from Ben which read "Heal the Bay," one with Boo's picture on it that I had made at a mall, one from the Volvo Car Clinic. She liked white mugs because she said, "They make better tea."

When I looked up to the second shelf where she kept the glasses, I identified my body's sensation. I felt stuck in one of the jelly jars that we used as milk and juice glasses when we were little, the ones with the cartoons painted on the outside that came with a purchase from McDonald's or the gas station.

From the moment I saw her body, I felt shoved into a tiny space from which I could see and hear the world around me, but everything was distorted by a thick plate of glass. The world and the people in it appeared and sounded inconsequential and distant.

I grabbed a chair from the kitchen table to search the corners of the top shelf, hoping she'd saved one of the jars from nostalgia. If I found one, I knew I'd feel better. When I didn't, I sat in the chair and cried, then crawled back outside to the blue plastic chair.

I felt like I could slip into insanity with a slight breeze. It scared me that my thoughts were crazy, but my spoken words sounded sane, too much disparity between them.

The years in therapy, hours in meditation and days and nights of study to find some link with this life and my inner world were lost. I fell back to one side of the chasm, which separated me from everything, everyone and myself.

It concerned me that I wasn't hot even though I had on a sweater, the same one I wore for Mom's first surgery. It was at least ninety-five degrees. I wanted to sweat or experience some normal bodily sensation. I wasn't hungry and hadn't eaten all day.

Over and over in my mind, I wished that Dad were dead so then Mom wouldn't be. I felt no consequence to my thoughts, no connection to anything. Even Boo looked like a stranger.

Old age hadn't given me time to detach from her. The womb that bore me died. I didn't exist.

I thought about tomorrow, because it was a different day and not yet destroyed by Mom's death. Sharon had called the house and offered me an appointment for the next day. I accepted.

As day changed to night, Dad panicked and ran around the house repeating, "I can't stay here alone." I didn't care. I had to get back to my space. To think, to smoke indoors, to cry without a witness. I was full yet empty beneath the fullness. Full of a feeling to which no emotion or thought fit, empty in a way that could never again feel full. It was like the opposite of joy but not despair or sorrow. It was vacant, cold and barren. I guess it was death. I felt dead.

Atiyeh, Raj's best friend who promised to find him came by and agreed to stay with Dad that night. Mom adored him. His sense of humor had warmed many of our family meals for over a decade.

Munju and Shipra Mashi heard the news from Kuntula Mashi and came by the house at dusk. Although Kuntula Mashi was a newer friend of Mom's, I'd known Shipra and Munju Mashi my whole life. The clang of their bangles and soft Indian manners reminded me of Mom. They were kind in that ancient way that doesn't impose itself.

I stood with them in the kitchen while they tried to feed me food that they had made. "I can't eat Indian food that she didn't make. I'm not ready," I said.

Their faces sank in understanding.

Around 8:00 p.m. under a bright red, angry sky, I told Dad I was leaving but would come back the next day. He tried to hug me but I backed away and ran to my car.

The radio jumped to life with its garbled nonsense. I quickly concluded that I couldn't tolerate the sound of anything but Yogananda's voice. I grabbed one of his tapes from the floor of my car and listened to it while I drove on the 10 West to Santa Monica.

Ahead of me, the downtown skyline swam in the late evening light. The colors muted and ran together like a dream. My car filled with the certitude of Yogananda's voice and I welled with a deep warmth. I felt protected.

Mom would watch over me. She wouldn't let me fall. I wished that moment could've lasted for years, but like all moments, it dissolved before I passed the La Brea exit.

At home, I checked my messages of which there was one from Scott 10:30 a.m. "Hey, I have a strange feeling. Just wanted to make sure you and your Mom were okay." I could see from his dark window that he was not yet home from whereever he was.

I sat at my kitchen table by candlelight. Lamps were too harsh. I heard Scott's truck around 10:45 p.m. and scurried down the backstairs, trying not to trip. The stairs were narrow, I couldn't feel them beneath my lifeless feet.

When Scott walked toward his apartment stairs, he saw me. "My Mom died."

"What?" His kaleidoscope eyes pierced the darkness. "She died this morning."

He followed me upstairs and sat on my chaise, while Boo and I sat on the sofa. Scott stayed until 2:00 a.m.

I slept but awoke with a jolt at 5:25 a.m., the same time I'd woken when she left her body the morning before.

Out of bed at 6:30 a.m., I concentrated on breathing through the pain, which threatened to overtake me. A block into Boo's walk, I lost it.

I heaved and howled just like I had in the Emergency Room when I'd been alone with her. I scrambled back to my house and pulled Boo before she was ready. I ran to the bathroom. Leaning over the toilet, I begged God to help me not throw up. If I started, it wouldn't stop for days.

I wanted to be strong. If I fell apart, nothing could put me back together. I had too much to do. I had to plan the funeral, write the obituary, take care of Boo. Telling myself that, I only dry heaved.

I left Boo at home, because I planned to go from Dad's to Sharon's. Back on the 10 East, I couldn't believe it had only been 27 hours since I had raced down it to find Mom's body. It seemed like months had passed.

At the house, I went into Mom's closet. I wanted to smell her. Her sweaters and shirts still smelled like her light, floral perfume. I put on some of her shoes and wiggled my feet around. Our feet were the same size but not the same shape. The curves in her Keds didn't match the contours of my feet.

"Mala, can I ask you something?" Dad said from the doorway of his den.

I threw off her shoe, closing the closet door. "Yeah, what is it?"

"Nandita Mashi called." He looked guilty. "She wants to come by, but I don't know what to do because your Mom didn't like her." Nandita Mashi was the woman who took her husband back after her daughters revealed that he'd molested them.

"It wasn't that Mom didn't like her. She–"

"I know, but I don't know what she'd want me to do." He was trying to live by Mom's rules.

"Do you want her here?"

"I don't know, no, I do want her here. We knew her a long time, since we came to this country."

"Well, Mom's gone. You've gotta do what's going to make you feel better." Dad's anguished face uncovered my compassion for him. He looked at me with a deep thanks that made me queasy.

Unprepared for the post-death process, I started a list that I carried around for comfort and read every few minutes. I stuffed the list in my purse when I rode up the elevator to see Sharon, wondering why I wanted to see her only the day after Mom died.

Had it just been an excuse to get away from Dad? Something to do until Tiff came over in the late afternoon? I felt overwhelmed, lost and confused and wanted to find my center. The center I'd worked so long and hard to find. Sharon had helped me the first time; I hoped she could this time.

I didn't usually hug Sharon before or after any of our sessions, but, on that day, I sobbed in her arms in the doorway of the waiting room.

Following her into her office, I noticed how cute she looked in her weekend wear, narrow khakis, crisp white hooded, zip sweatshirt and neat, clean tennis shoes and told her.

She tilted her head to the right, undistracted by my compliment. "How are you?"

"Not good or couldn't you notice out there." I tried to smile, but my bottom lip trembled. I wanted to make light of how I'd clung to her but couldn't.

"This is a lot to handle."

"You think so? I keep wondering whether I'm making it worse than it is. Like I'm over-dramatizing it or something."

"No, this is as bad as life gets."

She confirmed what I knew the day before standing over Mom's body. "I feel like who I was is gone. I don't know who I am again. Like when I started. It's all shattered into shards of glass on the floor under me. I can't move without cutting myself, I can't remember who I am. I can't feel me."

After an hour and a half, Sharon helped me hold the intensity of my feelings. She didn't back away, change the subject or probe. She let me talk, and I knew she'd remember everything I'd said.

I thanked Sharon over and over in my head on my way home to meet Tiff. We'd planned that she'd hang out with me for as long as I needed. When she arrived, she unloaded several grocery bags filled with our favorite snacks: Brie to bake in crescent roll dough, chips, French onion dip powder in the packet, sour cream, baby carrots, guacamole ingredients, mini candy bars to bake in the same roll dough and squeeze cheese in the can. Every year for the Oscars, we gorged on the same food, drinking some form of vodka throughout the night.

While she prepared it, I kept her company in my tiny, post-World War II kitchen. We ate but spoke only of the food. It felt good to eat junk and snacks, instead of a proper dinner or lunch. Like rules no longer applied.

We sipped our drinks and took breaks from the food to smoke. I sat on the floor and she on my sofa. "I'm so sorry. I don't know what to say." Like Mom, Tiff was stoic. When her eyes welled with tears, I broke.

"T, I'm so scared. I don't know how to get through this." Gulps of tears interspersed themselves between my words.

"Dude, I'm going to get you through it. I will be your rock now. I'm never going to leave your side. I'll be there for you as your mom was, forever. I know she would've wanted it that way." She sobbed when she said it.

I sobbed, because she said it with her heart in her hands. She was the only one who had reached me in my tiny, glass space.

The next morning, I awoke with the sun and left to take Dad to the mortuary. I washed my hair, an ordeal under the best of circumstances. It was long and thick and when wet, heavy and burdensome. That morning, I welcomed the distraction of my frivolous mane.

Boo and I headed down the 10 East. At the exit to the Norris hospital, my body bubbled. Hope crept into my chest. Even that moment of impossible hope, relieved my despair.

I remembered Dad's words about not being able to fix it. He was right. Death couldn't be solved. It was truth and purity, yet, like the largest of tidal waves, it swept you to a place of chaos, agony and suffering.

At the mortuary, Dad slumped in a chair. Whimpers escaped from him every few seconds. I'd never seen a human being so broken. A woman informed us about casket options and various other details for the funeral, which required decisions.

Dad shrank even smaller and curled into a corner of his chair. "Look, she's going to be cremated. I don't think she'd care about her casket. Can we just see some?" I said, wanting to get Dad out of there.

I chose the next Saturday for the service hoping that Raj would be found in time.

I chose a plain, pine casket.

"Now, what would you like your urns to say?" I gulped down a sob and wanted to run somewhere that I could cry and scream until she came back. I gripped the arms of the chair not wanting to lose it. "Just 'Mom,' my brother's and my urn can say just that."

I went into the office the next day, a Tuesday, because I had a session with Sharon in the Valley at 1:00 p.m. but shouldn't have. Every word spoken to me felt like salt on my raw and exposed sore.

I winced when the phone or fax machine rang. My mind dulled from the pain even as my nerve endings heightened. I'd never been so confused. I had either overestimated my strength or underestimated the trauma.

The pain embarrassed and humbled me. I couldn't function. I couldn't push myself with my will or resolve. My life was at death's mercy.

The next morning, Dad called around 11:00 a.m. The ring of the phone caught me wandering around my 400-square-foot condo without purpose. That distance between me and everything else created an immediate and unending feeling of jet lag. I didn't know what time it was, didn't care, wasn't tired but exhausted. It had only been four days.

"Mala?" Dad always started our calls with a sharp bark of my name. "What? What's up?"

"Raj called. He—"

"From where? Did you tell him?"

"In Switzerland. They're making arrangements to come home right away."

"Did you tell him?"

Dad didn't answer.

"Dad, did you tell him about Mom?"

"I couldn't do it. I told him she was in a coma." I ignored his crying. "What? God, Dad, can't you do anything?" Tears shot to my eyes.

I instructed Dad to have Raj call me when he gave Dad his flight information.

I hung up and lit a cigarette. What kind of a weak idiot was he? How dare he lie to Raj? Killing Mom was one thing but lying to Raj was sick. My phone rang fifteen minutes and two cigarettes later.

"Mom's in a coma?" Raj said.

"Look, I'm going to tell you the truth, because I love you and believe in your ability to handle anything life throws you. Okay?"

"What is it?" The silence that awaited my next words emphasized the thuds of my heart. My tongue stuck to the roof of my mouth. I swallowed a few times, prying the words out of my constricted throat.

"Mom died. She died on Friday morning."

"How?"

"She killed herself. I didn't stop her." I sobbed when I said it. "I'm so sorry, Raj. Please just come home quickly." My poor baby brother. Too far away to hear that his mom died by her own hands. I couldn't speak to him anymore. I didn't have the strength.

"Listen, we're coming home. Just hang in there until I get there." Strange words from him. I couldn't recall a time when he had soothed me. That had been Mom's job. I felt like I let Raj down. I had to tell him the whole story. I prayed that he'd forgive me and understand why I didn't drive home that night to stop her. I didn't care if anyone other than Raj understood my choice. Part of me knew it wasn't my fault or responsibility. God let her go home and didn't think of Raj and me. He was only 24 and I was 29.

We picked Raj and Kent up from the airport but spoke only of their trip in the car. Once home I left to pick up sandwiches from the same place we'd eaten from the whole week. After we unwrapped the white paper from our lunches, Raj said, "What happened?"

Dad gave him his version of the story. Dad's story revolved around the premise that "she accidentally overdosed on insulin." My ears shut off, my blood pressure rose. I saw red but kept my mouth shut. Raj listened and nodded throughout the story but said nothing.

"So, what happened?" My brother looked at me.

"She killed herself and I knew she'd do it and I didn't stop her." I sobbed. My hair spilled over my torso and I crumbled onto the table to hide my face in my hands. When I calmed myself enough to speak, I told him most of what happened on July 29th. "That's it. I wish there was something else to say."

Raj got up and knelt in front of my chair. "I'm so sorry no one listened to you." He held my hands in his. "Your whole life you've known when something was going to happen, but no one would listen. Now, you lost the thing you loved the most because of it. It's not your fault. You weren't the one who should've done something."

No one had ever or has ever spoken more beautiful words to me. I let it all go. I collapsed into my 6'2" little brother's arms.

"It's okay. It's all going to be okay," he said. Tears flooded over my whole being. Raj not only saw me, but forgave me. Mom had raised us, and she'd never see Raj shine as the way he did in that moment. It was all lost.

After a long while, I picked up my head. Dad had left the table during my tears, which gave me a chance to tell Raj how Dad put the insulin which killed Mom back into the fridge, drank so he couldn't stay awake and watched her slip into a coma.

I didn't share those parts when Dad was in the room, because I wanted to avoid any confrontation. I couldn't tolerate one of his tantrums. I knew if he pushed it, I'd kill him with the nearest available knife. I'd slit his throat before Raj could pull me off of him.

My rage was deep, and the only person who might have stopped me was dead. My lawyer's mind already considered my defense, which, of course, meant that the crime would be premeditated.

"Raj, Dad murdered Mom. He fucking finally did it."

"Yeah, I guess he did." Raj and I connected without a need for explanation. For decades, we'd watched Mom sacrifice her spirit for Dad.

I left the table to clean the dishes and check on Boo. I heard Raj's cries from his room and went to his door to find his giant body on his twin bed. He heaved and rattled from the pain of our truth. I sat down next to him and rubbed his back. He wanted his mom. I was all he had.

Dad stood in the door for a moment but fled down the hallway. Raj wiped his tears on his sleeve and pillow. "Remember how I used to wake up crying in the middle of the night when I was little, because I was afraid Mom was going to die?" he said.

I nodded.

"I think I always knew she was going to die really young." I held him until his tears stopped.

Raj stayed with Dad that night and for the following year.

CHAPTER TWELVE
Burn

The viewing was Friday, the funeral the following day.

I needed to deliver Mom's make-up, perfume and sari to the funeral home on my way back to Santa Monica. Mom's sisters made Dad promise to honor Hindu traditions for the funeral, especially that we cremate Mom in a sari. Dad asked me to choose one and take it to the mortuary. Only wearing her saris for Bengali events, Mom stored them in a large, light blue suitcase on the top shelf of her closet. Sifting through the stacks of bright-colored silk and linen, memories surfaced.

I pulled a green and purple flowered silk sari out, hugging it to me. Mom had worn it many times when I was young. I could almost feel the soft fullness of her legs when I sat on her lap, counting her eight bracelets at a Bengali party I wanted to leave.

I shook the memory away and chose a sari in her favorite color, a deep burgundy, with embroidered flowers in the same color along the border. Even though Hindu tradition required a sari, I would rather have seen her as I knew her.

Mom dressed in an understated manner and felt inhibited by her mom-like "stomach," which was softer and fuller than before she birthed Raj and me. Most days, she wore white Keds and a matching, lightweight sweater and pant outfit, with pockets in the sweaters that she filled with crumpled, unused tissue. Her closets were full of them, until a year after she passed when I gathered the strength to clean them out.

Dad and I decided that Mom wouldn't want her body viewed by anyone outside the family. Even though only we would see her, I gave the funeral home strict instructions on how she should look. The funeral home told me that they didn't have anyone on staff who could drape a sari.

"Could you dress her with us?" one of the staff asked me.

"Just do the best you can," I said running to my car. Dressing Mom's body was a test I couldn't pass.

When I got to the house to meet Raj and Dad on Friday, Raj appeared both strong and scared. Dad morphed into a self-pitying shell that I would see for a few years.

The mortuary staff directed us to the room where Mom's body awaited our observation. Walking to her, I felt suspended above ground although I heard the clomps of my wood-bottomed sandals on the tile floor. I worried about Raj. He hadn't seen her or anyone else's dead body.

We stopped at a room with a sign beside it that read "Dipta Mukherji." We went in together. Dimly lit, I paused in the doorway until my eyes adjusted. Dark carpet covered the ground and walls. Sparse bouquets of flowers perched on tables at either end of Mom's coffin.

Mom's open casket seemed to emanate the only light in the room. Raj walked toward her first. I peeked at her before Dad and I left to give him time alone with her.

The mortuary must've found someone who knew how to wrap a sari, which draped backwards so that the train covered her bloated midsection in crisp, symmetrical pleats. Her usual lipstick seemed like a different color. I'd seen an open casket before and anticipated her lifelessness. But, this was different. I knew her face as well as my own.

Raj raced out of the room in less than two minutes. "I don't think Mom wants me to see her like that," he said as large tears fell over his thick bottom lashes. I knew he was right and sat next to him on a small bench in the late afternoon sun while he wept.

Dad went in next, staying far longer than Raj. When he came out, he turned his face from us and walked a few steps away. He wiped his nose with a tissue he pulled from his pant pocket. I wondered what he thought about in there.

With a pat on Raj's back, I went to the door. I didn't know what I wanted in that room. I knew that it was just her body. I wanted to believe that she existed somewhere, everywhere at the same time.

A few steps from her, I knew what I wanted: a little more time with what would burn to ash the next day. Her beautiful hands with elegant, tapered fingers. Their long nails not painted in her usual dark burgundy but a lighter gold color. I hadn't thought to bring her usual polish so that the mortuary could have repainted them.

Her full, wide lips had none of their character without a smirk or suppressed emotion. Her dead lips sat stiff and uncomfortable without a thought behind them. I averted my eyes from her unopened ones, focusing on her arms that were uncovered.

No jewelry glistened from them. The cluster of bangles on her right arm and the three on her left were on the kitchen counter in Covina. One-inch oval scars from an illness she contracted at the age of two were sporadically sprinkled over her arms. She hated the scars so much that she had me vaccinated on my thigh, leaving my arms unmarked. I loved the scars because they were hers. I'd never counted how many there were and couldn't that day.

My beautiful, lifeless Mom. No one loved her as much as I did. Everyone, even Dad, knew it and had allowed the sacred space for us to commune since my birth. In so many ways, it was just the two of us.

I couldn't believe I'd never hear her smooth, lilting voice on my machine. "Hi Mala, it's your Mom. Give me a call when you get a chance."

I must have been in there a while, because Raj poked his head through the door. "You okay?"

"Yeah, just hanging with her."

"Okay, I was just worried." His eyes pleaded with me to keep it together so that he could. "Take your time."

I wanted to sleep there with her body. Instead, I waited with her long enough to pull myself together. I didn't want to frighten or burden Raj with my unchecked tears.

At home, we ordered in pizza. None of us had been able to eat the Indian food Kuntula and Shipra Mashi brought over.

I stayed the night but slept on the family room sofa, unable to face my old bed. Raj and I sat up and talked while the T.V. droned in front of us. Dad consumed two double scotches and passed out in his bed in front of a news magazine show. That night, I couldn't blame him.

I wanted to read a poem of mine at the funeral the next day, but, by the time I went to sleep, I hadn't tried to write one. At 5:00 a.m. the morning of the funeral, my eyes popped open.

Without a cup of coffee, I grabbed the nearest notepad and sat on my bed in the spot she died. This poem sprang forth:

mother's child

I am my mother's child nothing more nothing less
and for that privilege I have been blessed
I fell from your womb and into your arms
while you tried to spare me all life's harm
you are all I have known
from this life's start
your spirit now loud in my broken heart

I have begged God to let me see you again
and I believe I will but I do not know when
I would crawl on my knees over broken glass
to hold your soft hand one time last

although I know this will not soon be
I yearn to find your eyes watching me
quietly sitting and observing it all
so I believed I would never fall

as you were there with your strong quiet love
I will never be what I once was

you bore one daughter and one son
whose ties to childhood are today undone
we cling to each other in this deadly storm
reminding ourselves from whom we were born

our beautiful mother who was always there
is gone, our lives stripped bare
we scramble to find the parts you helped build
we pray we can keep going without your will

after nurturing us so we could bloom
you have returned home far too soon
around every corner and in every place
we will search and plead to find your face

our solace is that you fly free and high
although we will never know why
we will remember years after your death
the tears of blood that we have wept

despite this twist in our young stories
we promise to honor your soul and glory
nothing can change what you did give
we are that for as long as we live

we are our mother's children
nothing more nothing less
and for that privilege we are forever blessed

I read it over once, clutched the pages in my hand, grabbed Yogananda's picture box and went to Raj's room. I tapped him on the shoulder. "Hey, you want to go get Starbucks' with me?"

When we got home, I read the poem to Raj and Dad to make sure they'd be okay with me sharing it at the funeral. They were.

An hour or so later, Dad called for us from his bedroom.

"Is this right?" Dad pointed to the suit, shirt, tie and belt he laid out on his bed. Raj and I shared a look.

"I'm trying to remember which one your mom liked best," Dad added.

Raj showed compassion and said, "It's great." I went outside to smoke.

As I dressed, I noticed that grief had consumed my body. The scale told me I'd lost seven pounds in eight days.

Dad hired a driver for the day. We took Mom's car, because a limo seemed too unlike Mom.

Tiff was already there when we arrived. She sat in the front row next to me. I sat between Raj and her, Dad next to Raj and I imagined the rest of our row filled with Mom's brothers and sisters, who hadn't been able to come. I noticed Betty hadn't either.

Tiff insured that the handouts I'd written were available. She was much like Mom. I could count on her to do what needed to be done, better than I could have.

On the stage, Mom's body rested in the now-closed pine coffin, wrapped in red roses. I chose a smiling picture for Mom's memorial. Mom thought that she had too round a face to smile in pictures. In this rare photo, her smiling face rested on her right hand, with her gold bangles bunched below her elbow.

When I first saw the picture, I said, "Mom, that's such a beautiful picture of you!"

She giggled. "You don't think my face looks fat?"

People poured into the chapel on the Rose Hills grounds, many of whom I didn't recognize. Though Tiff called Ben to let him know Mom died, he didn't respond for over a week, until after the funeral. I didn't respond to his call.

Dad leaned to Raj. "All these people are from Mom's old work, her volunteering at the hospital, old family friends and neighbors."

I forgot how many other people Mom spoke to throughout her day. I always considered it my gift alone. Mom didn't talk about how many people's lives she touched at the Intercommunity Hospital gift shop, or the young women she kept in touch with from her work at the savings and loan years prior. She didn't display her talents or achievements. She only took pride in ours.

The Hindu ceremony required Raj, Dad and I to circle her casket and photo with burning incense in our hands. Shipra and Munju Mashi sang two Tagore hymns in Bengali. One of them was called "Remember Me."

Their angelic voices and Tagore's sacred words unleashed many tears in the chapel, including mine.

The Hindu priest announced that each family member would speak.

Dad did first. He shared how Mom had convinced him that he could become more than he ever believed. He spoke with calm and gratitude. I followed.

I brought Yogananda's picture up with me and held on to it, while I placed my crumpled poetry pages in front of me on the lectern. "I wrote a poem about my Mom and how much I love her." I didn't look up from my crumpled pages. "She always wanted me to share my poetry with people. So, I guess she's getting what she wanted."

I read the poem in a quiet voice, which I tried not to let quiver, looking only at Raj. When I finished, most everyone's hands were over their faces.

Tiff clutched my hand when I sat back down. Raj spoke next. He reminded me of JFK, Jr. who had just died, serene and dashing.

The funeral ended with a Hindu prayer translated into English. Raj, Dad and I stood to receive those who came to honor Mom. They shook our hands and hugged us. Even though I knew many of them well, I kept myself in a distant daze to get through it. I couldn't handle their pain and mine.

Almost everyone said the same thing, "Your mom would've been so proud of you. She was the most unique woman I'd ever met." Raj later shared his surprise at their words. Where Mom had been my mom, sister and best friend, Raj had only known her as his mom.

After the last person left the chapel, we went outside to our cars to drive down the hill to the crematorium. I stopped to smoke a cigarette with Tiff, while we watched in silence as the mortuary staff loaded Mom's casket into the hearse.

Our driver followed the hearse to a large building that overlooked rows of gravesites. Two people from the mortuary's staff, identified by their name tags and matching suits, led Dad, Raj and me to a huge barn-like door.

One of them turned to the crowd behind us and held up her hand. "Only family in the crematorium, please." I noticed the crowd from the chapel bunch together but stop a few feet from the door. A gap formed between them and us.

In the Hindu religion, the eldest son conducts the cremation. Dad suggested that Raj and I do it together.

I shivered inside the cold, dark, vast space. Mom's casket waited on a steel rolling table at the foot of what looked like a giant industrial oven. My brother and I stood on one side of her coffin and Dad and the priest, who was allowed in with us, on the other. The priest mumbled prayers in Sanskrit that none of us understood.

I stared at the red "on/off" button next to the left of the oven's door.

"Mala, I hope you don't mind," Dad said. "I brought her favorite rose from the garden to put inside with her." He held a blood red rose wrapped in a wet paper towel and tin foil.

He loved her, too.

I nodded, while tears overflowed onto my face.

I panicked. I couldn't do it. I couldn't let them burn Mom's body. Not her hands. Shallow breaths overtook me, like a panting dog.

I leaned on her coffin, then tugged at Raj's arm. "I know you don't want to see her body, but I have to one more time."

I pushed him aside so that I could pry open the top of the coffin. Unable to lift it, Dad came around and helped me.

I performed my first and last pranam to Mom. I touched each of her feet, my forehead and heart. I sobbed and stroked her hand. My teeth rattled.

Dad placed his rose next to Mom's hand. I whimpered.

When Raj put his arm around me and Dad lowered the lid, I screamed, "No, no, no, please, God, no!!!!!" Raj held me up, while I screamed "No" over and over.

Tiff later told me that outside it sounded as though someone ripped off my limbs.

Dad nodded to the priest, who motioned to the staff.

Nothing stood between the inevitable and me. The oven door slid open. They pushed Mom inside.

My shaking finger met Raj's. Together, we pushed the button to burn Mom into ashes.

With the sound of the gas igniting the oven, I bolted from the room and was met by rows of people and bright, hot August sunlight. I saw Tiff and fell into her arms.

I have no idea how long she held me. By the time I lifted my head, the crowd was gone. Dad and Raj stood waiting for me by Mom's car in the empty parking lot. My insides gone, my shoulders rolled inward. I couldn't stand up straight.

We rode in silence to my parents' country club where Dad had planned a gathering. After everyone left, the three of us went back to the house.

Boo met us at the front door with her innocent, unconditional wagging tail. She followed me to my room where I changed out of my forever-soiled clothes. Leaving Boo with Raj and Dad, I hurried to my car and the 10 West. I wanted to be alone.

In fading sunlight on August 7, 1999, I retreated into the depths of my soul from where I hoped never to return. Mom was gone, even her body.

CHAPTER THIRTEEN
Lost

Dad and I spoke more often in the two weeks after Mom passed than we did my whole life. We had no choice. Mom's ashes would arrive from the crematorium within two weeks and needed to be released. Both of us knew Mom's true home and decided she would want to be in India. Dad arranged for the three of us to travel there the first week in September.

Endless August, my least favorite month, loomed in the same way it did for me every year. Long, desolate, sticky and hot, anticipatory of September when school started and normal schedules resumed. Trapped between ceremonies, neither dead nor alive, 1999's August would be the worst.

Like a temporary dementia, spurts of pain prohibited coherent thought. I inwardly repeated the day, date, month and year to root myself in what I knew to be true. Doing it helped me shower, brush my teeth, drive, get back to work, clean my house, care for Boo.

I tried to focus on God, His will and my inner truth but found despair a more willing companion, especially at night. After work, I walked and fed Boo, then myself. I nibbled at macaroni and cheese, mashed potatoes or Chinese egg drop soup with difficulty. Boo fell asleep by 9:30 p.m. following her last walk. Hours passed with me in a trance on the sofa next to her or on the chaise with my cigarettes. I attempted to keep my second-hand smoke away from her and blew it out the window and into the trees.

By midnight each night, I huddled on the floor, knees to chest, beside my stereo in a corner of the living room. It was a one-and-a-half-feet square spot next to a floor lamp, which I turned off, too sensitive for light. Stacks of my CDs piled next to me, I listened to only one song.

Daria, Ben's and my old friend, gave me a CD a few days after the funeral. "I think you might like song number nine," she said as she handed it to me. "I'm not sure if I'm doing the right thing by giving it to you."

It was the perfect gift and became the flash point of my release. Heather Nova sang in a high, angelic voice:

> She carries a woman with her, as a ghost inside, in her shattered arms, she's still alive . . . could she be walking higher, could she be right beside her . . . does the spirit live on when the body dies.

With my headset hooked into the stereo, I sang with her, crumbling into sobs by the first line. I pressed the repeat button dozens of times.

Agony, despair, loneliness and confusion smothered me. It hurt so much I clutched the wall to bear the pain, which felt like thousands of pounds of sharp scrap metal crammed in my gut. I itched to rip my skin to shreds.

The weight of the suffering nailed me in place. I gritted my teeth. My heart physically ached. I cried out, gasped for air. Snot and tears drenched the front of my shirt. I couldn't smoke. Devastation unleashed itself without restraint. I was alive only when that song played. Tangible grief claimed my soul.

I chased after the grief, not wanting a serious physical illness years later to force me to face it. The thought of being sick terrified me. I couldn't imagine living in a body unable to function. I barely made it in one that did.

That corner was my medicine, my church, my truth.

Between 2:00 and 3:00 a.m., my body drained, I stopped playing the song and sat in silence and forced myself to accept that Mom was never coming back. Only after I was convinced that I had accepted it, I stumbled around my house, asking God how it all happened.

When my feet no longer moved, I passed out in my bed or on the sofa with Boo to the sound of her snoring. In and out, she breathed.

Sleep prevailed over insanity for a few hours, although it became more difficult each day.

Too early in the morning and always before 5:30 a.m., I awoke with a jolt from the shrill scream of reality. That scream woke me every morning for months.

I could bear that Mom was gone during the day. Daylight required me to function, get back to work. With my nightly ritual tucked into my pocket, I strong-armed my mind, gave it rationales for its tumult. I told myself that anyone would feel lost and abandoned if their mom committed suicide. I used the stock list of shock, trauma and stages of grief, although I could never remember their order or all five. I labeled myself as in "shock" or "denial," even if it felt untrue or hollow.

I saw Sharon twice a week, because it seemed like the best thing to do. I was too scared to tell her about my ritual, that I walked on the precipice of my sanity every night, with my toes curled over the edge in a corner of my house. Though probably the best place for me, I didn't want her to commit me to a mental hospital.

After the five and a half years of working with her, I consciously hid my truth, ashamed at how much I hurt.

Without the information she needed, Sharon tried to connect with me. "You must be very angry that she did this to you, especially because you were just getting stronger."

She thought I was angry, because a part of me was closed to her in a way I hadn't been. I bobbed my head in agreement.

She tried other tactics to reach me. "The loss of the mother is tremendous, especially at such a young age." My tears but not words responded to her.

Sharon told me stories of other young people she knew that experienced that loss and promised me it would get better with time. Again, I went along with her, although I didn't believe I'd ever feel better. No one could convince me I would, because no one could understand how close Mom and I had been. It wasn't the same as just losing a Mom. It wasn't just a death; it was suicide. She chose to leave me.

It was too raw, too insane a place for me to share with anyone other than that song.

Even though I shut Sharon out of the ugliest parts, I trusted her enough to release buckets of tears in her presence. After a teary appointment with her, I returned to the office shaken and puffy-eyed. Navigating the intersection of professional responsibilities and grief was a challenge. I felt my personal problems had no place at work, but I couldn't easily separate them anymore.

Wanting to appear calm for a conference call that Kevin and I intended to take together from his office, I went to the bathroom to splash cold water on my face and took a few deep breaths. It didn't help. I couldn't hide it that day.

In Kevin's office, I hung my hair over my face and sat in a guest chair across from him, hoping he wouldn't notice.

"Hey, MM, ready for the call?" I loved that he called me by my initials. No one ever had. I smiled at him, forgetting to hide my eyes.

"Were you crying? God, it's been almost three weeks since your mom died." He tossed his pen on the yellow pad in front of him, in frustration and almost disgust. "Don't you think you should be getting over it?"

First shame at my weakness flushed my face. Then, I remembered Sharon's compassion from a half hour before and saw red. "Are you serious?" I'd give him a chance to apologize.

"Yeah, you've got to move on with your life." He nodded his head for emphasis.

I gathered my things and stood. "Where are you going?"

"You're so over the line and such an incredible ass for saying what you did." He believed that I needed the paycheck enough to take his abuse. "Do you really think that my family would not support me if I chose to leave here this minute?"

He stared at me with his mouth open.

"I realize you have your own problems to even say this to me, but, God, this is too much. It's wrong."

"I'm sorry, I just don't see why, I mean, it's hard to see you like this. I don't know what. . . ."

I understood. He cared and couldn't handle seeing me in pain. So, he acted like an ass. I sat back down, forgiving him for not knowing what to say or do. I couldn't blame him. Other than in that corner, with that song, neither did I.

I no longer kept a journal, because nothing made sense. My trusted tool turned into forgotten blank pages. I missed Mom but questioned what she had taught me in ways I hadn't before.

I distanced myself from her, who she raised me to be. In the market, I chose different brands from those she used. I didn't send thank you cards for the flowers many people sent to the funeral and to me. I cut my fingernails to the quick. I drove without concern for others and rear-ended a few people on the freeway. I wasn't cordial to my neighbors. I didn't hide my disdain for law at work. At first, I became careless and rebellious in only those small ways.

My head flip-flopped between the terror of her absence and the freedom from her presence. All day, I picked up the phone once an hour to share trivial occurrences only to slam it down in frustrated agony.

She wasn't there. She never would be. How could she have done it? I clung to memories of her but rejected her voice in my head.

I contrived two goals: to survive the unbearable pain of her absence, and to figure out who I was without her.

The second goal granted me permission to explore worlds I never would have considered if she were alive.

I turned to Susanna. I reasoned that God had arranged for me to know Susanna before Mom died; thus, sending me a teacher to fill Mom's space and teach me things Mom couldn't.

The similarities in Mom's and Susanna's personalities comforted me, while their distinctions gave me hope. I decided that Susanna was like Mom, solid, smart and wise. When Mom was alive, I didn't need to know that much about other people, because Mom seemed to know everything about them. With her gone, I asked Susanna questions about her life, which didn't follow Mom's rules.

I knew Susanna lived in Brooklyn but not with whom. The outgoing message on her answering machine sounded like a younger girl. "Do you live alone?" I asked her in our first personal call.

"No, no, I wish. I live with my two daughters. One who is eleven, the other 20 and with my ex-husband," she openly answered.

"What's that like?" I'd never heard of someone living with their ex-husband. "It's okay. He's a good guy, we get along better as friends. Plus, we think it's best for Mary, our daughter, my youngest."

I argued with Mom's voice in my head that said "That's weird. Be careful." Who was she to judge how to live? I didn't want to share Mom's failed traditional view of what worked and what didn't.

"That's great she gets to see you both everyday," I said.

I liked learning about who Susanna was in her personal world beyond her intuition and encyclopedic knowledge of the occult, mysticism and various religions. I wondered out loud how she knew so much.

"I started when I was very little in Israel. I always cared more for the other side of life. The things we cannot see."

"But, how did you learn all these things you know about, numerology, symbology, religion, the tarot deck you use in readings, the people you quote?" She could quote from the Bible, New or Old Testament, Hindu Scripture, the Koran, Kabbalistic teaching, at will and length. Her wisdom and knowledge astonished anyone who spoke to her.

Susanna told me that she learned much of it from her teacher, Hilda Charlton who spoke weekly for years in New York until she passed. Hilda had studied with Yogananda when he was alive. We were all connected by a soul cord.

I saved my most important question for last. "How'd you start doing this work?" I wanted out of law and to put everything I'd studied for the past five years into practice.

"My friends knew I was intuitive and began sending people to see me. It grew from there." Susanna opened a door in my life. She embodied and practiced what I'd learned about. She never charged me for our phone calls, embracing me like a little sister.

Mid-August, in one of our now almost daily calls, Susanna told me she was coming into town at the end of August, staying for two weeks."

"Oh, but I won't be here. We're leaving for India to spread my mom's ashes the first week of September."

"I'll see you the first week."

"I know, but it's too bad that I wish I'd be here the whole time." I realized that my condo would be empty and offered it to her to stay when I was gone.

Susanna agreed and stayed in a hotel for the first week of her trip.

In exchange for her stay in my condo, Susanna gifted me with a reading. The Saturday before we left for India, I went to receive it. I only recalled that she said, "Your mom will communicate with you through rainbows. When you see one, it's her letting you know she's with you."

After the reading, Susanna, her friend Wendy and I went to dinner. Susanna seemed distracted, focused only on the bottom of each of her three Long Island Iced Teas. An alcoholic's daughter, I counted drinks.

A flush of panic filled my body. Part of me felt something wasn't right, while the remaining portion chastised the other for its paranoia. Only one day short of one month from Mom's death, my intuition couldn't be trusted.

When we rose to leave the table, Susanna wobbled, her eyes unfocused. I tapped Wendy's arm. "Does she always look like this after working all day?" Before she could answer, Susanna slumped to the ground. I froze as others ran to her. An ambulance, paramedics and a doctor in the restaurant attended to her.

She avoided the Emergency Room.

On the way back to the hotel, I said, "Don't you think you should go to the hospital?"

"No, they can't do anything. I'm fine." She sounded groggy.

"I think it was a shift in energy from the atmosphere. I felt it in the air." From my rearview mirror, I saw that Wendy looked pleased with herself. She continued, "You changed consciousness."

"It could've been," Susanna said, still out of it.

They sounded crazy to me. No one admitted that she fainted, because she drank three tall Long Island Iced Teas without eating all day, atmosphere changes or not.

I dropped them off in the parking lot in agreement with Mom's voice in my head. Nothing was simple.

I awoke the next day on the one-month anniversary of Mom's death paralyzed. I struggled to breathe and move. Every act labored against something I couldn't identify. The life force felt sucked out of my body.

In the bright warmth of the summer morning, I somehow walked Boo then, came upstairs, unable to move from my seated position on my sofa. I didn't open a window, drape or blind. I was terrified. I couldn't tolerate the weight from my body.

After a half-hour, I called in sick to work. I stared into my dining room. I couldn't ascribe any physical ailment to my condition and was convinced that I was dying. I waited, hoping to be dead by noon.

By 11:00 a.m., I realized I wouldn't die and yelled at God out loud, "If you're going to keep me in this fucked up place, I don't want to feel like this." I made a demand from the bottom of my soul. "I need a sign right now that you can hear me."

The cord to the blinds in the dining room swayed back and forth in the windless room. At first, it swung a foot from one side to the next; then, it swooped in three feet in long, emphatic arcs.

I giggled. "Mom dies, and that's my evidence you can hear me? A cord?" Years later, I understood God's deeper message: the cord between all of us, including Mom, was unbroken.

I opened the doors to my patio, lighting my first cigarette of my day. I sat on the warm wood deck to soak in its warmth. Still shaken, I called Tiff. She answered her work line with her standard "Hey, dude, what's up?"

"Dude, some weird shit happened to me this morning, I'm still kinda losing it." I told her about how I was unable to move my body, how I couldn't will myself to get up or take a deep breath. Telling her, I finally cried.

She listened with her endless kindness and shared some of the most profound wisdom I'd ever heard.

"Dude, you're going to be okay. You're a tiny, little seed in the ground right now. Tucked away and waiting to grow. You just had the most horrible thing happen. So, you're resting in there. But, on days like today, that little seed's going to make a big effort to sprout little shoots from its shell, and you're going to need to rest. Can you imagine how hard it is in there to use all your strength to send a teeny, tiny branch out into the world? I know you can do it and, when you think you can't, call me and I'll talk to you until you remember that you can."

CHAPTER FOURTEEN
Release

Recovered from my August 30th breakdown, our trip to India gave me something to which to look forward. I had detached from Susanna after she fainted. Her irrational justifications and humanity overshadowed my need for her.

I focused on Mom's family and hoped to find solace in their eyes, so much like hers.

We departed LAX on the Saturday morning of Labor Day weekend with the displaced look of refugees. After a slight hesitation about the cost, Dad paid for our business class tickets. I'd argued that we deserved to be at least physically comfortable when we could.

With few words exchanged, we started our journey with a Bloody Mary in each of our hands. A couple of them in my system, I fixated on the tiny movie screen attached to the arm of my seat. I couldn't sleep.

The plane descended into the dense orange cloud enveloping Calcutta (now Kolkata) following thirty-six hours of transit. A moment of elation hit me when my mind believed Mom might be in India on a trip that I'd forgotten, I reminded myself that she wasn't and that almost half of her remains were in Dad's suitcase. The rest was in California separated into three tiny urns for each of us and another metal canister awaiting release in the Pacific Ocean. I repeated those facts in my head so not to slip into denial or worse.

The familiar damp, humid smell of the airport brought me comfort, until customs. "Where is your visa, sir?" an officer said to Raj, who looked at me and not the officer.

I'd passed through before him but stepped back to the customs desk.

"Look again, he has it." I shoved Raj's passport toward him. "Do you think we'd come all this way without it? Do we look like we haven't been here before?"

Hearing my tone, Dad came forward. I held my hand up to him as I bored my eyes into the custom official's. When I wasn't sobbing in the corner of my condo or wandering through my days, I felt bulletproof. "Fuck you, my Mom's dead. What are you going to do to me?" I often thought.

The official didn't test me. "Oh, yes, ma'am, I see it is here. I'm terribly sorry." Before he finished his apology, I walked toward the exit door.

I spotted most of Mom's family through the glass doors. Boro Mashi and Munna (Mom's oldest sister and her son) now lived in Mumbai; Piu, my twin though my cousin, a year, six months and twelve days older than me, was in Dubai with a husband of her choice, who no one would have chosen for her. Scandal forced her into exile.

Dad's youngest brother waited to take him to their family home in Barakpur, a small town outside the city. Raj and I would stay with Boro Mama (the oldest of Mom's brothers) for a few nights without Dad.

Mejo Mashi (Mom's middle sister) hugged me first. She'd made the long, almost two-hour trip from South Calcutta where she lived with her husband, a rickshaw ride away from the family's old, grand house. Her hair was much thinner and far more gray, her eyes lined with years of life. She held my face in her hands. Her eyes softened in concern upon a closer look into mine.

"I'll be okay, Mashi," I said.

She turned to Boro Mama and said in Bengali, "I can't look at her. She's so broken. Her eyes. . . ." She stepped away from me. Boro Mama, who nodded his head with solemnity, hands jammed in his pockets. His face was most like Mom's. This trip, the light beneath his seriousness was absent.

Boro Mama's wife, Boro Mamima (my oldest maternal uncle's wife) wrapped her small body around me. She was under five feet tall, with stick-straight dark brown hair and the pretty, fair-skinned face of a Nepalese doll. Although she spoke little English, she'd always been my second favorite person in India after Piu. We both wept over the tragedy, understanding each other without words.

I waved a grateful good-bye to Dad, who acted too self-concerned to feel ashamed. He didn't seem to realize that he brought his wife home to her family in a canister. He had failed in the worst way possible but didn't notice. I shook my head at his back and caught a knowing look from Mamima.

Crammed into Boro Mama's tiny Fiat, we rode in silence to their flat in Dum Dum instead of the family home in Jodphur Park. A financial downturn in Dadu's (Mom's dad) fortune forced him to sell the home that we'd visited on prior trips. Gone were the fleet of large cars and drivers and the grandeur of their former life.

The family thought Dadu was senile when he bought property in Dum Dum, which was only known for Kolkata's airport. After Dadu's passing, Mom's brothers developed some of the land in Dum Dum, now a growing suburb. They built several buildings. The three brothers lived in the modest flats within one of the buildings and ran one of the remaining movie theatres Dadu had owned.

My middle uncle, Mejo Mama, had devolved into the family outcast as a result of his bi-weekly binge drinking. Although he lived in the building, he didn't see us on our trip. One night, I heard his drunken, profane shouts through the open window of his flat above Boro Mama's. He sounded like a wailing cat.

Inside Boro Mama's home, the Indian décor, faint smell of incense and loud horn honks from the street below filled my senses, relaxing my body. I smiled at the whir and snaps of the fan above my head.

It was around 1:00 a.m. their time on a Monday. They would return to their normal schedule the next day. After Mamima prepared their room for Raj and me, we went to bed. I slept for a solid six hours.

At some point during those hours, the jelly jar around me broke. My physical senses returned. Hungry again, I awoke to the smells of my favorite breakfast. Churida (shredded fried flakes) with fresh coconut, loochi (fried puffy bread) and my favorite Bengali misti (sweets). Mom's family remembered not only the dates of each of our visits, but our corresponding hairstyles and favorite foods. I followed the sound of oil popping and sat at the kitchen table, waiting for Mamima to feed me.

Dad came to Kolkata a few days later and the three of us went to stay with Mejo Mashi's. Her son, my cousin, Bubai had married the prior year and left their house quiet. It felt peaceful to be there and hear the familiar cadence of Mashi's voice.

Her voice was grainier than Mom's, but her words held the same familial thread. Mom had told Mejo Mashi about my spiritual studies and, under her watchful eye, I returned to my daily meditations.

The first morning, she stood guard by the closed door, while I sat in front of her altar. "Shoosh, she's meditating." I heard her whisper to the maids and her husband in half English and half Bengali.

After I finished, I said, "Mashi, if I truly knew how to meditate, silence would be unnecessary."

"I just wanted to help," she said with rounded eyes. She would do anything to take my pain away.

"I love your altar, with Mom, Dida and Dadu's pictures." I wanted her to say something about Mom, but she didn't. Instead, her face grew tight and she walked away.

No one wanted to talk about Mom. I hoped her brothers and sisters would be different than people in America, but it seemed that no one spoke of the dead. Another rule I'd never learned, another invisible wall I couldn't see.

My senses on high alert, I watched Dad's every move with disdain. He recounted the tragedy of his wife's passing to anyone who would listen, Mashi, Mesho, the maids and the visitors that came by to pay their respects.

After the first few times and within two feet from him, I said to the end table next to me, "Did you hear my father's wife died? Isn't it so sad for him?" I assume his hearing failed him, because he didn't stop.

Mom's family knew that I had little, if any, affection for Dad. I hated how, 15,000 miles away from anything "stressful," he consumed his two double scotches every night and had every trip we'd ever taken. He encouraged my uncles to drink with him. None of them hesitated.

Dad and I argued a bit, but I tried to keep it to a minimum so not to upset everyone in the household. I sat on my hands so not to kill him for putting the insulin back in the fridge, for ignoring my warning. With five years of therapy, I had healed a lot, but, after Mom died, I regressed.

A few days later back at Boro Mama's house sitting in the living room with our afternoon tea, I was dulled from the heat and depleted from weeks of emotion.

Dad sat on the sofa in front of me. Boro Mama and Mamima and I were in separate chairs facing him. Choto Mama (Mom's youngest brother) sat between all of us in a chair.

Dad said in Bengali to my uncles, "You know, Bachu didn't do much in America. She didn't work for many years." He placed his teacup back in its saucer. "I don't understand why she got so sick."

My ears buzzed, my dullness evaporated. I ran the tape of what he just said in my head. "Excuse me, what did you say?"

"It's true, she drove a Mercedes, we re-did the house, she had a maid–"

"Are you fucking kidding me?" I leaned towards him. My uncles put their tea cups down in unison.

Dad sat taller, an indignant look on his face. He looked to my uncles for support. I looked at Boro Mama, who gave me the same "Just let it go" look Mom gave me my whole life.

"No, I'm not letting it go, Boro Mama. He killed her, and no one wants to talk about it."

"Mala, please stop–" Boro Mama said.

"Oh, come on, Mala," Dad said. "You didn't do anything either." That day, he was brave and brazen without his scotch.

"Really? You killed her! For years and years and little by little." I was hysterical. Dad squinted. I knew his screams would follow. "That's enough. I don't have to listen to this."

Instead of saying anything, I leapt across the table and shoved my hands around his neck. Before I could snap it, my uncles pulled me from him.

Dad left the flat. I continued to cry, hands over my face.

Raj heard the yells from our room where he tried to nap and stood at the edge of the living room but did not enter.

"That's not going to help anything," Boro Mama said.

"Yes, it is. He killed her. You guys don't even understand in how many ways." I looked at all of them and Raj. "The police talked to him. We could've had him arrested."

"It wouldn't help anything, your Mom wouldn't want that," Boro Mama said, while Mamima shook her head. She looked confused and trapped. Because Dad was her elder, she couldn't stand up for me.

"I know. That's why I didn't help the police, but he isn't even sorry for what he did. He only feels bad for himself. It's how he's been our whole lives. This is what your sister had to put up with for all those years. Don't you see?" I waved my too-long arms in the small room. Years of memories racked my body. I looked insane.

"We see," Boro Mama said, but I knew he didn't want to see. I felt sick that he didn't want to understand what his favorite sister had endured. Like it was okay that she killed herself and didn't die naturally.

I went into my purse to grab a cigarette to smoke on the back balcony. Raj came out to join me. "You okay?"

"Yeah, I guess, it's just nuts, or maybe I am." My tears started again. I threw my cigarette over the balcony and watched the homeless men in the alley pick up the still-burning butt and smoke it. Nothing was wasted where so many had so little.

"They don't want to know. They can't understand living here so far away and they don't want to think of their sister like that," Raj said in a calm voice. He didn't surrender control like I did.

"You're right. I just lost it. I couldn't take Dad saying shit about Mom." I hated myself for dragging Raj into it. I should've protected him more. "Sorry it got ugly."

"Hey, no, good for you. Don't worry." He paused within his own thoughts.

"Now, I get why you acted that way all of our lives."

The morning we would release Mom's ashes, we left Mejo Mashi's house in South Kolkata where we'd been staying to meet my uncles by the Ganges River.

Once there, Dad got out of the car and looked around. "You know, your Mom and I used to meet at this exact place when we were secretly dating."

The Ganges flowed through much of India and all of Kolkata. Without knowing it, Boro Mama picked a spot familiar to Mom and Dad.

"It's weird, standing here now, for this, to do this," Dad said. His voice was passive, foggy. He stooped like an old man.

The hard metal of the canister pushed against my back through my backpack.

I fidgeted in discomfort.

"Shall we go over there?" Boro Mama said to Dad, pointing him in another direction.

Dad allowed Boro Mama to lead him down a narrow paved path to the edge of the water. The rest of us followed.

"I'll get a boat," Dad said to me. I nodded, overwhelmed and disoriented. I didn't expect to get in a boat to release Mom's ashes.

Boat and driver secured, Dad returned to our silent group. Mejo Mashi spoke first. "Do you three want to do it alone?"

Raj and Dad looked at me.

I took in a deep breath to think and sighed out my decision. "Yes, Mashi, I think it's best." Mom sacrificed for the three of us. It was our job to set her free. "Please then let us touch her one last time," Mejo Mashi said, tears breaking her voice. My uncles and Mamima gathered around me.

I reached around for the zipper on my backpack and took out the canister with care.

Back on the shore, I ran to Mejo Mashi and sobbed in her arms. We walked to a bench and sat together. I told her about the ash which blew all over me, showed her my skirt and my arms. I told her about the rainbow. I hadn't anticipated how much it would hurt to let Mom go.

Mashi grabbed both of my hands in hers. "Mala, please promise me you'll not do what she did."

She caught me off guard. I was transparent to her. "I can't promise you—"

"Your mommy wouldn't want you to." Her hands gripped mine. "Please, I'm begging you to promise me now."

Part of me assumed that it wouldn't matter to her if I killed myself. I saw them so infrequently. Then, I looked in her eyes. She meant it. She couldn't bear to lose a part of her sister.

I thought for a while. I didn't want to break a promise to her like Mom did to me the night she overdosed. "Okay, I won't."

We sat together with our complicated tears, hands entwined. After a while, we joined the others at the car.

Back at Mejo Mashi's, we went our separate ways to grieve. Raj and I shared a room and lay on our backs, on the wide, hard bed, with the fan's whirls as our only communication. We fell asleep and awoke in time for a dinner that no one could eat.

Dad planned for us to visit his family in Barakpur for two days and nights to say our good-byes. I didn't have the strength to protest.

With quiet reticence, I got in Dad's brother's comfortable, overly air-conditioned car and prayed for the best. A tremendous status symbol in India, the people who can afford air-conditioning overuse it. They keep their homes and cars as cold as their refrigerators.

The trip to Barakpur devolved into a disaster. Raw and vulnerable, I arrived at their adjacent homes a wounded animal, on guard, unsafe, claws ready. After a bland dinner at Dad's sister's house, we visited Dad's mom across the street. Dad told me that she was very ill, with two full-time nurses to help her accomplish basic life functions.

In the light of dusk turning to night, the fortress-like home still turned my stomach. I walked with heavy feet toward the room from where I heard the cackle of her voice.

"Ah, esho, esho," she said when she saw me in the doorway. Come here, come here. I walked closer to her bed. She looked the same, very skinny, gray, oily hair, which hung past her shoulders. "So sorry. Your mommy was a great lady," she said in reticent English and moved to hold my hand.

My blood boiled. She was lying. I'd watched her for years disrespect Mom with snide comments she thought I didn't understand. "You don't mean that," I said.

Raj and Dad moved closer to me. Dad's youngest brother stood from his chair close to the bed, but none of them stopped me. "You never liked her and I won't listen to you act like you did. It's not right." I cried hard at that point. "I really don't care if I ever see you again."

I raced out of the house to our flat down the street, ashamed that I'd lost control.

I didn't care if Dad and Raj were mad at me. Her lies punctured my heart. I went to bed before Raj and Dad returned. I avoided Dad's mom for the rest of our stay. Neither Raj nor Dad said anything to me about my outburst.

We arrived back at Boro Mama's flat the next day around noon. Afternoon tea with Mamima erased the memory of Dad's family. Boro Mama came home while Mamima braided my hair into two neat plaits. His face pinched like Mom's when she suppressed a smile.

"I have very good news for you." He pointed at me. "What?" I needed good news. "What's going on?"

"Your favorite person, your Piu Didi, is coming." Didi means oldest sister. "Coming where?"

"What? Did you get stupid in Barakpur?" he teased in Bengali. "Here, she's coming here tonight."

"Really? Are you kidding?"

"Enough silly questions," he said. I got up, screamed with joy and hugged him. It would only be one night, but I'd get to see her face. I couldn't believe it. She would be there in two hours.

We arrived at the airport at 6:30 p.m. just after her plane landed. I pushed my way to the front of the crowd outside the familiar exit, scouring the departing crowd for her face.

I jumped over the ropes when I saw her. "Hey, you're squeezing too tight," she said as I hugged her. We laughed. She pulled one of my braids.

"I can't believe you did this. You came." I looked into her deer eyes. "I needed to see you so much."

With mischief in her eyes, she said in Bengali "You better be prepared not to sleep tonight. I didn't fly all this way to watch you sleep!"

Mamima outdid herself. That night, we had more of a feast than usual. I kept up with Piu one for one of the puri (bread) stuffed with dry dal. Even Mamima, the force-feeder, waved her finger at me. "You can't eat like this. You'll get sick," she said.

Piu nodded in agreement. "Skinny girl, this isn't American food. Be careful," Piu added.

"But, I won't get this after tomorrow." My voice trailed, because, with Mom gone, I wouldn't eat like that again until I came back to them. "Just a few more."

I ate so much that Piu and I spent much of the night talking through the bathroom door. I rationed the soft toilet paper I'd brought from America while involuntarily excavating my over-burdened intestinal track.

Piu and I caught up on four years of life. It wasn't about Mom. It was about us.

Raj stayed up for a while with us. Then, she and I lay in bed and talked until morning. My heart broke when the sun peered through the slats of the wooden shutters. I wasn't ready to say good-bye.

We left for the airport after Dad arrived from Barakpur in the late afternoon. This departure was worse than it had ever been.

Once through Bangkok customs, we walked across the familiar corridor to the adjacent airport hotel. At the front desk, Dad said, "I'm getting you your own room. You need some rest." I must have looked destroyed for him to offer such a frivolous additional expenditure.

In my room, I enjoyed solitude and, after three weeks of not, smoking indoors. Raj rang after a couple of cigarettes. Dad had gone to the steam room. We decided to go downstairs for dinner. Both of us flu-ish, I suggested my symptom cure-all: Tylenol and sake. We ate some sushi and went back to our rooms.

The hotel room was like being nowhere. No death, no loss, no responsibility, no worrying about waking Raj or Boo or Mom's death, nothing but me. I slept deeply until my 5:00 a.m. wake-up call.

I followed Dad and Raj to check in for our flight without any desire to go home. I boarded the plane knowing nothing waited for me in L.A. I felt out of touch with my friends, even Tiff. Scott was only a distraction. I hated law.

My true job had been to be Mom's best friend and daughter. I wasn't anything else. I was nothing without her.

In the plane, we had our own rows, because the plane was barren. I peeked around my row of seats and saw that Dad and Raj were asleep in their respective rows.

After a re-fuel and a smoke in Tokyo, we re-boarded for the last leg of our journey. India, Piu and the rest of my family disappeared from my thoughts. Pain consumed me. I had to live without Mom.

I reclined in my seat with a blanket over my head. My heart drained its agony through endless sobs, which vanished into the sound of the jet engines.

PART THREE

Hope

CHAPTER FIFTEEN
Cornered

In the solitary cab ride from the airport, I hoped Scott wanted to continue what we shared for the prior months. I emptied my luggage, started some laundry. Routine tasks to ground. I knocked on Scott's door an hour later in search of relief. His voice was kind, his eyes cold when he said, "You're going through a lot. I can't . . . I don't want to do this with you."

Disappointment but not anger struck me. My life had changed forever, but it was still beach weather for him. No one should be dragged through death.

I ventured back to work and into the routine of life in a state of shock, which was evidenced by the fact that I couldn't recognize it. Mundane tasks sapped most of my energy. Introspection was impossible.

At night, I rested on the sofa with Boo in my arms, the T.V. on mute. My nightly hours of despair resumed that first night home, except I switched from Heather Nova's song to Natalie Merchant's "Ophelia" album, songs two through seven. Song number two promised that life was sweet. I asked Natalie's unresponsive voice when it would be. I slept where and when I could. An hour on the sofa, a couple in my bed.

Clear dreams of Mom filled my short sleep. I awoke startled with the fresh memory of her voice and face. She didn't bring fantastical messages from the other side, only herself. Most often I dreamt of the two of us on the sofa in the Covina house talking about the day.

The transition from those dreams to the truth tore off any scabs that could have formed while I slept. Pain met my open eyes and brought immediate tears. Mom was gone but wasn't, there and not here. Had Boo not needed me, I wouldn't have gotten out of bed.

I felt weak because I couldn't stop crying so hard, so often. I wondered if Mom felt weak or strong when she loaded the three insulin syringes and inserted them in her arm, one after the next. Was she scared when she drifted off to sleep knowing she would slip into a coma? I would've been.

Friendships lapsed. If someone spoke of Mom, I cried and felt too exposed. If they didn't, I resented their ignorance and selfishness. I avoided Dad after India. Raj was living with him. He didn't need me to ease his loneliness. Other than Tiff, I didn't burden the unencumbered with my heavy bag of sadness. Even with her I held back the worst.

I forgot to pay my September mortgage. When I told the woman in customer service the reason, she withdrew the late fees. "I'm so sorry. You sound so young," she said. I welcomed comfort from strangers.

Turned pages in my calendar revealed that my thirtieth birthday was ten days away. Somewhere weeks had passed. Thirty seemed far too young for how I felt.

Tiff called in mid-November to invite the three of us to her parents' for Thanksgiving. She honored her earlier promise and remembered that it was our first major holiday without Mom. Overwhelmed with basic tasks, I hadn't. Raj, Dad and I accepted. None of us knew how to make a turkey. We had nowhere else to go.

With a gaping hole in my heart and flowers on my front seat, I drove to Bel Air. I avoided looking at UCLA's entrance from Sunset Boulevard. There was no space in my mind for more memories.

I arrived before Raj and Dad, who followed within five minutes. Every year Tiff's mom, June, filled their home with Christmas decorations collected over the decades of her life. Hundreds of figurines created dozens of holiday scenes.

Every available flat space overflowed with fake snow, plastic and porcelain. The sounds of music, chimes and bells from each arrangement overlapped. The room hummed with holiday cheer, which contrasted their Japanese heritage.

I wanted to laugh at the absurdity and cry that Mom never tried as hard as June to create a sense of a true American home. My thoughts were interrupted when Dad introduced himself to June. He stood far taller than her yet more stooped than four months prior.

"Thank you for inviting us," he said and shook her tiny hand. "This is very tough. I. . . ." Tears stole his words.

We were in for a tenuous afternoon.

June smiled tightly. "Oh, okay, well, you're welcome. Come, come over here." She led Raj and Dad to the family room and waved to her husband. "Ronnie, why don't you get Ram a drink." June stayed far from Dad for the rest of the night.

Tiff's dad stepped forward. "I'm Ron," he said, with caring in his eyes. "What'd you drink?"

"Scotch, if you have it," Dad said.

My stomach lurched. Dad was drinking scotch at 3:00 p.m. "Do you like Johnnie Walker Blue Label?" Ron asked Dad.

At close to $200 per bottle, Dad's eyes lit up. "Oh, sure, my wife gave me a bottle last time she went to India." New information for me. Mom hated Dad's drinking yet enabled it.

Raj folded into Tiff's family with ease, as he did everywhere. I anxiously watched Dad, and did a lousy job of engaging anything or anyone else, except for smoking cigarettes outside at the patio table.

A few drinks into the Blue Label, Dad stumbled to each of Tiff's relatives to let them know that Mom died a few months ago. Tiff and Raj looked at me several times.

I didn't know how to stop him. If I tried to stop him, his sadness could turn to fury. Dad was more delicately balanced than ever.

June looked disgusted. I grew impatient with her lack of compassion. That night, I didn't blame Dad for his blatant alcoholism. Mom left us open to the shame. Or, perhaps I did by not stopping her.

The villains, victims and heroes in my mind melted together. No one was one or the other.

Ron kept Dad in a corner. They spoke of things Dad wouldn't remember. In horror, I noticed the tall empty bottle next to them. Dad had drunk every drop of Ron's full bottle of Johnnie Walker Blue Label Scotch. I wondered if I should send Ron a new one.

By 7:00 p.m., the pie had been eaten. The evening could come to a close. I said to Raj within Dad's earshot, "I'm going. What about you guys?"

He got up, jamming his hands in his pocket. He understood. "Yeah, we should get going, too. We've got a long way." He patted Dad's shoulder. "Obviously, he can't drive." Others overheard Raj's comments.

I lowered my voice. "Can you handle getting him home like this?"

"Yeah, just go." He pushed me forward. "You've had enough for one night." Raj had grown more protective of me after Mom died.

I said my good-byes with a fake smile. Before anyone could walk me to the door, I ran to my car, crying the whole way home. Dad humiliated himself, Raj and me, because Mom abandoned us.

Neither sleep nor tears found me that night. Instead, cigarettes in hand, I sat at my kitchen table in front of the window and watched the black shadows of the palm trees sway against the dark blue sky.

Thanksgiving made it clear that Dad had to be quarantined on the holidays. On December 23rd, Tiff tearfully informed me of June's retraction of her earlier Christmas Day invitation to her home. I told Tiff it was just as well and we all knew why.

In the late afternoon on Mom's birthday of Christmas Eve, I traveled the familiar 10 East to Dad's house. We decided not to go to a formal dinner, because that was how we celebrated our mom's birthday in the ten years that followed the Burks' break-up. Dad surrendered his American holiday dream and suggested sushi.

We eased into a booth at my parents' favorite Japanese restaurant by 6:00 p.m. I sighed relief. We didn't have to face other people. Dad didn't have to be contained.

The waitress came to our table. "Hi, Merry Christmas." She looked at Dad's side of the booth. "Your wife's not joining you tonight?" Nowhere was safe. I flinched in anticipation of Dad's tears.

"My wife passed away a few months ago. . . ."

"I'm so sorry. I didn't know." News of death never dropped with a light foot. "It's okay," Dad said and looked up from his menu.

"But, she was so young," the waitress said under her breath.

After she took our order, Raj touched Dad's arm. "You alright?" They were forming more of a bond by living together. I was grateful they didn't need me.

"Yeah, it happens a lot. Everywhere I go, people who don't know ask how she is." I was surprised at how calm he was about it.

Back at the house, Raj and I stayed up and watched a movie together, like we would have done with Mom. But, we didn't talk about her.

After the movie, I went to my room. I hadn't slept in it since she died there and brought Boo in to sleep with me. I slept a few hours.

At sunrise, I let Boo out in the back yard and went to Starbucks.

Dad and I read the paper together when I got back. He saw my white and green cup. "I think she had a coffee maker somewhere. I could've gotten you coffee from the store."

"It's okay, I like going to get it," I said in truth.

When Raj woke up, we opened presents at the kitchen table. We forewent a tree for that year and those that followed. It didn't feel right.

We opened gifts and made breakfast. By early afternoon, I wanted to flee to the safe corner by my stereo, to Natalie Merchant convincing me that "Life is Sweet." Instead, I made dinner and left later in the evening with enough time left in the night to mourn. Tiff and I had met every Christmas night for a drink or coffee since I'd know her. That year, each of us too embarrassed by the reality of June and Dad, we didn't mention it.

Around the New Year, Susanna called. "Long time no talk, how are you?" she said. I'd pulled back from her after the fainting episode and my trip to India. In tune with the unspoken, she'd honored our distance.

"I'm okay. You know, the holidays, this year . . . it's been tough." From speaking to Mom several times a day to no one. I was hungry for conversation.

"I know it has. There's nothing anyone can say." Her voice reflected that she understood.

I opened a door within myself and spoke some of my true thoughts. "I get that there's nothing to say. It is what it is and always will be."

"Time will change it. You'll see. It won't take away the pain, but, after the first few years, it lightens." She said things that other people didn't.

"Gosh, it's good to talk to you. I forgot how much your words help." I still saw Sharon twice a week but didn't receive the same type of wisdom.

"You too, kiddo. Listen, I'm coming to L.A. in January. I'd love to see you." She paused for a second. "There's something I want to talk to you about before I come."

I got nervous that she'd ask me why I'd pulled away. "Sure, what's up?"

"I got guidance that I need to start asking to be called by my new name."

"No problem, what is it?" I knew that people changed their names but didn't understand why.

"Orlana."

"That's pretty. What does it mean?"

"It means lamb of God."

"Can I ask you? Why do people change their names?"

"Names create NLPs. NLPs are neuro-linguistic patterns. Like, if you were yelled at when you were little, your name holds the energy of the shouts or anger." In my head, I heard Dad screaming my name, my nerves rattled, but I couldn't imagine changing my name.

Orlana's imminent arrival brightened my days otherwise spent on the internet researching painless and successful ways to end my life. What worked, what didn't, pill combinations. My sadness overrode the promise to Mejo Mashi, like Mom's pain overrode her promise to me.

Unlike my earlier years, the desire to die consumed most of my thoughts, both day and night. The highest rate of suicide victims is found in suicide survivors. They show us the road and tempt us to follow.

My favorite suicide plan was to go to the shooting range to blow my brains out. My concern was that I'd slip or miss. Although I visualized it often, I didn't know if I had what it took to place the barrel of a gun to my temple and pull the trigger. I imagined the cool metal against my head but not the pull of the trigger by my finger.

My second favorite plan was pills, except I couldn't get enough information on the best cocktail. Scared of needles, I couldn't overdose on insulin. My plans of suicide relieved my grief. They offered me moments in which I believed I might escape the unbearable, endless abyss of Mom's death.

In January, pain seeped out in paintings I did. Sad abstract flowers symbolizing family portraits of Mom, Raj, Dad and me. One dead flower and three lost ones.

I was thrilled to see Orlana. Wendy came with her again. They stayed in the same hotel they were in when Susanna, now Orlana, fainted.

A couple of days after she arrived, Orlana and I went to lunch alone. "You know, you can do the type of work that I do." Orlana offered many kinds of sessions, tarot readings, numerology workshops, energy work and combinations of all of them. Her work was intense but nothing like therapy. It acted like a sharp surgical knife, instead of a sculptor's chisel.

"You really think so. I mean, I wouldn't know how to start, or what I could actually do." My body vibrated with the hope of not practicing law.

"You could start by giving astrology readings. You know a lot about it."

"No, I really don't, only the tip of a very deep iceberg." Several years of studying astrology humbled the part of me that thought I could learn anything with enough effort. The more I read, the more there was to know. "Besides, I studied it to understand myself, not to make predictions. That's the stuff people like."

"Not always. You didn't come to me for that." I smiled at the accuracy of her insight. "Just keep an open mind."

She was right. I had nothing to lose. That night, instead of crying for hours in the corner, I asked God to send me a specific, unmistakable and impossible sign that I could work as a healer. My isolated months of mourning and not sleeping left me demanding of God. I felt like He owed me.

I said to Him, Yogananda and Mom: "If I'm intended to work as a healer, I'll run into Neen within one week."

I'd met Neen in the summer of 1996 at my Century City office, just before Mark and I began our sad, futile dance. I entered the copy room in Jerry's office, noticing the bottom door of the machine opened, I said, "Big shock, it's broken again."

A short, muscular man, with dark, brown skin stood. His eyes registered surprise when he saw me.

We introduced ourselves. I gave him a tight smile and wondered if I should run my letter through the copy function on the fax machine.

"So, what'd you do here?" he asked.

"I'm an attorney." I was on a deadline, with no time for the small talk.

"Oh, wow, okay, pretty big deal."

"No, not really. What about you?" Embarrassed, I said, "Or, I guess you're working right now."

"Yeah, I do this during the day, but at night I work on people." He got my attention. "Yeah?"

"I'm a healer. I work on people's bodies." He puffed in pride of his work. "I'm legit, a Chinese Medicine doctor, certified, licensed and all that."

At the time, Neen was the first person I ever heard use the term "healer."

"What do you mean?"

"Make an appointment and find out." He stood up in a relaxed pose, like his body was made of liquid. "You've got all kinds of chi stuck in your shoulders."

He smiled with knowing confidence. "That's why you walk around with them glued to your earlobes."

I knew chi meant life force. Due to Mom's training, no one found fault with my posture. My face registered the offense I'd taken.

"Hey, I'm not trying to insult you, it's the truth."

My secretary went to Neen first and said he was helpful. A few weeks later, I made an appointment to see him. A massage table was up in his living room, which left little room to move around.

I removed my shoes and lay on my back on the purple table. "What're you going to do?"

He grabbed a large stick that looked like a flare and lit it. "This is a moxa stick. It brings energy to where you need it. You're going to hold it over your stomach, while I move energy through the points and meridians on your body that are blocked." He held the stick closer for me to see it. "People get sick from blockages."

The points he poked on my body surged with heat and pain. I squirmed in discomfort for what felt like hours. After a few moments of stillness and a mumbled prayer, he said, "Take a few deep breaths. Get up when you're ready."

Upright, I felt clearer and centered. I respected his enormous gift.

We had a few more sessions and even went to dinner and lunch. I enjoyed his company. He spoke about martial arts, his open-weight World

Kick-Boxing championships in Thailand, Eastern philosophy and alternative medicine. In 1997, I'd never met anyone like him and soaked in what he knew.

He wanted more. "Look, I don't mean to sound crazy, but you're the One for me."

The blood left my head. "Why are you saying that?" It felt wrong, intrusive and inappropriate.

"A long time ago, years actually, I was electrocuted and passed out for a while." His eyes welled with tears. "From my dream state, a woman, who looked and smelled just like you, woke me up. I knew it when I first met you. That's why I was so surprised."

"Um, I don't feel the same way. . . ."

"Hey, it's cool. I'll back off." Although he acted unhurt, his face closed in rejection. "I just thought you should know."

We hadn't seen or spoken to each other in the three and a half years since that conversation.

That's why I picked Neen as a sign. He was the only healer I knew other than Orlana. It would be almost impossible to run into him.

CHAPTER SIXTEEN
Punishment

On January 23, 2000, exactly one week following my request, Wendy, Orlana's friend and I went to brunch in Venice at Rose Café, which I frequented often. We sat down at a table outside, because we both smoked. As I turned to put my purse in the chair next to me, I spotted Neen. I couldn't believe it.

"Hey there, I haven't seen you in so long. How are you?" I said walking toward him.

"Good." He was cold and dismissive. "I'm here for a business meeting."

"Oh, okay, I don't want to keep you." I backed away.

"No, it's alright." He relaxed a little. "They can wait." He checked his pockets, held up his empty hands. "Why don't you give me your number, I'll call you later." I was grateful to see a familiar face after the secret months spent mourning in the corner of my condo. In my lonely eagerness and request for a sign, I forgot what he said three years prior.

He called that afternoon. I resided in almost three years of celibacy in the name of love and God. When I rang him back, I had no intimate interest in him, but craved his sharp, vast mind.

I invited him to meet Daria and me for dinner a block from his house in Venice the following Friday. That night, I walked to his house from the restaurant's valet. "Wait down here," he said with a strange look.

I waited for him in a large living room, empty of furniture, but for a young woman who sat at a small table scowling at a computer screen. Earlier that week, Neen told me that he was trying to move his tai chi, kick boxing and healing business to "the next level" and was creating a website. I assumed the young woman was working on his site.

"Hi, there," I said to her, despite her glower at me.

"Did Neen tell you that I went to India with him last summer?"

Her random comment was not only aggressive, but bizarre. "Did Neen tell you that I am Indian?" I loved the rush I felt from my haughty flippancy. I'd missed it.

When Neen and I left to meet Daria, I didn't say good-bye to the young woman. Neen did. "Be back later. You know the drill. Let yourself out, leave the key under the mat." His voice sounded business-like, removed. I didn't ask him about her but relished in a sense of superiority. I took strange pride in the fact·that he chose me, not her.

Neen and I went to a few more dinners. I warmed to the thought of being with him. Years since Mark's rejection, I liked that Neen thought that I was his "One." My thick, hidden despair acted as an opaque yet invisible shroud. I couldn't see my own hand in front of my face, let alone anyone else.

I loved learning about the things Neen said he'd mastered: commanding his breath, his body and mind. Photos and eyewitness accounts evidenced him bending swords on his abdomen. Whereas Orlana's teachings were intellectual and emotional, Neen's were physical.

I fell for it. I wanted out of the corner in my condo, the mourning and the pain. I was tired of researching how to kill myself. Mark wasn't going to find me. Mom was dead.

The first night we had sex was a catastrophe. I let myself into his place through the unlocked front door, because he was expecting me. He met me on the staircase from his ground-level basement, kissing me with a very open mouth. We hadn't kissed yet and I hadn't in a while. I swallowed a gag from the intrusion of his meaty tongue, chastising myself as out of practice or stuck in my pattern of wanting those who don't want me, as Sharon had said.

On the climb of stairs to his loft bedroom, I was hysterically crying, crazed from anguish. He took his clothes off. I kept on most of mine and hid my face from his naked body.

My mind scrambled. I searched for a reason for my hysteria, unable to hear my soul's screams of protest. Sharon and I had worked on my "severe intimacy issues" for years. I told myself that they were surfacing that night.

Here, someone adored me, and I acted like a lunatic. My sobs and shaking didn't stop for a moment.

Neen quit what he was doing in and around my body, got out of his bed and dressed. I watched him pull a fresh sweatshirt out of his closet, feeling sorry for both of us. He had looked ridiculous in his attempt to pleasure a hysterical woman. I wanted to go home to Boo and dressed in silent shame to do so.

As I put on my shoes, the sky opened with torrents of rainfall. Giant drops smacked the roof. I wondered how the earlier clear sky had given way to such heavy rain.

"I don't want to live if there's no chance with us," Neen said from the stairway outside his bedroom.

"What?" I thought I must have heard him wrong. He knew how Mom died. "Look, all those years that we were separated, I had a bad car accident, I've been through so much. I just thought that God brought us together, because I survived all of it." He sounded like I felt until our dismal attempt at sex.

I didn't want to lie to him. He looked so ugly on the stairs. I watched the rain through the skylight.

He continued. "That's why I thought I saw you at the café. I wanted God to bring me the miracle of love. I've been praying for it." His voice was somber. My sobs returned when he mentioned God again.

"You can't give up. You have all these students who need you. You've made it this far. . . ." My voice gave out when I heard what I was saying to him. I hadn't driven home to say those same words to Mom.

"Is there a chance with us?" He pulled me from my regret.

"Yes, of course there is. I've been through a lot too. I mean, I wanted to run into you. I asked to run into you." I ignored the reason why and morphed into his story.

"You did?" His tears dried.

"Yeah, I didn't tell you before, because I felt so silly and—"

He interrupted my words with a hug and another intrusive kiss. I wiggled a little. "I've got to get home to Boo. She must be scared, I'm late . . . the rain and everything."

He smiled. "I feel better. Yeah, go home, take care of her."

He walked me to my car parked on the street outside. I jumped over the water that rushed by the curb to get to my car door. Once inside, I exhaled, started the car and waved without a look to him. The car clock read 3:04 a.m. Hours had passed in the haze of his house.

My head felt heavy, detached from my body. My eyes filled like the streets when I realized that one call to Mom would have clarified all of it. A call that could not be made.

I drove home in a fuzzy, sober dream through a foot of water. I wanted Boo and hurried on tiptoe up the stairs so not to wake my neighbors.

I opened my front door. Boo was on the chaise, curled up asleep. I didn't know what I would do without her. She was all I had left.

We ran through the rain to a patch of grass where she dipped her butt for a quick potty. Back inside, I dried us both off, climbed into my bed with her and pulled the covers over our heads.

I awoke a few hours later from my heart's humiliated, anxious pounds, different from the months before. The prior night rushed forward. I replayed it in the light of day but still couldn't see how my pain was playing out with Neen. Grief seeped shadows into my mind. Like when your eyes adjust to a dark room, my perspective of reality contorted. My murky mind yielded little light with which to find my way out.

Without knowing it, I thought I was tainted, the daughter of a mother who committed suicide, the shameful survivor who could've stopped her but didn't for reasons I no longer understood.

Neen called from his cell phone around 10:00 a.m., ignoring the prior night. The familiar denial of reality, like Mom after Dad drank too much, threw plates or verbally abused me or like her family ignoring the circumstances of her death. Not wanting to face the night prior, I was grateful that he didn't bring it up.

He invited me to lunch after he finished teaching. He taught tai chi classes at gyms around the city to recruit new students to his private classes. A few hours later, I met him in front of his favorite Ethiopian restaurant. He shared his endless life stories, while I only half-listened, distracted by my bizarre response to sex. I reasoned that in my almost three years of celibacy I had forgotten what it was like.

A beacon of forgiveness for my hideous behavior, I saw Neen as God's gift to me to fill the void left six months prior. I completely forgot why I'd asked to run into him. Terrified to spend one more night crying in that corner, I did anything to avoid it. Like a hungry, street dog, I ate the first thing I found.

Neen didn't believe the lies I told myself. He felt something I couldn't admit and retaliated. "You're just like that first night," he said after sex a week later.

"What'd you mean?" I didn't think that I was doing anything wrong in bed. My heart beat fast from his tone.

He rolled onto his back to stare at the ceiling in the dark room. "You're just emotionally and sexually repressed. Look, I love you a lot. I can get over it, but it's hard for me." His passive tone demanded pity. "I mean, I've had a lot of experience, in lots of different situations."

Then, he played superior. "I can tell you haven't. So, this, with you, is just really limited."

I defended my pride. "Sorry you feel that way, I've never had any complaints." Neen unleashed a part of him I hadn't seen coming. "Right, with all those white boys you've wanted your whole life." I winced at the cruel nastiness of his tone.

"Come on, they can't fuck properly. Why do you think women run to us?" I knew he meant black men. I couldn't respond. He was right that I'd only been with white men.

On a winning roll, he kept going. "I don't think it's something you can get over. I guess we can try, I'll just have to get used to being limited in this part of our relationship." I stammered an apology in acceptance of my ineptitude.

He said some variation of the same thing every night for weeks. I tried to overcome his words, to find out what was wrong with me when we had sex. It didn't work. His disgust for my sexuality grew.

Every time we had sex, he complained of my inadequacy. I chose the dark cavern of my bedroom over that corner of my living room.

I believed Neen's words. He was one of the most brilliant people I'd ever met. His ability to synthesize information was similar to Orlana. They both could relate mundane events to ancient texts, metaphysics and science to point out the hidden truths that I missed.

If Neen said that I had severe sexual repression, I agreed. I couldn't see that he wanted retribution for that first night, maybe even the prior years. I couldn't see I wanted to use him to destroy myself so that I didn't have to break my promise to Mejo Mashi.

Over the next few months, he dismantled me with brilliance. I lost every ounce of self-esteem that I'd built working with Sharon, meditating, studying and filling dozens of journals.

My body betrayed his authority. Four weeks into our sexual relationship, I felt a deep ache in my lower abdomen. I called Orlana, even though Neen was the Chinese medicine doctor.

"I think I have a bladder infection, maybe a yeast one, too. I don't know."

"Do you want to go to a doctor?"

"No, they'll just give me antibiotics."

She recommended some alternative remedies, which I wrote down. I heard the click of her lighter and a deep inhale. "Kiddo, are you okay with what you're doing with Neen?"

"Yeah, why do you ask?" I hadn't told anyone, not even Sharon, about the nightly verbal assaults. Shame invoked silence.

"When a woman gets a bladder infection, it means her body is rejecting the sexuality that's being brought to her, yeast represents shame," Orlana said.

"Oh, um, I'm okay with it. Thanks for the advice, for listening to me. I'll let you know how it goes." I hurried off the phone unable to admit that I was scared to be alone. I'd never been alone in my life. Mom had been only a phone call and forty-five-minute drive away.

Later that night, I told Neen about my infections in hopes that he wouldn't initiate sex. "See, I told you that you hate sex. You'll do anything not to have it. Allison was so cool with shit." He enjoyed his memory with a fulfilled expression.

"What?" Allison was the young woman who'd gone to India with Neen. "Nothing. Forget I said anything." Neen didn't say anything by accident. He wanted me to probe.

"Is there something you're not saying? I mean, is that why she's always so cold to me when I see her?" He lured me into the next layer of my humiliation.

"She's just having a hard time that we're together." Self-satisfaction gleamed in his eyes.

"Why?"

"I thought you knew that Allison and I hung out for a while?" His false innocence made me sick. "What difference does it make what I did before you?" He smiled like a snake before it bites you.

"How would I know that? You hid it from me." I played into his hand.

"Why are you making such a big deal out of this? This is why you're not right in bed. You're too insecure." He struck my button, his favorite target. I calmed myself down.

"How long did it go on with her? When'd it stop?"

"I don't know how long, but it stopped when I hooked up with you again." I hated when he said "again." We weren't together before.

"No wonder she was a bitch when I saw her at your house the first time."

"You don't need to call her that." He shook his head at my poor behavior. "Look, she was really good to me after the accident. I couldn't have made it without her." That accident. He used it when he needed it.

"What exactly did she do?"

"She invested in the business."

"How'd she invest? With what?"

"She invested $100,000 in the business. She's my main business partner." Pieces of the odd world I'd entered fell into place.

The alternative remedies Orlana suggested didn't work. Most nights, the pain in my abdomen woke me. I crawled to the bathroom, crouched in the dark to ease the pain. If I sat with my feet flat on the floor and let my pelvic bone open to the floor, the pressure relieved. I cried in a different corner of my house. Physical pain far easier for me than emotional.

I continued to have sex with Neen despite the endless infection. I never denied him the sex he requested at least twice a night. Not wanting to prove my frigidity, I clenched my teeth through the pain.

The more brutal his behavior, the more I could embrace the pain and confusion I felt over Mom's death. Neen became the tool to strip myself of my dignity. I just didn't know it.

When my urine contained drops of blood, I decided I'd suffered enough and took the antibiotics that my doctor prescribed over the phone.

Neen spent every night in my condo. My entire personal world was filled with him. I saw Neen, before, after and between the classes he taught and my work. His life became my routine. Distracted during the day, I chased Mom in a reoccurring dream.

My dream started with me driving in a frenzy to see her in Carmel. Mom loved it there. She and Dad had visited its quaint town every year. In that dream, I knew she would only be there for twenty-four hours, most of which had passed. I drove miles and miles thinking of what I'd say to her, the questions I'd ask in the short time I had. Part way through the dream, I began to doubt I'd see her. What if she didn't wait? I just wanted to get to her, to follow her home. I awoke with longing and defeat, because I hadn't made it in time.

At the end of February, Orlana moved to Los Angeles for a six-month stay. I compromised my Neen-focused routine to see her for lunch a couple of times and made appointments with her for sessions when Neen taught classes on the weekends. She didn't give me any direct observations but offered support. The subtleties of her concern were lost on my stupor.

Through the infections, degradation and powerlessness, I moved forward with Neen, even introducing him to the few people left in my life. Tiff met him once at her house. I ignored the rude and ridiculous manner in which he spoke only of himself. I reasoned that his father died when he was young, the luxury of manners not a priority in his childhood.

Orlana, Wendy and I went to dinner, where he behaved the same way. That time, I reasoned that he was intimidated by Orlana's brilliance. My need to demolish myself didn't allow for truth.

On Easter Sunday, I arranged for Raj to meet him. We went to lunch alone, then, to Neen's place. Neen showed off his vehicles to Raj: his unique Italian motorcycle, his 1968, re-built Camaro, his Mercedes military concept vehicle.

I asked Raj what he thought of him on the drive back to my house. I knew he'd tell me the truth.

"He's a kid with cool toys."

"What'd you mean?"

"Look, if you say you're happy and want to be with him, I support you, but he's not who I pictured you with." As with Orlana, I couldn't hear his dissuasion.

I didn't introduce Dad to Neen before we moved in together. I just didn't know where to place Dad in my life. I couldn't forget what he did and didn't do on the night Mom overdosed. After everything, I couldn't convince myself that Dad was someone I could trust to help me.

Mom had been so direct that I couldn't avoid her insights even if I'd wanted. No one could understand how scared I was not to be with Neen. I'd hidden too much. The six months of tears and terror never left my secret corner.

Underneath the law degree, polished exterior and articulate delivery was a little girl who had lost her world.

In early May, Neen received thirty-day notice to vacate his town home which pushed us to find a place together. He found a home for us in Malibu, high up in the canyons.

The house was pristine, overlooking the endless Pacific Ocean. I swore I could hear the surf hit the sand two miles below. The rent was $3,000.00 a month. The landlord required a $6,000.00 deposit.

Neither Neen nor I could afford the monthly rent on our own. We'd have to split the responsibility. Mom's traditional view of a woman's role crumbled to reveal what I hoped to be a more "unconventional" and progressive approach to a relationship. I told myself that it was okay for a man to need my monetary contribution.

A couple of months after Mom died, Dad gave me $30,000 from Mom's life insurance. Dad instructed me to pay off a chunk of my student loans. I paid some but kept $10,000 "just in case." I felt vulnerable with Mom gone. I always knew that if I were in trouble, she'd help me. I didn't trust Dad to do the same.

Orlana agreed to sublet my condo for June, July and August, until she returned to New York in exchange for some sessions and reduced rent. When she moved back to New York, I planned to lease it out.

Neen had poor credit and no extra cash. So, I signed the lease on the new house after I wrote the $6,000.00 check for the deposit.

CHAPTER SEVENTEEN
Standing

My move to the new house set the tone of my stay. Although Neen promised to help me, I spent the first two days of Memorial Day weekend alone. Several of his students helped him disassemble his town home. I stuffed my things in bags and boxes and drove up the canyon that I began to resent for its inconvenience.

On Monday, Neen arrived at my condo with some of his students to help move my furniture. His first words were, "We're leaving anything that's too much trouble."

"You're kidding, right?"

"No, you're too attached to your stuff."

Boo loved the new house. She sniffed every inch of the yard, rolled on her back in the grass. She was happier at that house than in our condo. Neen wrestled and played with her. His students filled the house in the afternoons. She was no longer by herself until I got home from work.

She became a dog, instead of my rock.

Neen changed tactics after the move and avoided me. If I was home, he wasn't. Most nights, I looked out the window, not at the ocean, for the single light of his motorcycle to turn the last hairpin corner a few minutes from the house. I went outside every hour to smoke while Boo sat with me. I watched for him for hours every Friday, Saturday and Sunday night. The other nights he taught class in Malibu and one of his students picked him up and dropped him off.

He never left me a message about his whereabouts. Sometimes, I called his cell in feigned concern, which hid my true agitation and rage. He answered none of my calls.

I felt trapped away from everything familiar, alone and apart. High up in an outskirt canyon, miles from a decent restaurant or anyone I knew.

Three weeks after the move, Neen said, "Hey, I'm not coming home after class." It was unusual for him to tell me his plans for the day. His tone was off-handed.

"You never do. Why are you telling me now?"

"I just wanted you to know." He smirked. "I'm trying to be considerate."

"I appreciate it." His eyes dared me to ask where he'd be, so I did.

"I'm helping Allison move. She found a really cool little place in the canyon over."

Cold fury but not surprise swam through me. I bet he was still sleeping with her. "Thanks for letting me know," I said and went downstairs to play with Boo in the front yard.

I felt powerless. I couldn't forbid Allison to live in Malibu. I had to accept it with the little dignity I had left. Besides, how could I blame him when I couldn't satisfy his needs, of which he informed me every night when he got into bed.

I called Orlana and Wendy and asked them if I could hang out with them for the day and left to do so within half an hour.

Neen's motorcycle was gone when I arrived home around 6:00 p.m. to feed Boo, who waited in the front yard for me. I walked up to the house with her and a soft smolder of anger. In the yard, Neen's weight equipment had killed the grass. A concrete plateau above the grass transformed into a mock boxing ring, the punching dummy in its center a forgotten warrior.

Neen's belongings made the pristine house ugly and cheap. His carnage of Hindu and Buddhist spiritual regalia, Indian tapestry rugs and wall hangings, cinder-block T.V. stand and jimmied stereo equipment maimed the majestic view of the Pacific Ocean.

After her move, Allison arrived at our house each morning to "work" as I left for the office. Her haughty stare prickled my spine, although I said nothing.

I spent much of my time at home on our bed feeling like a victim. The first anniversary of Mom's death loomed. The surgeries from the year before played out in my mind, memories of Mom struggling in pain, lifeless with a tube hanging from her mouth.

Neen heard my tears one morning. "People die. You gotta get over it. Move on," he said.

Ashamed at my weakness, I moved my tears to the bathroom.

By early July, Neen slept on the sofa, we barely spoke. I went into town every night after work. I'd call him in the afternoon to ask him to feed Boo and race to my condo to spend time with Orlana.

My life a mess, I gave up any thought of working as a healer. Suicidal fantasies consumed most of my inner thoughts. Knowing I'd never have the strength to shoot myself or overdose, I willed myself to die. I visualized that a big truck in one of the canyons I traversed each day would lose control and push me into a chasm.

Sharon devolved into an expensive excuse to leave my law office for an hour and fifteen minutes two times a week. The language we shared for so many years didn't work. I blamed her for my relationship with Neen, for not saying something to wake me up and to stop me from seeing him. Like she had with Mark.

The third week of July, Neen asked me to talk before I left for the day. His face looked solemn.

"I'm not going to make rent this month," he said. "I'm short on cash. It's all just flying out the door for the business."

"I don't get it. You teach class seven days a week. You don't buy a thing." I bought every ounce of food in the house.

"Forget it." He pouted. "I should've known you wouldn't help me."

"Look, I don't have a choice but to loan you money. It's going to come out of my pocket anyway." My indirect reference to my name on the lease escaped him.

"Don't do it if you feel that way." There was nothing uglier than his sad face. "What other choice do you have? I imagine I'm the last person you wanted to ask." I was being cruel. The months that he had attempted to break my spirit rose and opened a window of truth: He was a complete loser, nothing more than a charlatan.

"You know I don't have anyone."

"That's not really true, is it? You've just tapped all of them out." I looked at the clock in the kitchen. "How much do you need? I've got to get to work."

"I think about $5,000 will tide me over. Um, but can I also use your credit card to charge some parts for the Camaro?"

"You're joking, right? Why is it important when you can't even pay your bills?"

"When I got in the accident, the only thing that made me feel better was working on that car. I just think it'll help." I stared at him blankly. "I'm so stressed. I mean, I can't sleep or eat." The great master was losing his shit or acting like he was.

I wrote him a check out of my condo's equity line, which I waved in his face.

"I don't have that much left in this. So, I can't keep doing this for you." I met his eyes like I hadn't in weeks. "Let me know when you need my credit card number." I bought back some of my power.

"Hey, I really appreciate it. You know, I've got your back on this as soon as my settlement comes in from the accident."

"Right." I didn't expect to see my money again.

I leaned down to grab my purse off the sofa, he said, "Oh, and can you just leave your card today? I want to get those parts and they come from the south somewhere," he said.

I put my credit card on the counter and left. On the way to work, I realized Neen was a brilliant healer. He'd helped burn away my pride, ego identity and false sense of self during the months of humiliation. His need of my money released my need of shame and self-destruction.

By then, I no longer hid the hideous parts of my relationship and told Tiff and Daria a lot of what went on in the house. I shared my new story about the money with Daria as soon as I got to the office.

"You might say no, but there's this guy at the gym. I think he's really nice." Daria spoke rapidly so she could speak before I stopped her.

"Dar, I–"

"Just listen. He's Indian."

"Gosh,–"

"I know you don't like Indian guys, but he's pretty cute, I think. I've known him for a while, he doesn't seem crazy. He can't be as bad as Neen" She paused to get my attention. "I'm sure he won't need your money."

I laughed. "I'm not there yet, but I appreciate you trying to help." I didn't refuse her offer on moral grounds. Indian guys, other than Dad and Raj, looked uncomfortable in their own skin.

I was worried about the anniversary of Mom's death the next week and wanted to honor her before I dealt with my mess. Tiff, Daria and Orlana each asked me what I planned for the anniversary, whether I needed to be alone or with them. I wasn't sure. Other than spurts of tears in the bathroom, I'd become distracted from Mom's death by Neen.

Mid-week, I said to Neen, who was now all smiles from the money I gave him, "Everyone wants to know what I need on Sunday for my mom's anniversary. I don't know what to tell them." I tested him.

"It's just a day. You've got to treat it that way." He donned his Wise One voice. "It's the first anniversary. It's more than just a day," I said.

On July 30th, I went to Dad's house for a brief Hindu ceremony and came home to a giant bouquet of flowers from Tiff, who sends me flowers every year on that day. Neen didn't acknowledge the anniversary or the flowers.

The next day, I left Daria a message on her work line to give her the go ahead on the Indian guy.

Timmy rang me at work two days later. His voice was silky and smooth. We arranged to meet for tea that Sunday. He'd pick me up from my condo.

Orlana, Wendy and I smoked and talked about Timmy while I waited to meet him.

"I hope he's a good guy," Orlana said.

"It sure would help right now. . . ," I mumbled.

Timmy left a message letting me know he was running late. I began to get nervous. Orlana and Wendy waited in covert positions on the balcony, while I paced inside.

"He's here," Orlana said through the balcony door. I waited a second to open the door. When I did, I saw the top of his shiny, almost bald head at the bottom of the staircase, turned back and slammed the door shut. "I can't do this. I don't like him. He's bald."

Wendy looked concerned. Orlana said "Don't go if you don't want to."

"Oh, my God, I have to. Daria set this up, it would be rude to her."

I took a deep breath and walked down the stairs. He smiled when he saw me. His smile made him handsome. Wide smiles compelled me, but I still didn't want to go. "You know, it's gotten a bit later than I would have liked. I really do need to get home, but I'm glad we got to meet," I said.

"Come on, take a few minutes, at least grab a quick tea."

I wanted to kill Daria. How could she not tell me that he was almost bald? "Fine, I'll drive."

We sat at a small table in the window of a Jamba Juice on Montana Avenue. I concentrated on my Peanut Butter Smoothie.

He was kind. When he rested his arm on the window's ledge, I noticed that he had a beautiful body. I still didn't want to see him again. I asked God to forgive me, to bless Timmy, because he wanted love enough to meet me for tea.

I watched the clock. After a half an hour, I said, "Look, I'm really sorry. I thought I could do this. I know that Daria told you that I'm living with someone.

I feel like a jerk meeting you this way. It's not like me to do this." I'm sure everyone says that when they cheat.

"I understand." He put his berry smoothie on the table. "It's a difficult situation, but Daria told me the guy you're with is a real jerk and meeting you, I know you deserve better than that."

"You're sweet to say that, but I do need to get going." He couldn't know what I deserved.

I brought him back to his car. "Can I see you again?" he said. His earnest face turned me off even more.

"Why don't you e-mail me?"

He leaned to kiss my cheek. I gave him my hand to shake. I didn't call Daria. I knew my anger toward her was misdirected. She only wanted to help.

I drove up the PCH for the thousandth in my life and wondered with some clarity what I was doing. I couldn't figure anything out, but the question felt more real than it had in months. I knew I had to do something. At home, Boo and Neen greeted me with such warmth that I felt like an asshole.

On my work voicemail the next morning, I heard the most articulate message I have ever heard. Timmy had called early that morning. "I wanted to thank you for meeting me yesterday. The fact that you were conflicted because of your living situation shows that you're a wonderful and kind person, and I just hope you weren't too upset with yourself later, because you clearly don't mean to hurt anyone. Listen, I enjoyed meeting you and would very much like to see you again. I'll be at my home office all day. You have the number. Thanks again."

The perfection of his voice, words and tone comforted me. That comfort changed my decision. I saved that message for a couple of years, listening to it many times.

I called him a few hours later.

"Hi, hey, I had to call you, because, when I got home, I figured out that I didn't have your e-mail address," he shared.

"Yeah, I know. I didn't want to talk to you again." I laughed to lighten the sound of my truth. "But your perfect message in your perfect voice changed my mind." He chuckled with confidence. "I did have my own radio show in college." We spoke for a few more minutes. He shared his business travel plans. I enjoyed the sound of him and knew that I wanted to at least speak to him again.

Timmy and I talked everyday whether he traveled on business or not. I liked the distance and enjoyed his special attention a couple of times a day. I felt pretty and flirtatious and didn't want to lose that.

When I agreed to see him for a quick dinner after work, I responded to his baldness the same way but willed it away. He was a way out of my mess with Neen, a guarantee that I wouldn't drown in my isolated tears in that corner in my condo.

Orlana planned to drive back to New York with Wendy on September 1st. Although I placed a small ad in a local paper to rent my condo, I rejected all of the prospective tenants.

I was ready to move out of Malibu. Timmy's smooth voice and consistent calls brought me hope. I no longer wanted to die in a canyon. It would be too much like Mom's death. A way out of what seemed impossible, the impossibility of surviving her death.

I didn't let Mom go to follow her in the same way. I didn't want to give up. I wanted to survive the horror of the prior year. Survive to say that I did it, to prove to myself that I was strong, not because everyone said I was. If I needed Timmy's presence, then so be it.

I dug in deep and began to believe that my life could go on without her, without crying in the corner of my condo every night, without Neen's abuse to distract me from my devastation.

I didn't know how to get out of that house in Malibu. I feared Neen's reaction and believed I'd lose the $9,000 that I'd loaned him.

Within minutes, I decided that I didn't care about the money. I'd make more one day. $9,000 was too small a price for my sanity.

Neen sensed something. Sometime in August he started to sleep in our bed again. One night as I slipped into bed around 1:00 a.m. after dinner with Timmy and a long talk with Orlana, he said, "Who are you fucking?"

"No one. I'm not you." I hadn't lied. Timmy and I had not even kissed. Neither of us felt right about it until I moved out.

I planned to tell Neen on Friday, September 1st. I'd pay rent for September and hire movers to come that day.

A week or so prior to September 1st, I called Dad from work to tell him my plans. "Why don't you let me pay for your mortgage in September so that you don't have to pay rent on that house and your mortgage."

"God, that would help a lot." My eyes welled from the sincerity of his support. "I really appreciate it."

"You don't have to. Your Mom would've done the same thing."

"I don't know if I'd be in this situation if she were alive." The weight of the truth silenced both of us for a few seconds.

Dad started to cry. "Probably not, but I'm proud of you."

"Why? Because I've made a mess of my life."

"No, because you made a mess, and you're not too proud to say it. Most people can't admit their mistakes. You can. I wish I'd been like you when I was your age." His voice faded. "My life would've been a lot different."

His words sank into my soul. Dad had never given me a greater compliment. "I'm just trying to do my best."

"You always have, and you've always done great. There's nothing you can't do. Just remember that. Your Mom used to say that. Now, I will. You can do anything."

From that conversation, I believed that Dad and I could have a relationship based on something other than rage, disappointment and disgust. I understood what all the psychology books I'd read meant: I wouldn't create abuse from other men if I healed my relationship with Dad.

I didn't know how to forgive him for my childhood and the night he let Mom die, but his support and words that afternoon opened a possibility I never believed existed.

Miraculously, on Thursday, August 30, Neen's auto accident case settled. He gave me $9,000 in cash the next morning.

Cash in hand and through inexplicable tears, I told him I was leaving. "Hey, girl, I understand. It's just not like that for us," he said. "Go on, go live your life." I was grateful for his blessing. It was as if he'd known his role all along.

It was 12:30 a.m. when I shut the door behind the movers after a long, grueling moving day. I sat on my sofa, lit a cigarette and peeked at that corner of my living room.

I didn't need it anymore. I didn't need to sit in that corner alone in the dark and weep for what was lost. I didn't need to run from it in to the arms of self-destruction.

I could do what Mom couldn't.

If I could survive Mom's death, I could live.

Dirty, exhausted and shaken from the emotions of the day, I believed in myself.

CHAPTER EIGHTEEN

Steps

Timmy called early the next morning to invite me to dinner that evening. I accepted, giddy with relief to be home. Singing "My Favorite Things" from *The Sound of Music*, I walked Boo around our familiar neighborhood. I wanted to hug every tree.

Tiff came over to unpack my kitchen, like Mom had every time I had moved. Neither of them consulted me on where they placed things on the shelves, in the drawers and fridge. Two years prior, I tried to give Mom my input.

"You don't think I know where things go in a kitchen?" she said amidst the pile of newspapers that she pulled from around the dishes. "Oof, stop being so bossy." She'd made a good point. I left her alone, as I did Tiff that day. I no longer needed false authority over my plates and utensils.

At dusk, with a skip in my step, I got ready for my proper date. A date with someone more traditional like Ben, but Indian. Hopefulness replaced the terror I'd felt with Neen. Like maybe I could live a normal life, despite Mom's choice.

I saw Timmy arrive from my balcony and floated down the stairs to meet him. Across from him in the restaurant, I appreciated his Indian face. His brown skin shined in the dim light. Compassion filled his large, almond-shaped brown eyes, which I found more soothing than green or blue ones. His refined manners transcended time. There was a soft, old comfort between us, even in the way he gently took my menu after I closed it.

Following dinner and a bottle of wine, Timmy came home with me. We walked Boo together in the cool September night, chatting with excited energy about nothing of substance. Boo asleep on the couch, we made our way to my bed.

I'd lost confidence during those months with Neen. Nervous, I didn't know what to expect from Timmy. He climaxed after the few, sad thumps he gave my body. It was over before I started.

"Wow, that was great," he said, laying himself next to me. The pride he took in his accomplishment silenced my immediate desire to ask him to leave. I needed the sex to be satisfactory to believe we had a chance. Timmy's hasty performance dashed my hopes, until I rested my head on his shoulder and slept more deeply that I had in months.

I spoke to Sharon about the issue in our appointment a few days later. "Many men are, well, quick the first time," she said with a playful smirk. "You guys spoke on the phone so much. He probably had a lot of anticipation."

"But, he's also. . . well, I can't really feel it when it's, you know, inside."

"Neen had a large penis, right? He was quite proud of his prowess?"

I nodded.

"Seems as though that didn't create what you needed. So, how do you know this won't?" Her satisfied look told me that she had solved the problem by making a good point.

"I guess I don't. But, I–"

"It doesn't hurt to give it a chance," she said.

"Maybe. I mean he's really nice, gentle. I love his voice." I wished Timmy had acknowledged the issue. He had to know.

"Wouldn't you say that you tend to shy away from men who treat you well?" Sharon continued.

Neen and Mark marched to the front of my mind. "It seems so."

"Try and see whether being treated well helps you re-consider how to connect through sex," Sharon said. "It may be different than what you've thought of as 'good' and doesn't mean it can't be satisfying."

It didn't make sense to walk away from a great guy because of such a superficial problem. However, I took immediate precautions and got on the pill. I didn't trust the pull-out-in-time method with him.

The first real relationship I had since Ben, I hurled myself into it. The faster I went, the farther I fled from Neen.

Dad wanted to forget Neen, as well. Only a few weeks into my relationship with Timmy he offered to cook us dinner. Dad, with the help of Kuntula Mashi, learned to cook after Mom died.

"I feel closer to her when I'm in the kitchen, like she's standing next to me showing me what to do," he said to me months earlier. Dad connected to Mom through food, like I connected to her in my dreams, where we converged despite the confines of my earthly existence.

The smell of his cooking met Timmy and me on the driveway when we got to the house in the late afternoon. "Mala?" Dad yelled from the kitchen hearing me open the door. "Come in, this will burn if I stop stirring." Dad's cooking tasted as good as it smelled.

I led Timmy to the kitchen. He shook Dad's free, left hand. "It smells great in here. I'm impressed," Timmy said in that voice, with those perfect manners. I played with Boo outside to give Dad a chance to talk to Timmy.

From the patio, it was strange to see Dad with Mom's round stainless canister of spices, doling tiny spoons of yellow powder into sizzling pans. I could almost see Mom next to him, sizing up Timmy.

Raj joined us with some friends, including Atiyeh who I thanked profusely each time I saw him. "I don't know what I would've done, how we would've gotten Raj home," I said, remembering those chaotic days. He shook off my words with a giant hug.

The house filled with easy laughter. Boo pestered each of the guys to pull her rope toy. Atiyeh obliged, lifting her off the ground while her powerful jaw gripped her toy. She dangled a foot or two in the air with complete trust.

At dinner, Timmy interacted with ease. Dad asked him about his MBA, his start-up company, his parents. Timmy listened well, answered easily and made insightful observations about everything from sports to politics to the American corporate structure.

Raj slid his chair close to me and said, "He seems nice."

"He really is, isn't he?"

"After the last one, I don't know if it's saying much." None of us spoke Neen's name.

"Well, what'd you think?" After the mess I'd created, I vowed to remain receptive to the opinions of those I trusted, especially Raj. He had Mom's way of knowing who had good intentions and who didn't. "He wears his pants awfully high," Raj said.

It was his way of telling me that Timmy was not hip or cool. "I know, but maybe all that doesn't matter in the end."

"If you really feel that way, great. But,–"

"I mean, it's time for me to grow up. Don't you think?" Raj tilted his head and watched me twist my hair around my finger. "Mom's dead. She's not coming back and, I don't know. . . ."

"Right, Mom's not coming back. Doing what's not right for you won't change it." Despite my vow, I ignored Raj's warning and only heard that he thought Timmy was nice.

Timmy had traveled to France every year for the prior twelve. He had good friends in a small town above Cannes and planned a trip for the last two weeks of the year. As a Christmas present, he gave me a ticket to join him.

"We'll spend five days in Paris, then fly into Nice for New Year's with Gerard and his family," he told me a month before to give me time to clear my office calendar. I hadn't been back since high school and it felt fairy-tale-ish to go back with Timmy.

Following a quiet Christmas morning with Raj and Dad, Timmy and I boarded our plane. I huddled into the large seats. In one hand I held a champagne and, in the other, Timmy's hand. The picture was perfect, yet my insides quivered.

I recalled the last time I'd sat in a plane on our way back from India. Images and memories of Mom's soft, beautiful hands, her Christmas Eve birthday, the corner of my condo and her closed eyes on the hospital table engulfed me.

Crawling into Timmy's seat, I wept on his chest for most of the flight. He held me and whispered, "It's going to be okay," over and over. I couldn't have prayed for a more perfect response.

I wanted to fall in love with him. I wanted to want him forever. I wanted to forget about the bad sex, which hadn't improved. I wanted to be someone who could choose him.

We checked into a small, discreet hotel in the part of Paris he liked.

"Do you like it? I stay here all the time."

"I think so." I felt disoriented from crying so hard on the plane and not smoking enough cigarettes.

He opened the room's thick curtains. "Look outside."

I poked my head out. To the left, Sacre Coeur sat on her hill above the city, to my right, Christmas lights illuminated the elegance of Paris. Tears of joy filled my eyes, slid down my face. So many different types of tears in one long day.

Despite the cold December weather, I felt the same way I had thirteen years prior. France filled me. It wasn't any one characteristic of the country but the natural combination of all the things I loved: long afternoons with coffee and dessert, ready access to the greatest works of art in the world, layers of history in one building or city block, indoor smoking.

Timmy and I only fought about my smoking. He refused to be present when I smoked. I resented his indignation and smoked less than I wanted, especially being in Paris.

Although the sex between us was no different, I lied and told him it was "fantastic." I hoped that my encouragement would lengthen his performance. I still couldn't understand why he didn't say something about his difficulty with performance. My journal pages filled with my efforts to discern my truth about my feelings for Timmy. I was afraid to make another mistake.

A few nights into our trip, we snuggled together for warmth in line for the Ferris wheel across the street from the Louvre. "I wouldn't have brought you to my favorite place in the world if I wasn't serious about us," Timmy said.

My cheeks flushed hot in the stinging cold air. "I know, I appreciate it so much."

"No, I mean it. Look, I just turned forty. I want a family." He tilted my head up to his. "I never thought I'd meet someone I liked this much, who's Indian too."

I thought of the simple comfort of the ticket taker at the Picasso Museum who knew we were together, although standing apart. The laugh we shared when we loaded my camera and he imitated how Indians say "film" in two syllables, emphasizing the "l." I'd never shared those easy moments with anyone. "It's pretty nice," I said and wrapped my arms around his narrow waist, laying my head against his broad chest.

With Ben, so much of our relationship revolved around how I was different from what he wanted for his family and own children. With Timmy, I belonged.

Timmy made dinner reservations at his favorite restaurants for our stay. Later that night, we walked a few cobblestone blocks to Buddha Bar. I loved it. The dark wood, candlelight, Middle Eastern music and eclectic crowd. A satisfied smile filled my face.

"I knew you'd love this place," Timmy said, once seated at our table.

"I can't believe this is in the middle of a quiet Paris street. I wish it were in L.A." I looked from the fifty-foot Buddha statue into Timmy's eyes, which shone from excitement.

"Listen, I want to talk to you about our future. I–"

"Let's order drinks first." I was terrified he was going to ask me to marry him. "Sure, wait, I'm not asking you to marry me tonight. But, I want to, soon."

I didn't know what I wanted and didn't want to hurt him. "I don't think it's right. My mom just died, I'm still not in a good space." I fiddled with my cigarettes in my purse. I hated that I couldn't light one in front of him. "Shit, look how much I cried on the plane ride here."

Before he could respond, a prism of rainbow colors from an invisible source covered his heart. I pointed but couldn't say anything. Timmy knew what the rainbow meant to me.

"I think your Mom's trying to tell you something." He held my hand over the table. "I'm not going to rush you, but listen. You don't trust anyone, because your whole life everyone's disappointed you, even your mom." He put his other hand over mine. "I won't."

That night, I told myself that the sex was better, that I would marry Timmy, that I deserved some stability in my life. Our trip to the South of France reinforced the beautiful life I could have with Timmy.

We stayed with his friends in their home overlooking the Mediterranean. We shared long, engaging, many-course lunches and dinners. New Year's rang in with joy and warmth at a party high above the city lights of Nice.

The feeling didn't last. France and the rainbow prism faded once home. Timmy made comments about the tiny pimples, which had sprouted on my forehead. "Are you going to see a doctor about that?" he asked. "My sister's forehead looked like that when she was a teenager."

A week later, he addressed the issue of our sexual difficulties. "You know I finally figured out why it's difficult for me to get an erection and keep it with you," he said.

I froze mid-way in putting my purse down on his dining room table. "The smell of cigarettes in your hair turns me off."

I opened my mouth to retort but shut it. He made my decision. I wasn't going to accept blame for anyone else's sexuality. I hadn't left Neen to hurl myself into a funeral pyre.

I wanted to think about my decision for a few days before I did anything. Around that time, Raj had not only been accepted to the MBA program at Pepperdine but also bought his first condo with Dad's gift of a down payment. I was thrilled for him to move out of Dad's house. He'd served his duty and could create a life with a clear conscience.

A few days before I planned to end it with Timmy, Dad and I shopped with Raj for furniture for his new condo. Raj wandered ahead of us, sitting on many sofas, reclining in his easy manner. "Mom would be so proud of him, huh?" I said to Dad.

"So, how's Timmy?" Raj in a good space, Dad wanted to get me settled, off his worry list. "I really like him. He's got a good edu–"

"I'm breaking up with him."

"What? Why? He's so much better than that gross guy you lived with."

"Dad, I don't want to talk about it." I flipped my hair, which I'd cut from my waist to above my shoulders the prior day. I couldn't hide behind it anymore.

"Your Mom's gone. You have to talk to me." His eyes watered with tears. "I'm your only parent. I know we're not close, but you can talk to me."

"Okay, you're not going to like it."

We'd stopped in the middle of the aisle. Raj joined us. "Um, well, the sex. . . . His penis doesn't work for very long. He blames me, my smoking."

Dad stood his full height. "Eesh, you should've said so. You don't deserve that." Raj's jaw dropped alongside mine. "You're young, smart, beautiful." He wiped his hands together as if to clean them. "No, let's not speak of him again."

It turned out that I could run things by Dad that I wouldn't have discussed with Mom.

Dad's encouragement in my pocket, I broke it off with Timmy over drinks the next night. Almost simultaneously, I received a gift from an unexpected source.

Neen had watched me pour over my astrology and psychology books, before and while we lived together. He asked me questions about different theories, why I studied it, what it meant to me. One morning before I left for work, his insight astounded me. "When unused, a gift becomes a burden," he said and closed the door to his office before I could ask what he meant.

His wise words haunted me. I had a passion for the intersection of western psychological theory and eastern philosophy. I believed the western therapeutic process could be enhanced by ancient eastern technique. The years I'd spent with Sharon helped but seemed like a sluggish, almost barbaric, way to peace and Self. The combination of my eastern studies, hours with Sharon and thousands of pages of journal entries led me to something I didn't know how to explain, let alone use for the benefit of someone else.

Three months after I'd moved out of our house, Neen pushed me into action. The first Saturday following my break-up with Timmy, Boo and I sat on my chaise surrounded by my books and notes, as we had countless other evenings and weekends.

I climbed over the piles and Boo to answer my phone when it rang. "Hi, I'm Dina. Neen gave me your number. I'd like to make an appointment with you."

"I think you have the wrong. . . . Wait, I'm not sure what you mean."

"He told me you could help me. That you do astrological readings and other stuff. I need your help. I need an appointment." Her voice forced me to ignore my insecurity.

"Um, how about next Wednesday?" I had decreased my schedule with Kevin and didn't work in the office on that day. She scheduled a time after her workday and gave me her date, time and place of birth.

I prepared her Natal Astrological Chart, studying it for two days. I meditated for a half-hour before she arrived, prayed for help and lit candles throughout my house. I'd kept my spiritual practice private. To open them and my home felt strange.

What transpired with Dina unlocked a part of my being I'd wished for my whole life. In our hour, I interpreted her chart with an emphasis on her nature and character.

She nodded, teary and open to my observations.

I identified the psychological issues holding her back. The vilification of her mother, the pedestal upon which she placed her father and the eating and weight issues she manifested in search of comfort within that conflict.

Her mind and soul were transparent to me. Our time passed in a flash. "No one's ever seen me like this, seen my life," Dina said. "I want to work with you, I mean I don't know how you do this, but I'd like to see you next week."

I let her talk since I'd done most of it.

"I want to get over this stuff, the roots of it." She touched her midsection. "I don't want to live like this anymore."

I scheduled an appointment to see her the next week. Without realizing it, I had my first counseling client.

Other than calling Neen to thank him, I didn't tell anyone. Part of me was embarrassed. Even though I respected Orlana, a "reading" conjured an older woman sitting at a small card table in a long, bright-colored caftan and big crystal jewelry. From a lawyer to a psychic astrologer. The snob in me, the snob in Mom reared its head. I shook away the nasty voice but didn't tell Orlana because of it. I judged us both.

I didn't tell anyone else either. It felt like a fragile gift from God that could break in the wrong hands or ears. A gift so unusual I didn't know what to call it.

For days, I swallowed the sobs that gurgled from a need to call Mom to talk to her about it. I fantasized that she'd encourage me.

When Dad called to check in with me later that week, I told him instead. "I don't know how to bring this up. I really want to tell Mom but I can't do that—"

My throat constricted.

"What is it? Are you okay?"

"Yeah, I'm actually really okay. I mean, I miss Mom a lot but the neatest thing happened. Neen—"

"I don't want to hear about him." Like me, he ignored those months by not speaking of them.

"No, no, listen. He had someone call me to get a reading."

"What? What reading?" Dad's words clipped in agitation.

"Well, you know how I've been studying astrology and that kind of stuff for a long time, how I've been in therapy for seven years."

"Your Mom didn't like that you were in therapy." He used Mom's opinions as codified laws after she died.

"I know that, Dad." I felt myself getting angry with him. "She didn't want me to look at all the stuff she couldn't." I hesitated to finish what I wanted to share.

"You're right. I'm the one who got you into therapy. It's helped you a lot."

"Right, that's what I'm saying. Someone called for a reading, and she wants me to help her with her problems." I kept it linear for his engineer's mind.

"How can you do that? You don't have a degree or license?"

"I'm not sure, but there can't be a law against helping people. I know I can do it." I wanted to explain it to him, to myself. "Dad, I could see into her soul. Like a math equation, you know? It just came to me."

"When Raj studied psychology in college, Mom didn't like it. She didn't want him taking on other people's problems."

"Mom's not here." Dad's reaction reminded me of the reality of how Mom would've reacted. I gave thanks that she couldn't stand in my way.

"You're having strange people in your house? Is that safe?"

"Boo's here. I know I'm safe." I looked for my cigarettes in frustration. "God's not going to let something bad happen to me for doing this. I just know it."

My conversation with Dad solidified the miracle. The opportunity to explore a whole new life on my doorstep, I took responsibility for my misery. Law made me miserable, always had.

I shared the news with a few people, including Sophia who had resurfaced a few months prior. She floated in and out of my life like an angel when I needed her and no one else.

As before, she generously shared what she knew. She pointed me in the direction of a Jungian analyst, Marion Woodman and encouraged me to pursue a way of life that seemed impossible.

Orlana was thrilled, Raj calm and hopeful, Tiff supportive. Sharon's reaction was quite different.

For months, I'd analyzed and re-analyzed whether I needed Sharon's influence anymore. I examined her the first time I saw her after my appointment with Dina. "So, I met with my first astrology client, who seems to want to work with me weekly," I said.

Sharon's left eyebrow raised. She lowered her analytical gaze. "Well, that's exciting." Her voice flattened. She didn't mean it.

"It is, actually. I'm not sure what it means, but I'm trying to follow the breadcrumbs." Sometimes, I saw my life's road like Hansel and Gretel's forest.

"Do you want to go back to school for a license?" She crossed her legs. "It can be dangerous not to have the proper training and supervision."

My insides lurched in momentary defeat. I'd always played by the rules. Mom taught me that rules kept us safe, beyond reproach.

This time, I wanted to color outside the lines. "Hm, I'm not sure. But, as a lawyer, I'd like to think I'm sensitive to the issues, at least of confidentiality and liability."

"Of course, I'm sure you are." She felt like an adversary. I didn't want anymore of those, not at the magical moment of change.

I dropped the subject, finished the session and accepted that, after seven years, I no longer felt safe in her office or under her care.

I slept on my instinct for a few days and left her a message that I'd be taking a break from our work for a while.

She called me back, in the ten minutes before the hour between clients. We spoke for a few moments.

"I really think after all these years, all we've been through together, we should have a closure session," Sharon said.

The years of study outside her office, beyond the territory of Western psychology congealed with the love she'd given me. "With everything you've helped me with, from my Mom's death to believing in who I am, you're burned into my heart." I paused to see if she wanted to speak.

She didn't.

"How can there ever be closure? Our work will be a part of me and everything I do forever."

With a heartfelt goodbye, we parted ways, leaving me free to rely upon my own counsel for the first time in my life.

CHAPTER NINETEEN

Jump

The first place I went was to the pool. I hadn't swum since Mom died but knew the water would keep safe what I'd learned and provide me strength. Despite that, I was also scared it would destabilize me. Mom connected me to the pool, the hours of driving to and from workouts, the swim meets in obscure places, the sacrifices only she knew she made so that I could feel strong and whole.

I'd joined the Westside YMCA a few years prior and swam in several of their organized workouts. When I'd told Mom, she said, "Good, you always feel best when you swim."

I stepped onto the pool deck and backed away, as if a strong wind pushed me toward the locker room. The smell of chlorine reminded me of her. The Mom from when I was little, waiting for me on the pool deck where I could see her.

I told myself that I could do it, that Mom gave me the pool for just this moment. Dipping my toes in the water, I sighed relief at its warmth. Ignoring its yellow color and the unidentifiable chunks floating through it, I dove in.

Once in the water, my body unwound in a sensual, divine joy. I moved without effort or thought.

I re-created a routine that nourished me, like I had prior to July 30, 1999. I still worked with Kevin but focused on the few more clients referred by Neen. I kept my body and mind strong and clear through swimming, meditation, my journal and books.

Although I'd never been so alone, I grew to love it. I craved the silence of my condo. I no longer sat in the corner crying but on the sofa or chaise. I read, thought, petted Boo and watched basketball through the May playoffs, the Grand Slam tennis tournaments until Labor Day.

The grief evolved. I still grabbed the phone most mornings at 7:30 a.m. to talk to Mom. Waves of pain hit, less often and with more force. I learned to breathe until it passed. Sometimes, I called Tiff, Orlana or Sophia for help.

I thought about my time with Neen more than with Timmy. I sifted through those six months. Although the humiliation waned, my curiosity about my own sexual identity grew, especially after I ran into him and Allison.

I'd wandered around the Bodhi Tree book store for years, during which it became the destination for Los Angelenos on a "path," its patrons glancing at one another as much as the books. Lost in the Jungian section, I smelled Neen's Egyptian Musk oil then heard Neen's unmistakable baritone voice, "Hey, girl, long time no talk."

Allison stood next to him. Other than thanking him for his referrals and leaving Boo with him for visits, I'd kept my distance.

Hand on her hip, blue eyes wild with aggression, Allison stepped toward me. She'd waited a long time for the opportunity. "You know that Neen and I were together the whole time you were there, right?"

Even though I'd known, I felt punched by the confirmation. "Well–"

"Come on, we don't need to get into this. It's history," Neen said, stepping between us.

"Is it true?" I asked him.

"Yes, tell her," Allison urged. Neen grabbed her arm and pulled her beside him. "It's true," Allison said.

I pointed my words at him, not her. "Well?"

"It is. I–"

I cut him off. "Enough, I don't want to hear anymore." I grabbed my keys from my purse in an exaggerated manner. The dark side of my character wanted the drama. A sort of gift with purchase, it felt like a messy outlet for the recent months of good behavior I'd strung together.

Neen followed me to my car, pleaded for my forgiveness. "You know I always loved you. We just had all those problems with—"

I put my hand in front of his face to spare myself. "I don't want to talk about all that, ever again." I wasn't the broken little girl anymore. "Look, it's done. It's fine."

"But I want us to be cool."

"We are. Boo'll still come up and hang. It's all good. No worries." I used his language to help him hear me.

"You sure?"

Back to my senses, I said, "Listen, we've both lived through a lot in this life. This isn't all that in the big picture. Just let me go and sort it out."

A few days later, we spoke on the phone and made some sort of peace for Boo, who continued to stay with him when I traveled to see Orlana. None of it made sense in the context of how I was raised. But, that was okay with me.

Confirmation of Neen's cheating prompted me into action. If I wanted to be authentic when I worked with clients, I needed to hold myself account-able to my sexual history. Ben and I had enjoyed sweetness and lovemaking. Mark and I had bursts of sexual brilliance, but mostly false starts. Then, I was celibate for three years, allowed myself to be sexually degraded by Neen and lied to Timmy about the inadequacy of our sex. It was time to explore what interested me outside of a relationship, like college with a little more awareness.

Tired of swimming through water clouded by the urine of children, I decided to join a new gym. I knew the 90s "it" gym had a glorious indoor pool. It happened to also be where Ben and Mark worked out. Knowing nei-ther of their schedules would've changed, I avoided them.

The new gym was the perfect environment for my sexual research. The women were groomed to be noticed, the men athletic and looking for sex. The air was charged, like UCLA during spring quarter.

New to gym mating practices, I observed for the first few weeks and nod-ded as opposed to smiling upon eye contact. The men who were undeterred by my nod approached. Ninety percent of them were African American, active or retired professional athletes, mostly basketball players.

A long-time sports fan, I loved it. My ego swelled with the attention. I allowed it to do so. Something had to be healed so that I could stop choosing celibacy or the extremes of abuse or dysfunction. Therapy, meditation and my journal hadn't worked.

I accepted a couple of dates from men inside and outside that gym. By August, I was dating Marcus, an intelligent, sexually adept, thirty-five-year-old ex-basketball player. My attentions were scattered, as were his. Marcus' "ex" girlfriend was pregnant with his second child. I was far from where Mom had left me.

On a restless Sunday afternoon in early September, I decided to break my routine of errands and Self-Realization Fellowship or the Bodhi Tree. I never went on Sundays, because it was Kids Day from 11:00 a.m. to 2:00 p.m.

Yet, I needed to release some of my nervous energy. I wanted something I couldn't identify. Marcus was out of town on business. Yet, it wasn't him that I wanted. The usual places of the pool, my journal, the SRF temple or books didn't sound good either.

My intuition pulled me to the gym. Unfocused, I walked on the treadmill for ten minutes, rode a bike for five. I wandered downstairs from the cardio machines to the weights looking for something unspecified. I shook my head at myself for wasting precious time and gave up.

On my way to the locker room, I felt Rick before I saw him. He turned the corner, after I knew he'd be there. A two-foot glow surrounded him. I raised my eyes to 6'7" and met his, which were green mixed with honey. He smiled, wide and white. Dimples flashed. His skin looked like warm caramel.

Two equally regal children walked on either side of him. Shaken by his physical presence, I took a long, hot shower in the now-quiet locker room. The man's beauty shocked me. Still warm from my shower and his eyes, I stood in the gym cafe's line with macaroni and cheese on a tray. I felt like I was in grade school. I hoped that I'd imagined him.

His glow preceded him again. His young son in search of a cookie, Rick said to me, "The cookies are good here. You might try one after lunch." He sounded like Smokey Robinson.

Unsure how to engage with his son between us, I said to his son, "If you get the chocolate chip, let me know how it is."

I sat at a table by myself. I wanted to eat and leave as quickly as I could. His children ventured into the gym's clothing boutique. I braced myself.

He stood next to where I sat. "I've never seen you here before," he said. "Are you new?"

I raised my gaze to his full lips. "No, well, a few months."

"When are you here?" He wasn't hesitant.

"Every other late morning, never usually on Sundays." I didn't know how to handle him.

"That can't be. I'm here then." He unnerved me further with his step closer. "I would've noticed you."

"Well, I've been here." I shrugged, hoping he'd go away. "You know, we'd have amazing children together."

I laughed at him. "That's the worst pick-up line I've ever heard." He was more gorgeous than smooth. "Besides, you already have children."

"Yeah, I guess that sounded silly, but I mean it." He dipped his head, a little embarrassed. "You're really beautiful."

"So are you." I was cautious, not flattered. "You must be a Libra to say something like that."

"I am." He held out his giant palm, offering me something invisible. "You must be to know that."

"I am, as well." Uncomfortable, I changed the silly subject I'd raised. "Do you get to see your kids a lot." I assumed he was divorced or never married, like most of the other professional athletes I'd met.

"Yeah, they live with me." Their mother must have passed or moved away. I didn't probe.

"Oh, that's great. Usually, well, . . ." We both noticed his kids approaching. "I'll make sure I find you tomorrow," he said and smiled wide.

At home, I scrubbed the French doors to my balcony, which hadn't been cleaned in at least three years. I played an old L.L. Cool J CD that reminded me of college. I danced a bit, to Boo's surprise. Life was a little brighter.

Rick found me the next morning. We first exchanged glances, giggles and then numbers.

The next day at my law desk, thinking of him not my work, I realized I'd seen him before months earlier during the basketball playoffs. I'd flipped channels between games and said out loud to Boo, "That's the most beautiful man I've ever seen. God, I'd like to meet him." Once again, God heard me.

A few mornings later, I answered my phone far too early in the morning for our first call. "Hi, gorgeous," Rick said. He didn't follow rules.

I asked whom it was to keep him on his toes and agreed to meet him later that day. We didn't talk about much, sharing few life facts. He guarded his privacy and seemed to be testing me. He was twelve years older than me, like another man I'd been seeing. He divulged that he'd played in the NBA for many years and now commentated on television and radio. I didn't mention that I'd seen him on T.V. He kissed my hand good-bye.

We continued to see one another. One late morning, we ended up in my bed. We shared an intense, awkward passion and talked afterward, cozy in my tiny bedroom. He asked more about my life. I shared my passion for my therapeutic work with clients, my theories on healing, my distaste for law.

"I went to therapy once," he said.

"You did? When?" I was surprised by his admission. Therapy wasn't what I'd expected from very male athletes.

"After I retired from the NBA. It's a big adjustment going from 20,000 people screaming your name to the quiet of nothing." I savored the glimpse into his mind. "I didn't know what I wanted to do. I had a mixed career. High personal stats, no championships, no real success with one team."

He tightened his arm around me. "And, by that time, my wife and I only had two kids and—"

"Wait, what'd you say?" The way he said it implied the present tense.

"Well, yeah, I'm married." He said it like I should've known. I searched my brain for the clue I'd missed. His children lived with him. My romantic assumption about death or abandonment proved false.

"How can you be here then? What're you doing?" I pushed myself into a sitting position, sheets covering my breasts. "Does she know?"

"Yeah, she does." He pulled me down next to him. "She's alright. She gets it. Don't worry about it."

I was worried about myself. The implications of my actions. Before our next planned encounter, I experienced my first ocular migraine. But, I didn't stop seeing him.

Neen opened the door and Timmy's Indian blood pushed me along, but, in the tangle of my white sheets, I healed an old wound with someone else's husband. Our skin the same color, we melded into one being. The reflection of his exquisite physicality drowned out the old voices, repairing what had been broken on the playground at Badillo Elementary in my Brownie uniform and so many other times until college.

No one but Tiff really knew about him, and she only knew a little. I spoke about the other men I dated but not him. He was my secret for years.

Fourteen months after my first client, I had a few more. Most of them came more than once, but I wasn't clear about what type of work I wanted to do, astrological readings or counseling. An appointment made by a friend of Neen's student clarified it for me.

Rachel knocked on my door on a cold, sunny February Saturday. Her bright, happy red hair contrasted the worry in her deep blue eyes. Like me so many years earlier, her shoulders were pinned to her earlobes. I explained her astrological chart, while she made notes. Halfway through the session, the worry hadn't left her eyes. I pushed the chart to the side.

"Are we done?" she asked with worry, looking at the clock on the table. "Nope, what's up?"

"What do you mean?" She grew more agitated by my question.

"You're totally stressed out. What's going on?" It was a risk to ask such a direct question; my gut told me she would open.

"I'm, um. . . I don't want to live with my boyfriend anymore. I don't think I love him, but I don't have the money to move out. I know it sounds like I'm using him. I'm not. I love him so much as a friend, he's my best friend. I'm just not happy. I work as a make-up artist but I'm an actor, well a comedian." She stopped for a minute. "Maybe I'm nuts."

"Keep going." She needed to get it out.

"That's pretty much it, in a nutshell." We laughed at her reference to nuts. "You're not, you know, nuts. You're asking great questions of your life. It's not about your boyfriend. It's about the road that led you to feel unhappy. Then, making some small incremental choices to change that."

We spoke long past her hour session. I knew she needed more help. Although I encouraged her to try therapy, my fuzzy intentions about my own work hadn't invited her to sit with me on a regular basis.

I couldn't stop thinking about her anxious eyes the next day and admitted to myself that I didn't want to see people once and send them back into the world unsettled. I wanted to work with them for as long as it took for them to find steady feet to walk forward.

The effort it took to switch my brain from clients to law every other day tore me in two. I couldn't find a rhythm. I didn't know how to create more room in my world for the work that called to me.

Practicing law two days a week, I made almost $60,000 a year. I needed it. My few clients couldn't support my monthly overhead. I was stuck.

One morning before my drive to the office, Dad called. We didn't speak often, but no one else could understand my fears about money and career. He and Mom had taught them to me.

Dad asked how I was. "I don't know, Dad. No, I do know. I can't do this anymore."

"Do what? What's wrong?"

"I hate it. I can't do it anymore but I can't quit because I've got to pay my mortgage."

"Honey, I just quit Enron, you know I can't help you." He made it about him.

"I know that Dad. I'm not asking you to." I blew my nose and sat down at my kitchen table where I saw clients. "What would you do?" I couldn't have asked Mom that question. She'd never had to pay her own mortgage.

"How bad is it?"

"I cry in my car for fifteen minutes before I can force myself to go inside."

"Life shouldn't be like that, not for you, not for anyone. I always liked what I did, even if I didn't like the people." He exhaled an "Oh, gosh."

"What? Say it." I wanted his opinion.

"I don't like to say anything negative about your Mom, but I have to. I guess it's my fault too."

"What is?"

"She pushed you into law. You always wanted to do something to help people, but she made you choose between being a doctor or a lawyer." Priceless clues to my truth. "I think it's because she never could've done those things. She wasn't a good student like Mejo Mashi. She wanted you to be what she wasn't able to."

Dad had kept a lot to himself. "Honey, it's your life. Do what you want. I can't give you money, but I'll support you every way I know how."

Those few sentences from Dad freed me. For a few more months, doubt and faith wrestled within me without mercy. I replayed the visceral sensations of when I'd leapt before. When I didn't stop Mom from killing herself. A calm greater than me slowly claimed my body. A calm that couldn't be faked. I trusted that I'd know when I felt the right time to jump.

I stopped struggling to find a balance between therapeutic clients and law and accepted the discomfort. Urgency never worked for me. So, I gave myself permission to remain in that difficult space for the rest of my life. I told myself the riddle never need be solved.

Months after that conversation with Dad, the quiet found me at my desk. I was ready to remove the invisible shackles. I told Kevin I'd be leaving in two weeks. The words floated from my mouth with ease. He said he was proud of me.

The first six months without my law income I wrote checks out of my condo's equity line to supplement my income from clients. Exhausted from the effort it took to find and act upon my truth, I wasn't scared. I slept, exercised, dated and wandered without purpose.

I also stopped returning Rick's phone calls. I wanted purity.

I craved stillness after a life of striving. I'd always wanted to be something I wasn't, what Mom wanted or more than I was.

I embraced the void of space and time and tried to accept who I was in those moments. Without an identity of Dipta's daughter, lawyer, girlfriend.

Boo next to me, I spent hours in silence on my giant sofa. I allowed my consciousness to drift deeper and deeper into myself, the Self of a greater consciousness, to accept the reality I'd chosen. Knowing I had no outward control over the influx of clients, I had to trust that I'd followed my instinct to a safe place. After a few months, it wasn't easy.

I was the eldest child of an immigrant who came to America with $13 in his pocket. Dad's frugality enabled him and Mom to gift me with a down payment that left me with over a $100,000 in equity on which I lived to take a chance on my dream.

As I felt more rested and capable of putting my mind to what I wanted to create, Boo got sick. A month and a half before her ninth birthday, labored breathing from lungs filled with fluid revealed an enlarged heart. She had between one and six months left to live.

I stayed with her most every moment of the next three weeks. I wrapped her myriad of medications in cheese and made her low sodium meals. She still brought me her tug toy. She curled against me when I wept, now over her.

By the third week, she didn't bring me her toy and began to turn her head away from the medicine. She didn't want it anymore. A visit to the vet confirmed that her lungs were free of fluid, her heart less fragile. The medication worked, but she no longer wanted it.

Despite her progress, I decided to give her what Mom chose and what I would want. Hugging the nurses who'd known us her whole life, I made an appointment to put her to rest at noon the next day. I called Dad and Raj, who promised to be with me when I took her.

Raj didn't wait and came to see her that afternoon. She used all her strength to get up, tug toy in her mouth. We both cried at her effort.

After sitting with her for a few hours, Raj picked her up and carried her down the stairs to go potty under a twilight sky. She walked ahead of us on her long leash, paused and raised her face to the fading sun. "She knows," Raj said.

I could only nod. I wasn't ready to lose her.

After Raj left, I made a bed on the couch to spend our last night together. She was agitated and irritated until 2:30 a.m., when I gave up and went to my bed alone. She deserved rest. I listened for her soft snores but within ten minutes heard her gasping for air. Somehow, within twenty-four hours and though taking her medication, her lungs had filled again. I raced to her.

Boo's eyes begged me to do something. She couldn't sit up or lay down. She fell against the sofa, lungs rattling.

Three hours ahead, I called Orlana in New York.

"You've got to take her now. She doesn't want to wait until tomorrow. She wants to leave without Raj and your Dad seeing her like that."

"Oh, God, I can't do this alone. I can't watch the only other person I love die." I sobbed in the kitchen so not to upset Boo further. Her labored breathing grew worse each minute.

"You have to. You can't leave her to die like this. Mala," she snapped, "You can do it!"

"Okay, I will. I'll take her to the emergency room down the street." I sobbed. "Just pray for her, please pray." I hung up the phone, without a goodbye.

I put my keys in my pocket and gathered Boo in my arms.

In the car, through my tears I spoke to her. "We're almost there. I'm taking you to that emergency room that you went to when you swallowed the raw hide. Remember? They're going to help you." I looked into her eyes, not at the road. "The next part's important. Okay? They're going to put you to sleep, there's going to be a bright tunnel. Go through it. It'll let you off at the beach where your grandma will be waiting for you." Boo loved the beach and knew the word so that her tired eyes flashed with excitement. "Yes, my baby, the beach. Grandma can't wait to see you. Remember to tell her that I miss her, as much as I'll miss you everyday we're apart."

I didn't wait until they injected her. I told myself that she wouldn't want me to watch and drove the vacant streets to my empty condo, where I sat next to her dog bowls and wept.

Boo passed away three and a half years after Mom, to the day. There was no one left to die.

CHAPTER TWENTY
Found

Boo and Mom had been my world. Worried, Dad called me everyday. "You're not going to hurt yourself, are you?" he asked a few days after Boo died. I hadn't stopped crying and didn't leave the house, except to walk to the corner market for cigarettes and food.

"No, Dad, I'm just hurting. There's no way I'd do that to my clients. They trust me with their hearts and their lives. I'm not going to abandon them, like. . . ." I didn't finish my thought. Dad knew what I meant. He called me every morning by 9:00 a.m.

Raj drove up from his condo in Orange County to check on me the first few weekends. Boo's stuff was gone, her toys stored in a box in the garage, her bowls thrown away, her collar on my altar awaiting her ashes. My tiny condo was barren without her. "Why don't you renovate your kitchen?" Raj scowled at my kitchen. "My sister can't live like this."

The kitchen and bathroom hadn't been updated since 1948, when it was built. Without Boo, I wouldn't have to worry about the workers in and out or her safety. "I don't know. I'd love a real kitchen, but I'm not working that much." I was more embarrassed than proud of the risk I was taking. "You know I'm mostly living off my equity line."

"You're going to be fine. You wouldn't have quit law if you didn't have a gut feeling about it." Again, my little brother was more of a big one when I needed it. "I'll talk to Dad to pitch in and give you some too." Raj said. He saw my life in a way I couldn't.

Dad agreed to pay for half of the cost of renovating the kitchen. Living on borrowed money, I decided to roll the dice and re-did the bathroom and flooring, as well. The endless choices about fixtures, finishes, materials, costs and timing filled some of the hours I would've been sitting with Boo. Like Mom's death, Boo's left a space in my home, in my life that yearned to be filled.

Over the next few months the condo in which I'd lived through so much rebirthed itself. The kitchen and bathroom gleamed brand new. My energy and heart lifted.

Within weeks of completion, my schedule filled with new clients. I had a waiting list every week. The influx of activity after a year of sparse work invigorated me.

Unlike law, I loved my work and felt protective of my clients, energy and time.

Peripheral friends, who had filled my empty days and evenings, fell away. I focused on what I wanted: to make a living counseling and caring for others.

I spoke to Orlana a few times a week. She encouraged me but seemed to want to guide how I worked with clients. In a call with her one Sunday after a busy workweek, I called her. "You're not working today?" Orlana asked.

"No, not on Sundays, my Sabbath, I guess."

"In the beginning, I worked seven days a week." She sounded disappointed in me.

"I can't, I have to have at least one day for me, to recharge, sleep, wander around or something." I changed the subject and shared some general facts of a new client whose father had been diagnosed with brain cancer.

"You should tell her to do remote healing–"

"It's not like that, her dad's a medical doctor, so is her mom." Although Orlana was trying to help, I bristled.

"It's very effective if the cancer's caught early," she said.

A wall descended in me. My work flowed from the purist part of my soul. I didn't want anyone's interference. I couldn't hesitate or doubt myself in session with them.

"Look, we have different theories on therapeutic work. You give incredible, deep healings. Mine's different. I believe that psycho-spiritual change takes thousands of tiny steps to undo subconscious patterning."

I'd never disagreed with her like that. My heart beat fast in my chest.

She didn't say anything. I heard the click of her lighter, then a deep inhale. "You know so much about things I'll never understand," I said. Maybe I was making a mistake, but I needed some distance from her to discover myself as a practitioner, my style, techniques and rhythm. "You've helped me so much. I mean, I wouldn't even be here with this work if it weren't for you."

"I get it, kiddo. I think you're graduating." We didn't speak for a long while after that call. I was too busy and focused to regret it.

A significant portion of my clients had at least one deceased parent. Some of them were living through the terminal illness of a parent. As a whole, my practice was deep and extreme, because each of my clients was in crisis or in a significant transformation. I couldn't imagine it any other way. Their stories reflected and utilized my life experiences.

I tried to pass on what I'd discovered. Death was a traumatic way to explore your relationship with yourself, God and those who passed.

The first fall after Boo's death, one session encapsulated the grief process I understood. A young woman had been referred to me by her long-time friend, who was a few degrees separated from Neen. Denise had been in Western therapy for almost two years throughout the terminal illnesses that killed both of her parents, three months apart. She began seeing me one month after the first anniversary of the first death.

Because she worked some distance away, our weekly sessions began at 7:00 p.m. Long after Boo would've had her dinner and been asleep on the sofa. Long after I would've escaped from any remaining work on my law desk.

Waiting for her one evening I lit candles to fill the room with luminous light and waited for her soft knock at my door. Her face was stiff when she sat down at the kitchen table where I saw clients. As we talked about her week, her discomfort with her peers, her fear about the approaching holidays, she relaxed in the chair. The gentleness of our exchange reminded her that she was safe. I let her sit in peace for a few moments before I delved deeper.

"Don't you think that it would be strange to not feel anxious and fearful right now?" I hoped the allowance of her anxiety would lift it.

She stiffened. "Why? You mean because my parents are dead," she said. "Shouldn't I be getting over it by now? Isn't that why I'm here."

I said to her what I wished Sharon or someone had said to me. "No, you shouldn't be over it. They were your parents. You knew them your whole life. Don't chase away the grief. Let it have its time."

She began to cry. "But my brothers and sisters seem okay. They don't even talk about our parents."

"Your brothers and sisters have husbands, wives and children. Your life story is different. It allows you more time to reflect on what's happened and why God's given you your unique path." She'd been orphaned at twenty-seven.

With that, she broke. It's hard to remember God or anything light in the darkness of death. The same voice that stood up to Dad when I was little, told me not to stop Mom and when to quit law instructed me to say nothing more. Instead, that voice told me to let her sob as I had so many nights alone in my corner.

I inwardly asked for the strength to give her the space she needed to get some of the pain out. I wanted her to know that she would meet people who weren't afraid of her anguish, confusion or loss so that she didn't feel like she had to hold it by herself.

She sobbed for most of our session. I was sweating by the end of it. When I let her out, I touched her shoulder and said, "You know, there's no way around it, but I know you'll get through it."

Her footsteps faded on the sidewalk below, I opened my balcony door, breathed the fresh night air and wept in gratitude for what I'd been given.

The stream of clients through my weeks flowed with ease. On my days off, the weight of it physically depleted me. I saw with each session how Mom trained me as much as any of my books and seven years with Sharon to do what I was doing. Not only in her death, but in how she listened to me for endless hours on our phone calls, providing me a space to release and hear myself while feeling safe.

I made more money than I ever had. I was comfortable. That comfort led me to want to buy a house. I loved my renovated condo but wanted a home that didn't share walls and sat on the ground. I consulted Raj and Dad, both of whom supported my decision. I couldn't have taken the risk without their support.

The perfect, diamond of a tiny house found its way to me within a month. It was newly built by an up-and-coming, eco-friendly architect. Every corner of it gleamed with care, expertise and luxury. The second bedroom gave me a proper office for my clients. It was far more glamorous than most any house I'd ever seen. It humbled me.

I analyzed the numbers countless times. In the middle of the night at my kitchen table, with Raj and Dad twice a day.

In one such call to Dad, our calculators clicked in sync. "It can work," he said. "If you take the money from the sale and pay off more student loans and the credit card, your monthly overhead should be about the same."

"I don't know why I'm so nervous then," I said.

"Well, my only worry is that your work with the clients is so new. What if it stops?" Dad said.

"If it does, I'll find something else I love to do."

"Yeah, I guess you could always go back to law. That's–"

"No, Dad, I'm not going back to law. I won't need to." I said it with the heat of old anger and new certainty. I learned a lot in my leap. I believed I could create the world I wanted. "Dad, it feels like I finally get to go home. You know what I mean?"

"No, not really."

"The condo's always felt like I'm away at college, like the Covina house is my home." Even, without Mom there, I said I was "going home" when I planned to see Dad. "This house isn't like an apartment. It's a whole property."

"It is. It's a lot of work." I appreciated his practicality.

"I know, I hope I can handle it, with my clients and everything."

"You can. Your mom would've been so proud of you." He cried whenever he mentioned Mom.

"I think so, but, more importantly, I'm proud of me."

It took many months to get acclimated in my new home. Filled with all new furnishings, it turned out more beautiful than anything I could've imagined. I often sat in the tiny backyard and gave thanks. I sometimes wondered if Mom could find me there if she came back to get me.

One hot July afternoon in the warm sun on my deck, I "saw" the big, white backside of a bulldog tumbling down the steps. I had the same vision a few more times and knew it was time to invite a dog to complete my home.

Bubba bounded into my life with ease. I'd agreed to bring him home without seeing a photo. Eighteen and a half months after Boo died, Dad drove with me to Palm Springs where the breeder had brought Bubba from her home in Oklahoma.

He had the same large white behind I'd seen. His giant, twenty-two-pound, ten-week-old puppy body leaped into my arms. He looked directly into my eyes for a long moment, I knew Boo had sent him.

Bubba and I created a home within the perfection of that carefully crafted house. Far different from Boo, he made his way into another part of my heart.

We lived in harmony. Every morning I slid my bedroom door open, I gave thanks for the beauty that met me, for Bubba's sleepy look from the sofa. Companions and friends sprinkled through my limited free time. Tiff and I met for brunch one Sunday every month to catch up in person.

Clients came and went. I was satisfied with the world inside my home and heart. I didn't welcome intrusions. I wanted to work hard, throw the ball to Bubba and drape myself in luxurious sweaters.

In a morning meditation one and a half years after Bubba's arrival, a clear message from that voice found me in meditation: it was time to be open to sharing my life with someone. I remembered that Jung believed we only grew in relationship.

Although I'd found a new therapist to give myself somewhere to talk, my inner growth had slowed in the tranquility of my life. That voice told me that I'd rested long enough.

I imagined that I'd end up with someone similar to the men I'd dated, like Rick or Marcus but more available and honest. I mused that he'd been there all along and noticed Marcus at the gym, wondering whether I'd given him a chance. He'd seemed hurt when we lost touch the years prior. I fantasized a reunion.

A month later, Ben called, with an anxious, needy voice. We hadn't spoken or seen each other in years. I'd run into his brother, who told me that Ben no longer spoke to him or his family. Phyllis in drag didn't like them.

"Let me guess you're getting a divorce," I said.

"Yeah,–"

"Look, before you get into it, have you talked to your brother?" I was already irritated with him.

"No, I–"

"Why are you calling me before him? He's your blood. I'm hanging up." I did and shook my head at the phone, not wanting to help him through his crisis. He was a client I couldn't accept and didn't want.

He was the same Ben, confused and uncomfortable in his skin. I remembered something I'd bet he'd forgotten. Ben had called me a week before his wedding. He'd refused to continue our friendship when he got engaged but left me a message asking me to lunch. Although I hadn't seen him in many months, I agreed and met him at his office.

Thin-lipped and stressed through our lunch, he walked me to my car. "I just wanted to see you one more time, before I got married."

"Why?"

"I don't know." He bowed his head. "No, I do know." I let him talk.

"I love you, you know that."

"Yeah, I know you think that, but you won't be my friend, so I don't believe you."

"Just listen." He pulled me close to him, putting his hands in the back pocket of my jeans. I didn't wiggle away and tilted my head to look in his face. "Marry me."

"God, Ben, what are you doing?" I stepped back. "You're getting married next week."

"I'll call it off if you say 'yes.'"

"No."

"Why?"

"Because, I'm not Jewish, remember? Or, now that's not important." I hated him in that moment. "This is crazy. I'm going."

"Wait, don't–"

"Why not? What's changed?"

"I have."

"No, you haven't." I pushed his hand away that reached to grab mine. "How can you ask me this a week before your wedding?" I continued. "If you had called off the wedding and then asked me, maybe. But, not like this."

He stood still in silence.

"We all know that you don't love her, but, now, I feel like you don't love me." My eyes were dry as I said it, but my heart broke over him, again.

"I made a mistake seeing you," he said.

"There you go. Regretting anything you do with me." I found my keys in my purse. "This is why I said 'no,' before and now."

After Ben called, I sat with that memory, wondering why I'd forgotten about it, how different my life would've been if I'd said "yes" that day in the parking lot. I doubted that I'd have purchased my own home or would be working with clients. Yet, I knew I wouldn't have made so many mistakes after Mom died.

Three months later, Ben called again. I waited a few days to call him back. "Why are you calling me?" I said when he answered.

"Because you know me better than anyone. Because you were right all along."

He had changed. I soaked in the familiarity of his voice. Over our years apart, I'd called his work number at night many times to hear his outgoing message. He had a great voice, like a warm blanket.

"Are you there or did you hang up again?" We laughed. It felt good to talk to him. We spoke for over an hour about the very real things that had happened over the past almost nine years. He'd lived in the Palisades as planned, made partner long ago and had two young sons.

It felt like I'd spoken to him the day before. I agreed to meet him for dinner after we spoke a few more times. I was excited to have my friend back.

Late to meet me for sushi, I didn't recognize him until he smiled. His hair was more gray than black. Once at our table, he squirmed in discomfort.

"What's your problem?" I was my most honest self with him.

"I'm nervous, I haven't seen you in so long." With his admission, his broad, tired shoulders dropped. "You look exactly the same," he said.

"There's nothing to be nervous about. Listen, I'm never ever getting back together with you."

He didn't flinch at my words. "No, you made it clear a long time ago that you didn't want that." He smiled. Crinkles formed around his sage green eyes, his longer and deeper dimples creased his cheeks. "I just missed you."

I admitted I missed him, and we finished our dinner in familiar comfort.

I meant what I'd said to him. I hadn't worked so hard, for so many years to end up with him. What a crappy outcome, I thought in my car on my way home.

Our friendship resumed, we hiked every other Sunday, when he didn't have custody of his two sons. I hadn't been on those trails for ten years and huffed behind him, remembering how much I missed his easy company, our laughter and watching the back of his strong legs.

I looked forward to seeing him and our phone calls in between. One afternoon after a hike and lunch, he stood at my open car window. Without thought, I gave him my lips for a kiss for a good-bye.

"Cheek, please," he said, without a hint of shock.

"Oh, my God, I'm so sorry. Habit or something." I backed out of the parking spot before I finished speaking.

I drove down the PCH to my home eight miles from his, with the car radio off, shaking my head and smoking a cigarette. Why did I do that? I wasn't trapped in the past. I knew who I was and felt clear about whom he was.

"The grass isn't greener, it's just grass," I said to my car and God. In ten years, I'd laid on all kinds of grass, rolling around and everything else. Ben was still my favorite grass. He was the grass I trusted and loved.

I slept on my epiphany for a couple days to make sure it was real. I even discussed it with Dad. "I know this is weird, but I've been hanging out with Ben again, just as friends." I told him the story of how we'd reconnected.

I hoped Dad would remind me that Ben had broken my heart, that Mom thought he was weak.

"I always liked him." Dad wasn't helping me back away from Ben. "I know your Mom had doubts, but I left my family for her. She didn't know how hard that was. If it took Ben to make a huge mistake to learn, so what?"

I was still surprised by how easily Dad and I spoke and the wisdom he shared, how I included him in the important parts of my life. "You forgive him, Dad? For what he did."

"Look what we've lived through. We're both so different from it. I wouldn't be this kind of dad if your Mom was here. I wouldn't have learned about who you are."

Two evenings later, I called Ben. "Hey, look, I know what I said before about never ever and all that."

I heard him shut the washing machine lid. He'd always been obsessed with laundry, doing the smallest loads so it didn't pile up. I smiled that I knew that. Ben listened.

"Okay, here it goes. I've been thinking, and I'm pretty sure we're supposed to spend our lives together. I want to. I love you. I mean, I tried to love a lot of other people, but it wasn't real. Not like how I feel about you, about us. How I feel about myself when I'm with you."

Ben laughed.

"Are you laughing at me?" I asked.

"No, I'm laughing because of the 'never ever.'"

I paced my backyard without a cigarette. "Well, what'd you think?"

"I think, if you're serious, I'm the luckiest guy in the world." His voice grew quiet, more serious. "I've always loved you. You're the love of my life."

Our birthdays fell over the next two days. He picked me up to meet his brother and his family the following night. In the car, I was giddy, almost uncomfortable by what I'd said. Ben was at ease. He grabbed my hand, and I held his middle and forefinger, like I had a decade prior.

At the restaurant, his brother was surprised to see me. He gave me a hug, as did his wife and kids. "What's going on you guys?" Audrey, Ben's sister-in-law said. She'd been my favorite person in Ben's life, standing by me when his parents, sister and uncertainty drove us apart.

Ben sat on my right. "You want to say it?" he asked.

Around the table, eager faces waited. "Well, I love him. We're getting back together."

"You lucky jerk!" Audrey teased Ben with a smile and shining eyes. "Don't blow it this time."

"I won't, I promise," Ben said and squeezed my hand under the table. Audrey turned to me. "Mallzee (her nickname for me), are you sure? His life's a mess, the kids, the divorce, the whacked ex-wife. Do you need all that?"

I loved her for looking out for me. "I'm as sure as I can be of anything at this point. I only know that I want to try. I can't walk away from our history, what we share today and what we might share tomorrow."

That night when we went to bed, I sobbed. I'd missed his chest hair, his smell, the feel of his wide lips against mine, the way I fit under his arm. I wished Mom could see the man and woman we'd become.

"Get it all out," Ben said, lifting my face buried in the pillow to lie on him. "You've been through so much. Too much for one person."

Tears flooded his chest. I didn't hurry to dry them. Sorrow and joy escaped from the bottom of my soul.

I rested my head on his shoulder when I stopped. Holding his two fingers tight in mine, I thought about the long road back to where we'd always been.

—

Turns out that the crappy outcome feared wasn't the comfortable conclusion I craved. It had nothing to do with greener grass and everything to do with the fact that Truth and Love exist as one in my heart.

The End

Acknowledgments

Thank you Dad for teaching me to claim my truth and encouraging me to share it in these pages.

Thank you Raj Mukherji for allowing me to offer our experiences to others. Thank you Ken for the countless hours you read and re-read these pages, for believing in me and for holding my hand.

Thank you Cynthia Mukherji for your tireless support and effort.

Thank you Erin Tauscher for seeing something I couldn't see in my story. This book would not exist without you.

Thank you Beth Lieberman for teaching me the craft of writing.

Thank you Adrienne Stolz Johnson for gifting this book with your brilliance when it needed it the most.

70429675R00135

Made in the USA
Middletown, DE
26 September 2019